ASK THE VET

Behavior
of Dogs & Cats

Gary Landsberg DVM
Diplomate of the American College of
Veterinary Behaviorists

Debra Horwitz DVM
Diplomate of the American College of
Veterinary Behaviorists

Illustrations by Mike Buckner

D1114503

Lifelearn®

A Lifelearn Publication
Lifelearn Inc., Guelph, ON, Canada

Published and distributed by Lifelearn Inc., Guelph, ON, Canada

Toll Free in North America	1•800•375•7994
Elsewhere	519•767•5043
FAX	519•767•1101

INFO – info@lifelearn.com
SALES – sales@lifelearn.com
WEB – www.lifelearn.com

ISBN #1-896985-25-4

Printed in Canada

CONTENTS

Feline Behavior   ◆

<u>General</u> <u>Behavior</u>
Feline & Canine

What is aggression?

Aggression is defined as threats or harmful actions directed toward another individual. In animals, aggressive behaviors are a means of communication. Dogs and cats use aggressive displays, threats and attacks to resolve competitive disputes over resources (territory, food) or to increase their reproductive potential. "Aggression" describes the behavior, but does not give any information about underlying motives or causes. Aggression can have multiple motivations.

How is aggression classified?

Aggression can be subdivided into type based on intended victim, body postures during aggression, and other factors such as the animal may want, estrus status of animals involved, and location of the aggressive encounter. In determining the diagnosis, the factors surrounding the initial aggressive event are important considerations, since over time the effects of learning (consequences) including the actions of the owner and the stimulus (i.e. person or other pet retaliates or retreats) will affect how the aggression is displayed.

Ethologists, persons who study animal behavior, use the term 'agonistic' to refer to the behavior of animals (usually of the same species) that involves conflict or contest. These encounters can involve fighting, escape, dominant and submissive gestures and posturing. Aggressive behavior can also be divided into offensive and defensive aggression. In dogs and cats the supposed function of the aggression is most commonly used as the basis of classification:

Dominance (status related) related, possessive, protective and territorial, predatory, fear-induced, pain-induced, parental, redirected, play, intermale, interfemale, and pathophysiologic (medical) in origin.

Note that there is no one single cause of aggression. In addition, an individual pet can display one or more forms of aggression and that multiple factors and stimuli may combine to push the dog or cat to a point where aggression is displayed. For example, a dog may be territorial as well as fearful of children. This dog can only exhibit aggression however, when it is cornered or tied up and cannot escape, and a strange child comes onto the dog's property. When the dog learns that snapping or growls are successful at chasing the child away who has been hugging the dog, the dog may begin to generalize its aggression toward similar stimuli (e.g. other children) and similar situations (hugging).

Are aggressive dogs and cats abnormal?

Aggressive behaviors may be "normal", but when they result in human or animal injury, the behavior is dangerous and unacceptable. Human safety must always be a primary consideration when discussing aggression. More than two million bite wounds occur annually across North America and most people are bitten by animals they own or are known to them. It is important to be able to identify aggressive dogs and cats to prevent injuries wherever possible.

Some aggression in dogs and cats may have abnormal components and be the result of genetics, disease conditions ranging from hormonal imbalances to organ disease, environmental influences or experience and learning. However, even though health problems and degenerative changes may be present, they may or may not contribute to the aggressive behavior.

How do dogs communicate their aggressive behaviors?

By watching the body postures and facial expressions of dogs, it is possible to find an indication of what the dog may do. When a dog is reacting to intrusion, the first sign may be eye contact as when two dogs meet. In some cases, the more dominant dog will maintain eye contact, until the more subordinate dog looks away.

Prolonged eye contact may be considered a threat by both dominant and subordinate dogs. Dogs that are acting subordinate by looking away may feel threatened by continued eye contact and bite out of fear. A dominant and/or assertive dog can react to continued eye contact by holding the stare and escalating its aggressive threat. In some dogs a dark iris or hair occluding the eyes may make eye contact difficult to ascertain.

What happens next?

If the dog believes the intrusion is continuing, the dog may escalate the threat by exposing the teeth and snarling. Snarling is not always accompanied by growling and may only be an upward movement of the lips. Long pendulous lips, long hair or beards on the face may obscure seeing such lip movements. Ear position in dogs can also give clues to canine intentions. A subordinate dog will usually place the ears back as will a fearful dog. An assertive dog will have ears erect. Again, visualization of these positions can be inhibited by conformation, coat and cosmetic surgery.

Dogs will also attempt to change the way they position their body in reaction to a perceived threat. A dog standing its ground tries to look "bigger" by raising the hair along the neck and back, raising the tail in a high position and slowly wagging its tail from side to side. Other dogs attempt to look "smaller" by crouching down, tucking the tail between the legs and even rolling over. Crouching and a lowered body posture in dogs is an appeasement posture designed to decrease the aggressive threat. While maintaining either of these postures a dog may be growling, snarling or barking. These postures can result in a stand off, a decrease or an increase in the aggression.

What does an aggressive cat look like?

Often the first sign is a dilation of the pupils (the dark part of the eye) and rapid lateral movements of the tail. This may be accompanied by putting the ears back and hissing or growling. In addition, the cat may "swipe" at the intruder with a front paw, either with the claws sheathed or exposed. Sometimes the cat will gather its legs under and appear ready to pounce. If the intruder is not too close, or begins to leave, the aggressive encounter may end.

Cats have other more dramatic body postures that signal "go away". Cats frequently try to enhance their size and ferocity to make the threat more menacing. They will do this by turning sideways to the intruder, arching their back, holding the tail upright or straight down, and having their fur stand up. They may hiss, growl and yowl at the same time. In other situations a cat may crouch down, tail switching back and forth with the ears tight against the head, again with accompanying vocalization. A cat anticipating a fight may roll onto its back with claws extended ready to fend off a foe.

How should I respond to these behaviors?

The distance between the animal and the intruder can be influential in determining response. This is often called the "flight" distance. If the intrusion is far away the animal may choose to flee, but if the intrusion is very close the animal may choose to fight. If flight is inhibited, as in a dog or cat that is cornered or tied up, aggression or fight is likely to occur. Most dogs, and some cats, on their own territory are more likely to fight than retreat and dogs with their owners may also stay close rather than retreating. When approached rapidly, a dog or cat may go through the stages of aggressive behavior very quickly and bite without the intruder being able to react. This may happen in encounters between people and their pets because they may approach too close, too fast. On a similar note, dogs that are highly aroused may react with a defensive response almost reflexively in comparison to a dog that is calm enough to make a quick assessment of the approaching stimulus and "decide" on the appropriate response. Dogs and cats that are mildly fearful may calm down if the intruder shows no fear, waits until the pet settles, and then offers a food reward. Reaching for a dog or cat, while continuing to advance is most likely to lead to aggression. Standing still is often the best way to reduce aggression in the dog that is chasing.

Cats will often flee if given the opportunity. However some cats will stand their ground and will scratch or bite if reached for. Bites are most likely if the cat is cornered or restrained and cannot escape, but some bold, confident cats will exhibit territorial displays to intruders on their property in much the same manner as they might chase another cat off of the territory.

In some cases, despite standing still, avoiding further advance or retreating, the aggression continues. Since aggression depends on the situation, the pet's level of motivation, previous experiences and the type of aggression, it will be necessary for you to provide a detailed history to your veterinarian in order that an accurate diagnosis, and appropriate treatment plan be established.

BEHAVIOR – CAUSES & DIAGNOSIS OF PROBLEMS

What makes a pet misbehave?

Behavior problems can be due to medical or behavioral causes, or both. A clinical history, physical examination, and diagnostic testing will determine if there are underlying medical conditions contributing to the problem. Although there may be a single cause for a behavior problem it is often the combined effect of the environment and learning on the pet's mental and physical health that determines behavior.

For example, the pet that is fearful of children, may begin to become more reactive, irritable, and aggressive as diseases such as dental problems or arthritis make the pet more uncomfortable, in pain or less mobile.

Another example is the cat that had been exposed to other cats roaming across its territory, but only began to mark when it developed an overactive thyroid at 10 years of age. Correcting the thyroid problem as well as behavior modification techniques resolved the problem.

What are some behavioral causes of behavior problems?

Any change in the environment may contribute to the emergence of behavior problems. For example, schedule changes, a new member of the household (baby, spouse), moving, loss of a family member or pet, or the addition of a new pet can have a dramatic impact on behavior. Any medical or degenerative changes associated with aging may cause the pet to be even more sensitive to these environmental changes.

Learning (e.g. reinforcement, punishment) also plays a role in most behavior problems. When a pet's actions result in unpleasant consequences (discomfort, lack of attention) i.e. punishment, the chances of repeating the behavior will decrease. If the behavior is followed by pleasant consequences such as obtaining food, attention, or affection (rewards), the behavior is likely to be repeated. These consequences could occur unintentionally when the pet gets into the garbage and finds some appealing leftovers, or could be administered by the owners, when a reward is given following a behavior. It can be difficult to determine what might be reinforcing a behavior, but reinforcement maintains behavior problems.

Some of the most important causes of behavioral problems and the ones that might be most difficult to improve are genetic factors that influence or even dictate the pet's response to stimuli, and the environment that the pet grew up in during its most sensitive periods of development including a) the socialization period from 3 to 12 weeks b) prenatal and neonatal experiences and c) secondary socialization and development through to maturity. Lack of stimulation, lack of handling, lack of exposure, insufficient socialization, and particularly stressful or traumatic events can have a major impact on the pet's behavior.

What tests can be done to determine a behavioral cause?

A good history is one of the most important means of determining the cause of a behavioral problem. This involves an indepth analysis of the pet's medical and behavioral past including any training, as well as the circumstances surrounding the problem itself. Daily interactions with the pet and any changes in schedule need to be explored. Often the event that precipitated the behavioral change may be different from that which maintains it.

Based on the behavioral problem, the pet's age, and a physical examination, the veterinarian first determines if there are any medical causes or contributing factors. *Diagnosis of a behavioral cause can only be made after all medical factors have been ruled out.*

What medical conditions can cause or contribute to behavior problems?

A decline in the pet's hearing, sight or other senses, organ dysfunction (e.g. liver or kidney disease), hormonal diseases, diseases affecting the nervous system, diseases of the urinary tract (infections, tumors or stones), any disease or condition that might lead to pain or discomfort, and those that affect the pets mobility can all cause or contribute to behavior problems.

a) Any condition that leads to an increase in pain or discomfort can lead to increased irritability, increased anxiety or fear of being handled or approached, and ultimately an increased aggressiveness. If these aggressive displays are successful at removing the "threat" (and they usually are) the behavior is reinforced. Medical conditions that affect the ears, anal sacs, teeth and gums, bones, joints, or back (disks) are some of the more common causes of pain and discomfort. If the pet's mobility is affected, it may become increasingly aggressive, choosing to threaten and bite, rather than retreat. A decrease in mobility could also affect urination and defecation by reducing the pet's desire or ability to utilize its elimination area.

b) Sensory dysfunction: Pets with diminished sight or hearing may have a decreased ability to detect or identify the stimuli, and might begin to respond differently to commands, sounds or sights. Sensory decline is more likely to be seen as pet's age.

c) Diseases of the internal organs, such as the kidneys or liver, can cause a number of behavior changes, primarily due to the toxic metabolites that accumulate in the bloodstream. Organ decline and dysfunction is more common in the older pet. Any medical conditions that cause an increased frequency of urination or decreased urine control, such as kidney disease, bladder infections, bladder stones, or neurological damage might lead to an increase in house-soiling. Similarly, those problems that affect the frequency of bowel movements or bowel control, such as colitis or constipation might lead to house-soiling with stools.

d) Diseases of the nervous system (brain and spinal cord) can lead to a number of behavior and personality changes. Conditions such as epilepsy, brain tumors, infections, immune and degenerative diseases can all directly affect a dog or cat's nervous system and therefore its behavior. In the older pet aging changes can have a direct effect on the brain, leading to cognitive dysfunction and senility.

e) The endocrine (hormone) system also plays a critical role in behavior. Over-activity or under-activity of any of the endocrine organs can lead to a number of behavior problems. The thyroid and parathyroid glands (in the neck), the pituitary gland (in the brain), the adrenal gland (by the kidneys), the pancreas, and the reproductive organs can all be affected by conditions or tumors that lead to an increase or decrease in hormone production. Endocrine disorders are more likely to arise as the pet ages.

f) The aging process is associated with progressive and irreversible changes of the body systems. Although these changes are often considered individually, the elderly pet is seldom afflicted with a single disease, but rather varying degrees of organ disease and dysfunction. Cognitive decline and senility have also been recognized in older dogs (and perhaps cats). (see geriatric behavior problems for more details).

What tests need to be done to determine if my pet's behavior problem is due to a medical condition?

CLINICAL HISTORY AND PHYSICAL EXAMINATION

The assessment begins with a clinical history and physical examination. Remember the history that you provide may be the only way to determine if there are behavioral or medical changes that occur in the home, so be certain to mention any changes or problems that you may have noticed in your pet's behavior. If you can catch the problem on videotape, this can be a valuable diagnostic aid for the veterinarian. Based on the signs that you report and the findings of the examination, laboratory tests and a more comprehensive examination such as a neurological examination or sensory testing may be required. For some of these tests your pet may need to be referred to a specialist.

MEDICAL, SURGICAL, DIETARY OR PHARMACOLOGIC TREATMENT

Before beginning behavior therapy, any medical problem that has been diagnosed should be treated. A change in diet or a drug trial may be an important aspect of differentiating a medical from a behavioral cause (as a food trial or steroid trial might be used to rule out an underlying allergic cause). Surgery may also be indicated such as when a tumor is diagnosed or when castration is indicated to reduce male sexually influenced behaviors. Your veterinarian may commence medical and behavioral treatment for long standing behavior problems.

What products are available to help prevent undesirable behavior?
There are numerous products on the market that have been designed to help prevent undesirable behavior in pets. Leashes, harnesses, and head halters are needed to keep pets under control, especially when outdoors. A cage or X-pen provides a safe comfortable home for the dog, when the owners are not available to supervise. Alternately, child locks and child barricades can be used to keep pets away from potential problem areas.

Since dogs, especially young puppies are strongly motivated to chew, it is important to provide a variety of chew toys. A chew toy can also help maintain good dental health. Find a few products that are safe, durable and that appeal to your dog. Each dog is an individual. Many companies manufacture toys that can be stuffed or coated with food or treats or designed to require manipulation to release the food (Kong®, Kong® Biscuit Ball, Nylabone Crazy Ball™, Buster Cube™, Tricky Treats™). Interactive toys provide an opportunity for social play with the owner. The Mutt Puck™, Boomer Ball™, Water Kong™, and flying disks have been designed for interactive play with dogs. Cats are attracted by toys that are a moving target for chasing and pouncing (Feline Flyer™, Cat Dancer™, Tiger Toy™, and Laser Mouse™). The Crazy Ball for Cats™, has a flashing ball that is activated by movement and delivers food as it is batted. The Kitty Kong® can be chased and batted, has rubber whiskers for chewing and a catnip impregnated tail. Although some cats are chewers, they can usually be managed by keeping them away from problem areas, and by providing play toys or by planting a kitty herb garden (if the cat finds plants appealing to chew). For both dogs and cats, dental chew toys, dental snacks and dental foods can serve a dual purpose (to promote good dental health and as a good target for chewing. Another concern of cat owners is the damage that might be caused by scratching. By providing a scratching post with a surface that appeals to your cat, scratching can be directed toward the post, rather than a favorite piece of furniture. A product known as Pavlov's Cat™ delivers food treats each time the cat scratches the post. For scratching problems, plastic nail coverings, (Soft Paws™) are available that can be glued on to prevent damage (see 'destructiveness – chewing' and 'destructiveness – digging').

What type of training collar should I use for walking and controlling my dog?

The head halter is a quick and effective method of teaching the dog to respond to commands, so that a reward based training program can be implemented. The halter exerts pressure behind the neck and around the muzzle, rather than pulling against the trachea. With a pull forward and upward, the dog can be immediately prompted to sit and the tension then released as soon as the pet is performing the appropriate response. A favorite treat or toy can be used to reinforce and "mark" the correct response. The Gentle Leader® has been designed to be left attached for remote control with a pull on a remote leash. The Halti™ and Snoot Loop™ offer fits that might better suit some dogs, but have not been designed to be left attached. Body harnesses (K9 Pull Control™, Lupi™) will effectively stop pulling, but provide poor control.

What products are useful for house-soiling problems?

For indoor house-soiling you should purchase commercial odor eliminators to ensure that the pet is not attracted back to the spot by the residual odor. Your pet's sense of smell is extremely acute, so don't rely on commercial cleansers to do the job. Odor eliminators use chemicals, bacteria or enzymes to break down the odor entirely. Some products are available as concentrates, which can then be diluted so that there is a sufficient amount to saturate the entire area. Also available is Nature's Miracle® Black Light that can be useful for detecting previous elimination spots and a moisture sensor that can be useful for finding moist areas where the surfaces appear dry (see product list on p. 15). For cats, a synthetic cheek gland pheromone Feliway® is now available that can be sprayed on areas where the cat might be inclined to spray or mark, in order to reduce marking.

What products are available for correcting undesirable behavior?

Once behavior problems develop there are numerous products that have been designed to interrupt or deter undesirable behavior. This is one area where the quality and durability of the product is essential, and the type of warrantee may also be an important consideration. Follow the instructions carefully, and supervise the pet well. Punishment is intended to reduce the probability of a behavior in the future. To be successful, punishment must be administered during misbehavior, and must be sufficiently noxious to deter the pet. If a training device is not effective immediately, discontinue its use, and seek additional advice.

Why do some behavior products utilize shock?

For punishment to be effective, it must be sufficiently aversive to overcome the pet's motivation to perform the behavior. For this reason, some punishment devices use "shock" to deter the pet. When selecting a retraining device, you will need to consider the pet's motivation to perform the behavior, the severity of the problem, the type of punishment that is most likely to be effective, and the consequences to the owner or the pet if the problem is allowed to continue. While devices that use shock should be considered as a last resort, they may on occasion be the fastest, most effective, most economical, or most practical means of dealing with serious problems where the owners might otherwise have to "give up" their pet (e.g. excessive barking, destroying furniture). Shock devices also provide an alternative to confinement as they can be used to keep pets away from potential problem areas. Therefore, it might be argued that when a shock device causes minimal fear or discomfort, is immediately successful in deterring the pet, and there are no other practical options, then its benefit might be weighed against the discomfort (i.e. short-term pain for long term gain). In addition, products that pair a warning tone with the uncomfortable stimulus can minimize exposure since most pets learn to retreat when they hear the tone or learn to avoid the area. Whenever an electronic shock product is used be certain that the manufacturer is experienced and reputable and that the product is of high quality. It is important to note that even a highly noxious punishment may not be sufficient to overcome reflexive, innate or highly motivated behaviors. Consider, for example, the dog that continues to pursue porcupines after a faceful of quills.

What products are useful for training and punishment when the owner is present to supervise?

Physical forms of punishment should be avoided as they can lead to physical injury, fear and defensive aggression and seldom are effective at deterring the pet from repeating the behavior. In fact, physical punishment can serve to reinforce some behaviors by providing attention. On the other hand an owner-activated device can be used as an immediate undesirable consequence associated with a behavior (punisher) or as a means of interrupting an undesirable response (disruptive stimulus) so that an appropriate desirable response can be achieved and reinforced.

How can a device be used to train appropriate behavior?

The concept of a disruptive or inhibitory stimulus is that it is sufficiently startling to interrupt the behavior. Whether the disruptive stimulus is also a punishment will depend on its effect on the pet and the problem. Some pets may be sufficiently deterred by the stimulus in order to reduce the possibility of the behavior recurring, while others will be interrupted but will not be deterred from repeating the behavior or will habituate to the stimulus over time. The goal of the disruptive stimulus is to inhibit the undesirable response (with a minimum of fear or anxiety), and provide a window of opportunity to achieve the desirable response (which can then be reinforced negatively and/or positively).

What devices can be used for pets that misbehave in the owner's presence?

Direct punishment or disruption devices include audible trainers (Barker Breaker™, Sonic Pet Trainer™) ultrasonic trainers (Pet-Agree™, Easy Trainer™, Ultrasonic Pet Trainer™) or a citronella spray (Interrupt™). Rape alarms, water rifles, and compressed air may also be effective.

Why should the owner remain out of sight during punishment?

If punishment can be administered while the owner remains out of sight, the pet will not associate the "punishment" with the owner. On the other hand, if the pet realizes that the owner is administering the punishment, the problem may cease when the owner is watching, but the pet will learn that the behavior is safe when the owner is away.

What devices can be used to punish a pet while remaining out of sight?

A remote citronella spray collar and a number of remote shock collars are available. The remote citronella spray collar also has an audible tone that can be paired with a favored reward so that it serves as a remote form of reinforcement (as in clicker training). A water rifle may also be effective. A remote vibration trainer (Pet Pager®) has been designed for deaf dogs. For cats, placing a remote spray device on a surface and activating it remotely might teach cats to stay away from plants or counters.

Since it is imperative that pet owners use these devices during (not after) misbehavior, a pet monitor is another practical training tool. A small motion detector, The Tattle-Tale™ is capable of picking up the movement of a dog or cat on virtually any surface. The device can be set up in any area where the pet might "misbehave" (scratching, garbage raiding, climbing on counters, furniture etc.). Home security monitors can also be used.

What can be done when the owner is absent?

Environmental punishment (or booby-traps) may train the pet to cease the inappropriate behavior or to avoid selected sites even in the owner's absence. This type of punishment resembles the learning that occurs when pets are exposed to cars, predators, barbed wire, sprinklers, and other unpleasantries in their environment.

With a little planning and ingenuity it is often possible to design a successful booby-trap out of everyday items. A few strips of double-sided tape, a few tin cans set to topple or an upside down plastic carpet runner may successfully keep pets out of an area.

Outdoor devices: Electronic containment systems utilize either shock or citronella spray collars to keep dogs within selected boundaries. As the pet approaches the transmitter wire, there is first a warning tone, and then activation of the collar if the pet does not retreat out of range. Motion activated alarms (Critter Gitter™), ultrasonic deterrents (Cat and Dog Stop®, Yard Garden Pest Control®), The ScareCrow™ (a motion detector sprinkler) and pet repellents might keep the owner's pet out of areas on the property (e.g. garden) or stray animals off the property.

Indoor devices: Shock or citronella spray containment systems can also be used with indoor transmitters, to keep pets away from selected areas or out of certain areas in the home. The Scraminal™ is a motion detector alarm and home security devices may also be effective. Alarm mats (ScratcherBlaster™, SofaSaver™) and shock mats (ScatMat™, PetMat™) are available to fit on windowsills, furniture or around plants. The Snappy Trainer™ has a plastic end that fits over a mousetrap to deter the cat with minimal discomfort. A citronella spray motion activated device (Smart Cap®) is in development, to keep cats away from selected areas.

A number of dog doors have been designed to be activated only by the pet wearing the activation collar or "key". A similar cat product is in development.

What products are useful to control and deter barking?

For a bark activated device to be effective it must be sufficiently noxious to deter the barking, sensitive enough to detect each undesirable vocalization and specific enough that it is not activated by extraneous stimuli. The Super Barker Breaker™ and K-9 Bark Stopper™ are audible bark activated alarms that are designed to be placed on a counter or table in an area where a dog might bark (front hall, cage, etc.). Bark activated collars emit an audible or ultrasonic noise, a spray of citronella or electronic stimulation (shock) with each bark. The audible and ultrasonic devices are seldom sensitive, specific, or noxious enough to be effective. The most effective antibark collars have proven to be the citronella spray or the electronic shock collars. To ensure consistency and safety only products from reputable manufacturers should be selected.

PRODUCT MANUFACTURER INFORMATION

DIRECT INTERACTIVE DEVICES

Barker Breaker (sonic), Amtek Pet Behavior Products, 11025 Sorrento Valley Court, San Diego, CA, 92121, 800-762-7618, 858-597-6681

Interrupt / Direct Stop Repellent, (citronella spray), US: ABS Inc, 5909-G. Breckenridge Pkwy, Tampa FL, 33610-4253, 800-627-9447, CAN: Multivet, P.O Box 651, St-Hyacinthe, QC, J2S7P5, 800-303-0244, 888-456-2626

Easy Trainer (ultrasonic)/Ultrasonic Pet Trainer, Radio Systems Incorporated, 10738 Dutch Town Road Knoxville, TN, 37914, 800-732-2677, 865-777-5404

K-9 Bark Stopper/Sonic Pet Trainer (audible), Innotek Pet Products Inc., 1000 Fuller Drive, Garrett, Indiana, 46738, 800-826-5527, 219-357-3148

Pet Agree / Dazzer (ultrasonic), KII Enterprises, P.O. 306, Camillus, NY 13031, U.S.: 800-262-3963, 315-468-3596

MONITORING DEVICES

Tattle Tale, (vibration motion sensor), KII Enterprises, see above

REMOTE DEVICES

ABS Remote Trainer (citronella spray), US: ABS Inc, CAN: Spray Commander, Multivet

Pet Pager, Vibration stimulation remote collar, Radio Systems Inc.

Tritronics Inc., (remote shock), 1705 S. Research Loop, Tucson, AZ, 85710, 800-456-4343, 520-290-4204 and also from Innotek Inc., and Radio Systems Inc.

BOOBY-TRAPS (ENVIRONMENTAL PUNISHMENT DEVICES)

Indoor and Outdoor Pet Citronella Spray Containment Systems, USA: ABS Inc., CAN: Spray Barrier (Indoor citronella spray containment system), Virtual Fence (outdoor citronella spray system), Multivet Inc.

Indoor and Outdoor Electronic Containment Systems, Invisible Fencing, (electronic stimulation) US: 355 Phoenixville Pike, Malvern, PA, 19355, 800-538-3647 or Radio Systems Incorporated

Scat Mat, (electronic stimulation mat), ScareCrow, motion activated sprinkler, Contech Electronics, P.O. Box 115, Saanichton, BC, V8M 2C3, Canada, 800-767-8658, 250-652-0755

Pet Mat, Radio Systems Incorporated

Scraminal /Critter Gitter, Scratcher Blaster, Amtek Pet Behavior Products

Snappy Trainer, Interplanetary Incorporated, 12441 West 49th St., Suite 8, Wheatridge, CO, 80033, 888-477-4738, 303-940-3228

SofaSaver, Abbey Enterprises, 1130 Summerset St. New Brunswick, N.J. 08901, 732-873-4242

ELECTRONIC DOORS

From Staywell, Solo, PetMate, Cat Mate, Johnson, PetSafe: www.catdoor.com,

www.dogdoor.com, www.petdoors.com
Electronic or Electromagnetic – pet exits without a key but entry only by key which releases latch
From High Tech Pet Products – Power Pet Door- http://store.yahoo.com/hightechpet

BARK ACTIVATED DEVICES
A.B.S (US)/Aboistop (CAN). (Citronella Spray collar), ABS Inc. (US), Multivet (CAN)
Electronic stimulation bark collars available from Radio Systems, Innotek, and Tritronics – see above
K-9 Bark Stopper (audible bark activated), Innotek Inc.
Silencer Bark Activated Collar, (ultrasonic bark activated collar), Radio Systems Inc.
Super Barker Breaker, (audible bark activated) Amtek Pet Behavior Products, see above

HEAD HALTERS
Gentle Leader / Promise: (head collar), Premier Pet Products, 527 Branchway Rd., Richmond, VA, 23236, 800-933-5595, Canada: Professional Animal Behaviour Associates Inc., P.O. Box 25111, London, ON, N6C 6A8, 519-685-4756
Halti, Coastal Pet Products, 911 Leadway Avenue, Alliance, Ohio, 44601, 800-321-0248
Snoot Loop, Animal Behavior Consultants Inc., 102 Canton Court, Brooklyn, NY, 11229, 718-891-4200, 800-339-9505

NO PULL HALTERS
K9 Pull Control, Dog Crazy Co., 6640 Cobra Way, San Diego, CA 92121, 619-824-0400
Lupi, Coastal Pet Products, 911 Leadway Avenue, Alliance, Ohio, 44601, 800-321-0248

EXERCISE, PLAY AND CHEW PRODUCTS
Ask your veterinarian for suggestions on products that might be most suitable for your pet.

ODOR ELIMINATORS
Ask your veterinarian for suggestions on products that might be most suitable for your household.

C ounter-conditioning and desensitization are powerful ways to change behavior. They are usually used in combination. Desensitization provides a means of safely exposing the pet to the stimulus at a level at or below which fear is likely to be exhibited. Counter-conditioning is used to change the pet's attitude or emotional response to a stimulus. Differential reinforcement or response substitutions are techniques that can be used to change a pet's response from one that is undesirable to one that is desirable through the proper use and timing of reinforcement. Although counter-conditioning may also be used to describe the practice of teaching an alternative and appropriate response to the stimulus, for clarity we will use the terms differential reinforcement or response substitution.

What is counter-conditioning?

Counter-conditioning is changing the pet's emotional response, feelings or attitude toward a stimulus. For example, the dog that lunges at the window when the mailman walks by is displaying an emotional response of fear or anxiety. Counter-conditioning would be accomplished by pairing the sight, sounds and approach of the mailman with one of the dog's favored rewards to change the emotional state to one that is calm and positive.

What is desensitization?

Desensitization is the gradual exposure to situations or stimuli that would bring on the undesirable behavior, but at a level so low that there is no negative response. As the animal experiences the stimulus, but does not respond in the undesirable way, the animal becomes "less reactive" to the stimulus, and the pet can soon tolerate a somewhat more intense stimulus without exhibiting the undesirable response. The key to effective desensitization is to design a stimulus gradient so that the pet can be gradually exposed to progressively more intense levels of the stimulus without the undesirable behavior being elicited.

What is differential reinforcement?

Reinforcement of a response that is incompatible with the undesirable response is referred to as differential reinforcement of an incompatible response (DRI)) while reinforcement of any alternative response is known as DRA. There are a number of techniques that can be used to help the owner turn the inappropriate response into one that is desirable. If the dog is trained through reward based techniques to immediately focus on the owners in response to commands (settle, watch), the command might then be used to achieve the appropriate response (sometimes referred to as counter-commanding). Alternatively disruptive devices, head halters, and lures can be used to get the alternative or incompatible response that can then be reinforced. For many dogs, the head halter and leash is often the safest, most effective and most immediate method to obtain the desired response (e.g. sit, focus, heel), which is then reinforced by release (negative reinforcement) and positive reinforcement (the pet's favored reward). Regardless of the technique used, if the pet can be taught to display a new acceptable response instead of the undesirable response when exposed to a stimulus then response substitution has been achieved. Again, rather than attempting to overcome an intense response, the training should be set up to expose the dog with stimuli of reduced intensity to ensure a successful outcome. The task is not complete until the dog's fearful reaction to the stimulus is replaced by a response to the stimulus that is relaxed and positive (counter-conditioning).

How might these techniques be used in a training situation?

Take the example of the mailman. Begin by getting the dog to sit quietly by the window. Use food as an inducement to the dog to respond, and as a reward for performance. When the dog anticipates a food reward, the "mood" of the dog is usually happy, relaxed and not anxious or aggressive. These are behaviors that are incompatible with the behavior you wish to change, in this case lunging at the window at the mailman. This is counter-conditioning. It may take days or weeks for the dog to learn how to perform this task reliably on command. During that time phase out food rewards so that the dog does the task equally well with or without food.

Next, train the pet to perform the desired behavior in the presence of the mailman. Desensitize the dog, by presenting the stimulus, the mailman, at a low enough level so that the dog will still remain sitting and be relaxed, happy and not anxious or aggressive. Start by having someone the dog knows, WHO IS NOT THE MAILMAN, walk by the window. The dog gets to practice the good behavior when it is easy. Repeat this many times so that the dog does it reliably. Gradually progress to stimuli that more closely resemble the real life situation. Perhaps have the dog sit by the window when the mailman is down the street. If the dog could do this well several times, try when the mailman is across the street. It may be necessary to take the dog outside. Proceed slowly, so that the dog learns how to perform the desired behavior over and over before being challenged with the real thing, the mailman delivering the mail to his door.

What are other ways to design a stimulus gradient for desensitization?

In the example of the mailman the stimulus gradient was to begin the training with a family member and then progress with the mailman at varying distances. Stimuli for desensitization can be arranged from mildest to strongest in a number of ways. For example, begin desensitization from a distance and move progressively closer as the pet is successfully counter-conditioned. Sound stimuli can be presented in varying intensities from quiet to loud. A pet that is fearful or aggressive toward a man with a beard might be desensitized to young boys, older boys, men with no beards, a family member with a costume beard, familiar men with beards and finally strangers with beards. Distance can also be varied. Dogs that are aggressive or fearful as strangers arrive at the front door, could be desensitized and counter-conditioned to the doorbell being rung by a family member, a family member arriving in a car, a family member walking up the front walkway, a stranger walking along the path in front of the home (while the dog remains in the doorway or on the porch), a familiar person entering the home, and finally a stranger at the front door.

In order for desensitization and counter-conditioning programs to be successful, it is necessary to have good control of the pet, a strongly motivating reward, good control of the stimulus, and a well-constructed desensitization gradient. A leash and head halter is often the best way of ensuring control over the dog. Each session should be carefully planned. Pets that are punished for inappropriate behavior (fear, aggressive displays) during the retraining program will become more anxious in association with the stimulus. Owner fears, anxiety or frustration will only serve to increase the pet's anxiety.

Pets that are rewarded during the retraining program will get worse. Whenever a pet can successfully threaten and the stimulus (person, other animal) retreats, the behavior is further reinforced.

How might differential reinforcement be used?

For counter-conditioning to be successful each exposure must have a relaxing or positive result. This means that ideally exposure to the stimulus must be prevented unless a desirable outcome can be insured. Desensitization so that exposure is always below the threshold for fear allows for proper counter-conditioning. However when the exposure is slightly above the threshold for fear the options are to a) keep the pet in the situation until it habituates and then counter-condition with favored food rewards b) use any available method (that does not cause fear) to interrupt the undesirable response and achieve the desirable response (command, lure, disruptive device, head halter) so that an alternative acceptable behavior can be reinforced. If at the end of the session the pet is calm and relaxed and has received favored rewards in the presence of the stimulus, then counter-conditioning may have also been achieved.

How might flooding and exposure techniques be used?

Another technique for reducing fearful behavior is to continuously expose the pet to the stimulus until it settles down (habituates). This technique will only work if the stimulus is not associated with any adverse consequence, and the pet is exposed for as long as is needed until the pet calms down. Once the pet is exposed, the stimulus must not leave or be removed until the pet calms down. Similarly the pet must not be removed or allowed to retreat until the pet habituates. Once the pet settles, reinforcement can be given to ensure that the ultimate result is a positive association with the stimulus. The pet must not be rewarded until it calms and settles down as this would serve to reward the fearful behavior. Owner intervention or punishment must not be utilized as this would lead to an unpleasant association with the stimulus. Since exposure must continue until the pet settles down, flooding is most successful for fears that are not too intense. Beginning with a somewhat lower or muted stimulus may be best. In practice, keeping the pet in a cage or crate or keeping a dog on a leash and halter during exposure to the stimulus, will prevent escape and prevent injury to the stimulus (person or pet).

BEHAVIOR PROBLEMS OF OLDER PETS

It is not unusual for behavior problems to develop in older pets and often there may be multiple concurrent problems. It is also important to note that some of the changes associated with aging may not seem significant, but even a minor change in behavior might be indicative of underlying medical problems or a decline in cognitive dysfunction. Since early diagnosis and treatment can control or slow the progress of many disease conditions, be certain to advise your veterinarian if there is any change in your pet's behavior.

What are some of the causes of behavior changes in senior pets?

1) Many of the problems have similar causes to those in younger pets.

Changes in the household, changes in the environment and new stressors can lead to problems regardless of age. For instance moving, a change in work schedule, a family member leaving the home, or new additions to the family such as a spouse or baby, can have a dramatic impact on the pet's behavior. In addition, it is likely most older pets will be more resistant or less able to adapt to change.

2) Older pets are also likely to develop an increasing number of medical and degenerative problems as they age. Any of the organ systems can be affected and play a role in the development of a wide variety of behavior problems. For example, diseases of the urinary system and kidneys can lead to house-soiling. Diseases of the endocrine organs such as the thyroid gland and pituitary gland can lead to a variety of behavioral and personality changes. A decline in the senses (hearing and sight), painful conditions, and those that affect mobility may cause the pet to be more irritable or more fearful of approach and handling (see 'behavior – causes and diagnosis of problems for more details).

3) As with other organs the brain is susceptible to age related degenerative processes that can affect the pet's behavior, personality, memory, and learning ability. When these changes occur, the pet may show varying degrees of cognitive decline and in pets that are more severely affected, this might be referred to as cognitive dysfunction or senility. Many of these changes are similar to what occurs in aging humans. In fact, the amyloid deposits that are found in the brain of dogs with cognitive dysfunction are similar to what is seen in the early stages of Alzheimer's disease in people.

How can I find out why my pet's behavior has changed?

Regardless of age, every behavior case should begin with a complete veterinary physical examination and a clinical and behavioral history. In addition, blood tests and a urinalysis may be needed to rule out organ disease and endocrine imbalances, especially in the older pet. Sometimes a more indepth examination of a particular organ system may be indicated. Additional laboratory tests, radiographs, ultrasound, spinal tests, brain scans, or perhaps a referral to a specialist may all be appropriate. A decision on which tests are needed would be based on the pet's age, previous health problems, any ongoing drug or dietary therapy and an evaluation of all of its medical and behavioral signs and the findings of the physical exam.

My pet is quite old. Is there any point in doing these tests?

Unfortunately many pet owners do not even discuss behavior changes with their veterinarians since they feel that the changes are a normal part of aging and perhaps nothing can be done for their dog or cat. This is far from the truth. Many problems have an underlying medical cause that can be treated or controlled with drugs, diet or perhaps surgery. Hormonal changes associated with an underactive or overactive thyroid gland, diabetes, diseases of the pituitary gland and testicular tumors can all lead to dramatic changes in the pet's behavior and many of these problems can be treated or controlled. Degenerative organ systems can often be aided with nutritional supplementation or dietary changes. High blood pressure, cardiac disease and respiratory diseases may be treatable with medication, which may dramatically improve the quality and even length of the pet's life. And drugs and dietary therapy are also available that are useful in the treatment of age related cognitive dysfunction.

What are some things to look out for?

Changes in behavior (see cognitive dysfunction below), an increase or decrease in appetite or drinking, an increased frequency or amount of urination, loss of urine control (dribbling urine, bedwetting), changes in stool consistency or frequency, skin and hair coat changes, lumps and bumps, mouth odor or bleeding gums, stiffness or soreness, excessive panting, coughing, changes in weight (increase or decrease), and tremors or shaking are some of the more common signs that should be reported, should they develop in your pet.

What is cognitive dysfunction and how is it diagnosed?

It is generally believed that, as in people, a dog or cat's cognitive function tends to decline with age. If your dog has one or more of the signs below and all potential physical or medical causes have been ruled out, it may be due to cognitive dysfunction. Of course, it is also possible that cognitive dysfunction can arise concurrent with other medical problems, so that it might be difficult to determine the exact cause of each sign. Over the past few years the signs commonly attributed to cognitive dysfunctions have been described by the acronym DISH (Disorientation, alterations in Interactions with family members, Sleep-wake cycle and activity level changes or House -soiling). However this may not be a sufficiently complete list to describe all of the categories in which a decline in cognitive function might be seen. These might include:

a) Disorientation (such as getting lost in familiar areas such as the home or yard)

b) Social interactions might be altered between the pet and owner or pet and other pets – some pets may appear to be more clingy while others might be disinterested or even irritable when petted or approached

c) Anxiety might be increased

d) Activity levels often decrease so that the pet is seen sleeping more or is less playful and exploratory. However some pets also become more active and restless with pacing, or even stereotypic behaviors such as licking or bouts of barking

e) Appetite may be affected with some pets showing a disinterest in food and others having a more voracious appetite

f) Altered sleep cycles with increased waking or restlessness at night

g) Altered learning or memory as demonstrated by an inability to retrain, loss of performance (such as commands, working ability, or previous training) or house-soiling (no longer can remember where to eliminate or how to signal)

In one study of dogs that were 11-16 years of age, owners specifically questioned regarding signs of cognitive dysfunction reported that 28% of 11 to 12 year old dogs and 68% of 15 to 16 year old dogs exhibited at least one of the signs above. However, it's important to note that these are signs noticed by pet owners in comparison to when their dog was younger. Research has shown that if you were to try and train your dog on some new learning tasks, that after about 8 years of age many dogs may begin to show a decline in memory and learning ability around this age. Owners of older cats also noted many of these signs listed above but they tended to arise at a little older age (e.g. 15 years and older). Treatment options tend to be most effective at slowing or reversing decline when they are instituted early in the course of disease. Therefore, be certain to report any of these signs to your veterinarian immediately.

Do pets get Alzheimer's?

Many of the same changes and lesions associated with Alzheimer's disease in people have also been recognized in dogs and cats. Should multiple behavior problems develop and these changes progress to the point where the dog or cat is no longer a "functional" pet, the condition may be consistent with senility or dementia of the Alzheimer's type.

Can geriatric behavior problems be treated?

In many cases the answer is yes. Of course if there are medical problems contributing to the behavior changes, the problem may not be treatable. The key therefore is to report changes and bring in your pet for assessment as soon as new problems arise.

Dogs that develop behavior problems due to underlying medical conditions may need alterations in their schedule or environment in order to deal with these problems. If the condition is treatable and can be controlled or resolved (e.g. Cushing's disease, infections, painful conditions) then, as discussed, you must be prepared to retrain the dog, since the new habit may persist. For example, the house-soiling pet may have less duration of control due to its medical problems. If these conditions cannot be controlled, then the pet's schedule (more frequent trips outdoors), or environment (installing a dog door, paper training) may have to be modified. With conditions that affect a cat's mobility, adjustments may be needed to the pet's environment, litter box placement, or type of litter box, (e.g. a lower sided box).

In cognitive dysfunction, an increase in a neurotoxic protein called beta amyloid, an increase in damage due to toxic free radicals, a loss of neurons, and alterations in neurotransmitters such as dopamine may be responsible for many of the behavior changes. Both drug therapy and dietary therapy are now available that might improve these signs and potentially slow the decline. Again early diagnosis and intervention is likely to have the greatest effects.

Selegiline is a drug that has been licensed for the treatment of cognitive decline in dogs in North America. It is classed as an MAOB inhibitor but its action may be to enhance neurotransmitter function such as noradrenaline and dopamine, to help reduce free radical damage in the brain and perhaps as a neuroprotective drug (see 'drug therapy' for more details). Many of the signs listed (DISH) may be improved by treatment with selegiline.

Another method of managing senior behavior problems is a prescription diet that is designed to protect against and possibly reverse damage due to toxic free radicals. It is enhanced with a variety of antioxidants including vitamin E, selenium, vitamin C and fruits and vegetables. It is also supplemented with essential fatty acids in the form of fish oils and some factors to help the cell's mitochondria function more efficiently including carnitine and lipoic acid. The diet has been shown to improve learning ability and memory in old dogs and improve many of the clinical signs listed previously (i.e. DISH).

There are a number of other medications, some licensed for use in European countries (such as nicergoline and propentofylline). These drugs have been developed for use in human geriatric patients. They are behavior modifying drugs that might also enhance cognitive function by increasing blood flow through the brain or by enhancing neurotransmitter function.

It is important to note however that once new habits are learned, retraining and changes to the environment may also be needed to resolve the problem. For example, in addition to drug therapy, dogs that have begun to eliminate indoors will need to be retrained much like a puppy that has begun to eliminate indoors.

There are a number of excellent books and training guides available that are intended to teach pet owners how to apply the basic principles of learning and training in a humane, effective, and logical manner. At the other extreme, many training books and manuals have been written by self-professed experts who advocate techniques that may be scientifically unsound, inappropriate, or inhumane. Following these techniques will seldom lead to improvement of the problem and might even aggravate some conditions.

The best way to select a book, video or training manual is to seek the guidance or recommendation of a veterinarian, behaviorist, or obedience trainer who you trust and respect. It can also be useful to assess the background, expertise and, in particular, the education of

the author(s). Be certain that the book you choose covers the training techniques, products, and topics for which you are seeking assistance. In general the most recent publications will include the most recent advances in behavior, training, and products. However, some of the older texts are the best resources for obtaining a sound understanding of the psychology of learning and the basic behavior of dogs and cats. Although, inclusion in the reference list below is not intended to be an endorsement, the publications have been screened and are included based on the following criteria:

A. The author has a sound knowledge of basic canine and feline behavior.

B. Training techniques emphasize positive reinforcement, motivation, and shaping rather than punishment.

C. Correction techniques have been designed to train or encourage the pet to perform an appropriate behavior and set the pet up to succeed, rather than punishing the pet for inappropriate behavior.

UNDERSTANDING CANINE AND FELINE BEHAVIOR

1. Beaver BV (1992) Feline Behavior: A Guide for Veterinarians. W. B. Saunders: Philadelphia, PA
2. Beaver BV (1999) Canine Behavior: A Guide for Veterinarians. W. B. Saunders, Philadelphia, PA
3. Bradshaw JWS. (1992) The behaviour of the domestic cat. C-A-B International. Oxon, UK
4. Bradshaw JWS. The True Nature of the Cat. Boxtree, London, 1993
5. Coppinger R, Coppinger L. (2001). Dogs – a startling new understanding of the origin, behavior and evolution. Scribner, NY
6. Donaldson J. (1996). The Culture Clash, James and Kenneth Publishers, 2140 Shattuck Ave. #2406, Berkeley, CA 94704 (510) 658-8588
7. Donaldson J. (1998) Dogs are from Neptune. Lasar Multimedia Productions, Montreal
8. Dunbar I. (1999) Dog Behavior. Howell Book House, NY
9. Fox M. Canine Behavior, Charles Thomas, Springfield. IL, 1965
10. Fox MW. The Dog: It's Domestication and Behavior. New York, Garland STM Press, 1978
11. Houpt, K. (1998) Domestic Animal Behavior, 3rd edition. Iowa State University Press: Ames, IA.
12. Scott JP, Fuller JL. (1965) Dog Behavior. The Genetic Basis. University of Chicago Press, Chicago
13. Serpell, J; Barrett, P (Eds.) (1996) The Domestic Dog: Its Evolution, Behaviour and Interactions with People. Cambridge University Press, 268 pp
14. Thorne, C. (ed.) (1992). The Waltham Book of Dog and Cat Behaviour. Pergamon Press: Oxford, 159 pp
15. Turner DC, Bateson P (editors). (2000) The Domestic Cat, the biology of its behaviour, 2nd edition, Cambridge University Press, Cambridge, 244 pp

READING LIST FOR PET OWNERS: TRAINING AND BEHAVIOR PROBLEMS

1. Ackerman, L., Landsberg, G. and Hunthausen, W. (eds) (1996). Cat Behaviour and Training: Veterinary Advice for Owners. TFH Publications: Neptune, NJ
2. Ackerman, L., Landsberg, G. and Hunthausen, W. (eds) (1996). Dog Behavior and Training: Veterinary Advice for Owners. TFH Publications: Neptune, NJ
3. Bailey, G. (1995). The Perfect Puppy: How to Raise a Problem Free Dog, Hamlyn, London
4. Bohnenkamp G. (1990). Manners for the modern dog. James and Kenneth Publishers, Berkeley, CA

5. Bohnenkamp G. (1991). From the Cat's Point of View, Perfect Paws, Inc., Belmont, CA

6. Bohnenkamp G. (1994). Help! My Dog Has An Attitude, Perfect Paws, Inc., Belmont, CA

7. Campbell, W (1999). Behavour Problems in Dogs. 3rd edition. BehaviorRx systems. Grants Pass, OR

8. Campbell W. (1995). Owners Guide to Better Behavior in Dogs. Alpine Publications, Loveland, CO

9. Davidson D, Manning P. (1997). Canadian Dog Owner's Manual., Toronto, MacMillan Canada

10. Dodman, N. (1996). The Dog Who Loved too Much. Bantam, NY.

11. Dodman, N. (1997). The Cat Who Cried for Help. Bantam, NY

12. Dodman N. (1999). Dogs Behaving Badly. An A-to-Z Guide to Understanding and Curing Behavioral Problems in Dogs. Bantam, NY

13. Dunbar, I. (1987). Sirius Puppy Training. (Video). James & Kenneth Publishers, Berkeley, CA

14. Dunbar, I. (1998). Dog Behavior: An Owner's Guide to a Happy Healthy Pet (Owner's Guide to a Happy Healthy Pet) Hungry Minds, Inc.

15. Fisher, J. (ed) (1993). The Behaviour of Dogs and Cats. Stanley Paul: London

16. Fogle, B. (1990). The Dog's Mind. Viking Penguin Inc.: New York

17. Fogle, B. (1992). The Cat's Mind. Howell Book House: New York

18. Fogle, B. (1994). ASPCA Complete Dog Training Manual. Dorling Kindersley: London, 128 pp

19. Fox MW. (1996). Superdog. Raising the perfect canine companion. Howell Book House, NY

20. Heath S. (1993). Why does my cat...? Souvenir Press, London

21. Horwtiz D, Landsberg G. Lifelearn CD of client behavior handouts (62 titles), Lifelearn, Guelph, ON, 800-375-7994

22. Hunthausen W, Landsberg G. AAHA client behavior handouts (10 titles), AAHA press, Denver, CO

23. Kilcommons, B. and Wilson, S. (1994). Child-Proofing Your Dog. Warner Books: New York

24. Marder, A. (1994). Your Healthy Pet: A Practical Guide to Choosing and Raising Happier, Healthier Dogs and Cats. Rodale Press: Emmaus, PA, 216 pp

25. Neville P. (1991). Do Cats Need Shrinks? Contemporary Books, Chicago

26. Neville P. (1992). Do Dogs Need Shrinks? Citadel Press, NY

27. Pryor, K. (1999). Don't Shoot the Dog: The New Art of Teaching and Training, Bantam Doubleday Dell, 202 pp

28. Reid P. (1996). Excel-erated Learning, James and Kenneth, Berkley.

29. Schwartz S. (1996). No more myths. Howell Book House, NY

30. Scidmore, Brenda and McConnell, Patricia. (1996). Puppy Primer, Order from Dog's Best Friend, Ltd., PO Box 447, Black Earth, WI 53515, 608-767-2435

31. Rafe, S. (1990). Your New Baby and Bowser. Denlinger Publications: Fairfax, VA

32. Ryan, T. (1990). Puppy Primer. Legacy: Pullman, WA

33. Ryan, T. (1994). The Toolbox for Remodeling Problem Dogs. Legacy: Pullman, WA, 26 pp

34. Volhard J. (1994). Canine Good Citizen, Howell Book House.

35. Weston D, Ross ER. (1992). Dog problems: the gentle modern cure. Howell Book House, NY

36. Weston D. (1990). Dog training. Howell Schwartz S. No More Myths. Howell Book House, New York, 1990Book House, NY

37. Wright JC, Lashnits JW. (1994). Is your Cat Crazy? MacMillan, NY

READING & REFERENCES FOR VETERINARIANS

1. Askew HR. (1996). Treatment of behavior problems in dogs and cats. A guide for small animal veterinarians. Blackwell Science, Oxford, 350 pp

2. Beaver, B. V. (1994). The Veterinarian's Encyclopedia of Animal Behavior. Iowa State University Press: Ames, IA

3. Dodman NH, Shuster L. (1997). Psychopharmacology of Animal Behavior Disorders. Blackwell Science Inc., Malden, MA. 332 pp

4. Hart BL, Hart LA. (1985). Canine and Feline Behavioral Therapy, Lea & Febiger, Philadelphia

5. Hetts SA. (1999). Pet Behavior Protocols. What to Say, What to Do, When to Refer. AAHA Press, Denver

6. Horwitz H, Heath S, Mills D. BSAVA Manual of Canine and Feline Behavioural Medicine. In press, BSAVA

7. Houpt KA (editor) (1997). Progress in Companion Animal Behavior. Veterinary Clinics of North America Small Animal Practice, 27 (3), 427-697

8. Jackson J, Anderson RK, Line S (2001). Early learning for Puppies to Socialize and Promote Good Behavior. A Program Guide for Veterinary Clinics, Canine Trainers and Humane Societies. Premier Pet Products, Richmond, VA

9. Keltner NL, Folks DG. (2001). Psychotropic Drugs, 3nd edition, Mosby, St. Louis

10. Landsberg G, Hunthausen W, Ackerman L (1997). Handbook of Behaviour Problems of the Dog and Cat, Butterworth-Heinemann, Jordan Hill, Oxford, England. 1-800-366-2665 (US), in Canada

11. Lindsay, S. R. (2000). Handbook of Applied Dog Behavior and Training, Vol. 1: Adaptation and Learning. Iowa State University Press, 410 pp
12. Lindsay, S. R. (2001). Handbook of Applied Dog Behavior and Training, Volume Two: Etiology and Assessment. Iowa State University Press, 304 pp
13. Mills DS, Heath SE, Harrington LJ. (1997). Proceedings of the first international conference on veterinary behavioural medicine. Universities Federation for Animal Welfare, Herts, UK
14. Overall K, Mills DS, Heath SE, Horwitz D. (editors), (2001). Proceedings of the third international congress on veterinary behavioural medicine. Universities Federation for Animal Welfare, Herts, UK
15. Overall, K. (1997). Clinical Behavioral Medicine for Small Animals. Mosby, St. Louis
17. Reid PJ. (1996). Excelerated Learning. James and Kenneth Publishers, Oakland, CA
18. Schwartz, S. (1997). Instructions for Veterinary Clients: Canine and Feline Behavior Problems. 2nd edition, Mosby, St. Louis
19. Voith VL, Borchelt PL. (editors) (1996). Readings in Companion Animal Behavior, Trenton, NJ, Veterinary Learning Systems, 236 pp

BEHAVIOR ORGANIZATIONS

1. American College of Veterinary Behaviorists, executive director, Dr. Bonnie Beaver, Dept. of Small Animal Medicine and Surgery, College of Veterinary Medicine, 4474 TAMU, Texas A & M University, College Station, TX, 77843-4474, www.veterinarybehaviorists.org
2. American Veterinary Society of Animal Behavior, www.avsab.org/avsab
3. Animal Behavior Society. www.animalbehavior.org
4. Association of Pet Dog Trainers, www.apdt.com
5. Association of Pet Behavior Counsellors www.apbc.or.uk
6. Companion Animal Behaviour Therapy Study Group. www.cabtsg.org
7. European Society for Veterinary Clinical Ethology. www.esvce.org
8. International Society for Animal Ethology: www.sh.plym.ac.uk/isae/home.htm
9. The Society of Veterinary Behavior Technicians www.svbt.org/
10. National Association of Dog Obedience Instructors, www.nadoi.org

ADDITIONAL BEHAVIOR RESOURCES

1. American Animal Hospital Association: Behavior Pamphlets for Dog and Cat Owners (10 titles), AAHA, Denver, CO
2. Clicker training: www.clickertraining.com, www.clickandtreat.com
3. Dunbar Ian, Sirius Puppy Training. Video. James & Kenneth Publishers. Berkeley, CA, 1987

4. Hunthausen W. Learning to be safe with animals. Dogs, Cats, and Kids (Video). Pet Love. Partnership, LP P.O. Box 11331, Chicago, IL, 60611-0331, 800-784-0979

BEHAVIORAL DRUG THERAPY

How are drugs used for behavior modification in pets?

A number of drugs are now being utilized to treat pet behavior problems. In order to determine if drug therapy might be a consideration, it is first essential to determine the diagnosis and cause of the problem. Drugs might be indicated when behavior techniques alone are unlikely to improve the problem, or where it might be difficult or dangerous to proceed without the aid of drugs. Drugs might also be in the best interest of the pet and owner when there is excessive anxiety or when there are underlying neurotransmitter imbalances that might be contributing to the behavioral signs. For some problems drug therapy can be an essential component of the treatment program (e.g. urine spraying, compulsive disorders) or may be indicated due to medical problems (e.g. epilepsy, hyperkinesis). While drugs can help improve the outcome for many behavioral cases, it is the behavior management program that is needed to obtain the desirable behavior and ultimately resolve the problem.

Which drugs are licensed for veterinary use?

To date, few of the drugs used in veterinary behavior have been approved for pets. In addition to sedatives, only clomipramine and selegiline have been approved for use in dogs in North America. Most of the drugs utilized in veterinary behavior therapy are human drugs, so that doses, side effects and applications for animals have been extrapolated from human use. Such drugs can be used under the supervision of your veterinarian but you may be required to sign a form acknowledging your informed consent for such use. Each behavior case needs to be handled individually. Medications are specific for each pet and must not be transferred to other pets in the home nor, of course, used by owners.

Do all behavioral drugs act by sedation?

Many of the behavioral drugs that have been used in the past are sedatives that have broad effects and side-effects. Recently behaviorists have been turning to human medications, which have effects that are more specific. For example, using anti-depressant medications, we can often treat panic and phobias without compromising social, play or exploratory behaviors.

What tests are required prior to drug use?

Before drugs can be considered, the pet should have a full assessment to rule out medical problems that might be contributing to the behavior problem, and to ensure that there are no contraindications for drug therapy. Prescreening laboratory tests include a general blood profile, urinalysis and blood count. Additional blood work including a thyroid profile or an EKG may be needed if a problem is suspected. For some drugs, monitoring may be necessary throughout the course of therapy.

What are the side-effects and contraindications?

Except for those drugs licensed for veterinary use, the side-effects, adverse effects and contraindications are for the most part, extrapolated from human literature. Since the number of pets treated with these drugs is relatively small, new problems may yet arise and each pet should be closely monitored for any undesirable or unexpected effects on health or behavior. For some drugs, the physical and behavioral effects seen in the first few days, whether problematic or desirable, may be a temporary side-effect that could resolve with ongoing therapy.

Antihistamines: how are they used in behavior therapy?

Antihistamines may be useful in behavior therapy for their antipruritic and sedative effects. They have been used in pets for sedation prior to car travel, for pets that are waking through the night, and for some forms of compulsive scratching and self trauma. Antihistamines are sedating, especially during the first few days of therapy, and are contraindicated in pets that might be prone to urine retention (e.g. prostate disease), glaucoma, thyroid disease, heart disease, or liver disease.

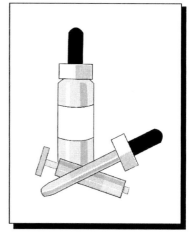

Anti-anxiety drugs

Depending on the type of drug utilized, anti-anxiety drugs may have an effect within hours of starting therapy, or may take a week or longer to achieve their effect. Side-effects vary with the type and class of drug being used, ranging from increased appetite and sedation to agitation with little or no sedation. Any anti-anxiety drug can reduce fear to such a point that some pets become more confident, bold and aggressive, especially with members of their own species.

What are benzodiazepines and how are they used?

For anxiety, urine marking, noise phobias, fear-induced aggression, generalized fear, waking at night, and some panic disorders, anti-anxiety drugs such as the benzodiazepines (e.g. diazepam, alprazolam) might be used. Because of their short onset of action and relatively short duration, these drugs are primarily used for situations that might produce temporary anxiety, and less frequently for long term on-going problems. Because of potential dependency effects, gradual withdrawal is recommended after continuous therapy. Liver function should be monitored prior to, and during therapy because of potential liver damage, particularly in cats.

Benzodiazepines may cause sedation and appetite stimulation, and some pets might even become more agitated or anxious when therapy is first initiated. These effects usually resolve within a few days. Be certain to report any unexpected behavior changes, or any medical changes such as decreased appetite or vomiting to your veterinarian immediately.

What is buspirone and how is it used?

This is a relatively new anti-anxiety drug that is used for some forms of fear, anxiety and urine marking. It is non-sedating, does not stimulate appetite and has not been associated with major side-effects. As with other anti-anxiety drugs, buspirone may remove the inhibitions associated with fear and could lead to an increase in aggression. Buspirone may take several weeks to take effect and is therefore not useful for the treatment of temporary situational anxieties but may be used on a "as needed" basis.

What is propranolol and how is it used?

Recently, in human medicine it has been found that the heart drug, propranolol can be useful at reducing anxiety without causing sedation. The drug works by blocking some of the physical effects that accompany fear. The heart rate is slowed, blood pressure is lowered, and the tremors, sweating, or diarrhea that might be associated with fear are reduced. The theory is that if the pet cannot exhibit the physical effects of fear, the behavior signs are less likely to be exhibited. Propranolol should not be used in pets with heart, respiratory or liver problems.

Antidepressants: when are they used?

Most anti-depressants work by causing changes in a brain chemical called serotonin. This chemical is vital in transmitting signals between brain cells (neurotransmitter). However antidepressants may also affect other neurotransmitters such as noradrenaline so that the uses and side-effects may be somewhat different among the antidepressants. The only antidepressant licensed for veterinary use is clomipramine. It can be used for separation anxiety as well as compulsive and repetitive disorders, phobias and anxiety disorders. It is also licensed in Australia for use in cats with urine spraying. Antidepressants have also been used for urinary incontinence, sleep disorders and some forms of aggression. Occasionally tricyclic antidepressants such as amitriptyline may also be used in chronic painful or inflammatory conditions such as feline interstitial cystitis. These drugs are generally used on a long term basis. They take from several days to several weeks to reach full effect. Side effects may include a dry mouth, urine retention, sedation or constipation especially during the first few days of therapy. Additionally they may cause tachycardia, an increase in heart rate. If your pet has any evidence of heart disease, an electrocardiogram may be advisable prior to use.

A newer class of antidepressants known as selective serotonin re-uptake inhibitors include drugs such as fluoxetine and paroxetine. They are most useful for compulsive, anxiety, phobic and panic disorders, urine marking and perhaps some forms of aggression. They seldom cause sedation and have few side-effects, but may occasionally cause restlessness, agitation, insomnia, weight loss and gastrointestinal upset in humans. They can take up to a month to achieve therapeutic effect.

Progestins: when are they used?

The female hormones, progestins, has been used to treat a variety of behavior problems. They have a general calming effect, and can be used in the treatment of aggression, urine marking, and compulsive grooming. They are also used to reduce male behaviors such as marking and mounting. Progestins may lead to serious adverse effects including diabetes and suppression of the bone marrow, adrenal gland and immune system. Therefore, they are generally used only in those cases where no other treatment is likely to be effective.

Sedatives: when are they used?

Sedatives have generalized effects on behavior, causing primarily as the name indicates, sedation. They can be useful for the treatment of excessive vocalization, noise phobias, sleep disorders and to control the anxiety and excitability associated with events such as car rides, nail trimming or veterinary visits. They are also effective in preventing nausea, as anti-nauseants. They should not be used in patients with seizures, liver disease or heart problems, and can lead to a dry mouth or urine retention.

Stimulants: when are they used?

Stimulants such as methylphenidate are used for attention deficit disorders in people. Although rare, some dogs that have short attention spans, are difficult to train, display repetitive behaviors, or are extremely active and have difficulty settling down may also have attention deficit disorders. Since these drugs are stimulants they generally cause an increase in heart rate and activity level. However in hyperactive pets, they actually have the opposite effect, leading to a calmer pet with a slower heart rate.

Anti-convulsants: when are they used?

Anticonvulsants such as phenobarbital and some benzodiazepines, are used to control seizures. Since certain parts of the brain control behavior, it is likely that a seizure in these parts of the brain could lead to sudden and bizarre changes in behavior that come and go without any apparent stimulus. If a seizure focus is suspected to be the cause of unusual behavior, anticonvulsants may be effective. Anticonvulsants have also been used on their own, or in combination with other medications for some anxiety, panic and sleep disorders.

Selegiline: when is it used?

Selegiline is licensed for use in dogs in both Canada and the United States for the treatment of cognitive dysfunction syndrome (CDS) as well as the control of clinical signs of Cushing's disease. This is a condition where an overactive pituitary gland causes the adrenal gland to produce too much cortisone. Signs of cognitive dysfunction may be considered to be those of senility disorientation, decreased responsiveness to owners, altered sleep-wake cycles and house-soiling. The drug known as an MAOB inhibitor may help neurotransmission of dopamine and noradrenaline, which may decline with age. It may also help cognitive dysfunction by protecting brain cells, and decreasing free radicals (see 'behavior problems of older pets' for more details).

Natural remedies and supplements

This is a broad topic that includes a variety of therapeutic options including herbal remedies, homeopathic remedies, neutraceuticals and supplements, as well as therapeutic touch and acupuncture. There are no controlled studies to show that any of these treatments are effective in pets. The same might be said for most of the drugs mentioned above, but most of these have been proven to be effective in human behavior therapy. In addition, because these products contain "natural" ingredients, there can be great variation in purity, quality, level of activity, and efficacy from manufacturer to manufacturer and from batch to batch.

Ginkgo biloba

Ginkgo biloba may alter a number of neurotransmitter systems in the brain, including acetylcholine, serotonin and norepinephrine and may have antioxidant effects. It may be effective at enhancing blood flow to the brain. It may be useful for senior pets with cognitive decline.

Kava kava

Kava kava may aid in the relief of mild anxiety. In pets there have been no controlled studies but it has been recommended for anxiety, as a sedative or muscle relaxant or as a sleep aid, and for the treatment of overgrooming in cats. Kava should not be combined with other anti-anxiety medications. It may cause gastrointestinal upset and should be avoided in patients with liver disease.

St. John's Wort

St. John's form has been suggested as a natural alternative to antidepressants. There have been claims of its use in dogs and cats, but no controlled studies. There are the same contraindications as with other antidepressants. In addition, there may be increased sensitivity to sunlight. It is said to sedate, reduce anxiety, improve mood and sleep and reduce inflammation and may be useful in compulsive disorders. As with pharmaceutical antidepressants it has been suggested that a period of three weeks or longer may be required to achieve therapeutic effects.

Valerian

Valerian has been used as a natural "tranquilizer" and muscle relaxant in animals, but controlled studies are not available. Valerian is not meant to be used long term, but may have benefit as a treatment for helping pets sleep through the night, exposure to periodic stressors, such as travel, thunderstorm phobias, and acute anxiety. Several weeks may be needed to achieve success.

Melatonin

Melatonin is produced in the pineal gland and is secreted into the blood at high levels during the night and at low levels during the day. Melatonin may be useful to help dogs with sleep disorders and in the treatment of fears and phobias such as thunderstorm and fireworks phobias. It may be used alone or combined with other medications such as antidepressants.

Diet and Tryptophan

It has been suggested that a change in diet can also alter behavior. Although some reports indicate that there may be adverse effects of supplements and preservatives in pet foods, there is no evidence to support this premise. For the most part these additives increase the nutritional balance and safety of pet foods. In addition, one would expect more signs (e.g. dermatologic, gastrointestinal) than just behavioral changes if there were an adverse reaction to the food or one of its ingredients. An elimination diet (i.e. one that did not contain the suspected offending ingredients) could be used to test this hypothesis.

One common suggestion has been that a reduction of protein in the diet may lead to a decrease in aggression, but this has not been validated. In a recent canine study, the level of protein (high vs. low) in the diet or addition of l-tryptophan had no effect on fearfulness or hyperactivity but a combination of low protein diets with tryptophan supplementation were shown to lower territoriality scores while high protein diets without tryptophan supplementation were most likely to lead to dominance aggression.

Homeopathic and Bach flower Remedies

The basic principles of modern homeopathy is that like cures like. The theory is that a patient's symptoms can be cured by a product that would produce the same behavioral or physical symptoms in a healthy individual. The homeopathic remedy is prepared by repeatedly diluting the substance to render it non-toxic. Although the substance may be undetectable after dilution, the remedy is said to contain the vibrational energy essences that match the patterns present in the ailing patient. These remedies may be made from plants, minerals, drugs, or animal substances. Bach flower remedies are intended to improve the emotional state of the pet, using minute dilutions of plant essences. Rescue Remedy is a combination of 5 flower essences intended to counter panic following emotional or physical stress. Calms and Calms Forte are also combination homeopathic remedies that have been recommended as an alternative to psychotropic drugs. Although there is no scientific evidence to support any claims of efficacy, the extreme dilution of the ingredients, are likely to render them entirely safe.

CHILDREN & PETS

The birth of a baby or adoption of a new child is associated with a great deal of anxiety, excitement, and stress for not only the family, but also the family pet. Some dogs and cats can have a difficult time adjusting to these changes, especially if this is your first child, but preparation and planning will help.

How is my pet likely to respond to the new arrival?

There are so many different variables that it is impossible to accurately predict the way that any pet might get along with children. However, there are considerations that give some insight into how your pet might react.

How much exposure has your pet had previously to children? How has your pet reacted when it has been exposed? The most serious concern is the pet that has previously reacted aggressively or fearfully with children. If there have been previous problems you should consult with a veterinary behaviorist to determine the situations that have previously led to aggression, and the safest way, if any, to make the transition. If the pet's previous problems were with a specific child, a specific age group or under specific circumstances, it may be possible to design a program so that the previous situations that resulted in aggression can be treated and resolved prior to the arrival of your new child.

The next most serious concern is the pet that has had little or no exposure to young children or babies. A lack of early socialization to children may lead to some initial anxiety or fear associated with the sights, sounds and odors of the new child. If there are no unpleasant experiences when the child first arrives, and the first few introductions are made positive, there may be no problems. Even if a pet has shown no previous problems when interacting with children, keeping all introductions positive will help to get the relationship between your pet and your new child off to a good start.

One final concern is the growth and development of your child. As your child progresses from being carried to one that rolls, crawls, and begins to walk, and so on through childhood, some pets may have trouble adapting to one or more of these changes. Fear, dominance challenges, possessive displays, and playful behaviors could result in aggression. Anxiety or fear could lead to anorexia, compulsive disorders (e.g. flank sucking, acral lick dermatitis), or destructiveness (e.g. house-soiling, marking, chewing, digging).

What can we do to prepare for the new arrival?

Behavior problems (destructiveness, house-soiling, compulsive disorders, increased demands for attention, generalized anxiety) may not develop directly from the arrival of the child, but rather from the changes in the household, associated with the new arrival. With nine months or more to prepare for a baby's arrival, the best way to minimize problems and help the pet to cope is to make changes gradually so that they have been completed prior to the arrival of the child. Consider any changes that you may need to make in the pet's schedule, housing, play, exercise, or attention, so that adjustments can begin to be made well before the baby's arrival. Set up the nursery in advance and if the pet is to be kept out of the room, access should be denied before the child's arrival. Otherwise, if your intention is to allow your pet to continue to enter the room when supervised, begin to accompany your pet into the nursery, so that it can adapt to the new odors and new setup. The dog should be allowed to investigate the baby's room, blankets, and new furniture, and praised or given a small food treat so that it can develop a positive association with each of these new cues.

For dogs, reviewing or upgrading obedience skills is essential so that you can safely and effectively control your dog in all situations. Obedience training should be reviewed every day, in a variety of locations and circumstances. Practice each command in different rooms of the home, in the yard, while out on walks, and when visitors come to the home. Concentrate on those commands that are presently the least successful, using prompts and rewards to achieve success and then gradually shaping the response so that the pet stays for progressively longer times, comes from greater distances and will heel and follow even when there are distractions. Any existing behavior problems should be resolved before the arrival of your baby.

Some pets might become anxious of, or fearful toward, any of the new and different stimuli associated with the sights, sounds, or odors of the new child. New activities associated with childcare can be practiced in front of pets so that they can become familiar with them. Tape recordings or videos of babies crying, holding a doll wrapped in a blanket, taking your dog for a walk beside a stroller or baby carriage, or even going through the motions of changing a diaper and applying baby powder will simulate some of the experiences to which your pet will soon be exposed. If there is any sign of anxiety associated with any of these situations, then more formal reward-based training should be practiced and repeated until the pet exhibits no problems in the presence of the stimuli. By providing a favored chew toy, giving a food reward, or providing extra affection during these activities, your pet may actually learn to enjoy these new stimuli.

Once your pet shows no fear or anxiety in some or all of these situations,

you may want to enlist the help of some friends or relatives with young children. Dogs can be taken for a walk while the child is rolled in the stroller or carriage. A baby can be carried around the home or nursed in the presence of the dog and children should be encouraged to play at the opposite end of a room or yard from where the dog is situated. The dog must be well controlled, preferably with a leash and head halter, and given food rewards and/or play to keep the association positive. A wire-meshed muzzle could also be applied to ensure additional safety, especially when being exposed to new situations. By the end of the visit it may even be possible to let the dog interact with the child but only if it remains friendly and shows no fear or anxiety.

For cats, the most important adaptation is to any changes that will be needed in the cat's home. Although fear and anxiety to the sights and sounds of a new baby are possible, adapting to changes in the household are often the most trying for cats. For example, obtaining new furniture, altering the cat's feeding, sleeping, elimination or play areas, and trying to keep the cat out of certain locations such as the crib, should all be considered before the arrival of the baby. To reduce the chances of the cat marking new furniture, the first few introductions to the new areas should be well supervised. Once your cat has investigated and rubbed against the new furniture, spraying is far less likely. Similarly, when the crib or cradle is first set up, the cat may wish to mark the area, or investigate, or even to sleep in the crib. booby-trapping areas (see 'controlling undesirable behavior in cats – the role of punishment') can teach the cat to stay away from the areas of concern, well before the baby arrives.

Remember, each of these techniques are intended to help the pet adapt to changes in the household or lifestyle before the arrival of the baby. Once the baby arrives, there will be far less time to deal with the needs of the pet, and there will be additional variables to which your pet will need to adapt. Even if your pet does begin to exhibit fear or anxiety, during this pre-arrival training, such anxiety will not be associated with the presence of the child. The cat will have no reason to develop animosity to the new child.

What should be done when the baby arrives?

Progress gradually, avoid any situations that might lead to fear, anxiety or discomfort in the baby's presence and make all associations and experiences in the baby's presence positive. Maintain or even increase the amount and type of training, exercise, and play.

Even a curious and affectionate pet may have some problems adjusting to the new arrival. Jumping up to greet when the baby is being carried, barking during the baby's sleep or nap times, raiding the diaper pail, licking the baby's face, or cuddling up to sleep against an infant who is still unable to shift position are just a few of the concerns and potential problems that pet owners may need to deal with. Keep your pet's nails well trimmed. Supervise all interactions between the pet and baby. Keep the pet out of the baby's room during nap and sleeping times. Ensure that your dog is well controlled and responsive to obedience training commands. For some dogs, leaving a leash attached (preferably to a head collar) is a useful way to ensure additional control.

The most important aspect of retraining is to reward the pet for obedient and relaxed behavior in the presence of the child. In many households there will be less time and energy available for the pet. While focused on the child, or attending to the chores associated with parenthood, the pet may be ignored, disciplined for approaching too close, or confined to a different area of the home. Your pet may still receive its play, exercise, affection, food and attention, but often not until the baby is finally asleep or is under the care of some other family member. Many pets soon learn that the presence of the baby is a time for inattention, confinement, or even punishment, while the absence of the baby is a cue for "good things" to happen. This must be reversed. Every effort should be made to allow the pet into the room for food, play or affection when the baby is present. Feed the pet when the baby is being fed, or have another family member give affection to the pet, play with the pet, or do some reward training (stay, go to your mat) when the child is in the room. Take your dog outdoors for play or a walk when you are taking the child out. The goal is to teach the pet that positives or "good things" are most likely to happen in the presence of the child and to avoid any negative association with the child.

What should be done if aggression arises?

Such behavior is very upsetting, regardless of its reasons. An immediate decision on whether to keep and work with the pet or remove it from the home must be made. Dogs targeting children may be motivated by fear, dominance, possessive, redirected, playful or predatory aggression. Such aggression (particularly predatory and fear) may arise immediately when the child is brought into the home, or may begin as the child becomes more mobile (e.g. fear, predation, possessive, play) or when the child grows a little older and begins to challenge the dog (fear, dominance, possessive, play). Cat aggression toward children can be fear-induced, redirected, territorial, or play/predatory. For most aggression cases, especially those directed toward children, the guidance and advice of a behaviorist is strongly suggested since it will be necessary to make an accurate diagnosis, determine the prognosis (the chances of safe and effective treatment) and guide you through a treatment program. Although some cases may be treated quickly and safely, most cases require extensive precautions to prevent injuries and a great deal of time, effort and commitment. Regardless of reason for aggression, biting dogs should be leashed (attached to the owner) preferably with a head collar, muzzled and closely supervised or crated in the presence of small children. Aggressive cats should be confined away from small children except when they are in a carrier, on a leash and harness, or well supervised and either calm or otherwise occupied with food or toys.

How can I teach my children to be safe around pets?

Although there are no rules that will guarantee safety, there are important guidelines that can be followed to reduce the chances of problems and the risk of injury. The first rule of thumb is to avoid doing anything to the dog that you might not want your child to do. This would include physical punishment, rough play, or teasing. Children must be taught how to interact with and handle their family pet including how to approach, pat or lift small pets. Wherever possible, play sessions and training should include the children with the supervision of a parent. This can begin from the time the dog is a puppy by attending puppy classes and obedience classes that include all members of the family. If the pet has not previously exhibited possessiveness of food or toys, the adults can practice with the children approaching the dog at its food bowl, patting and giving favored treats, along with teaching the give or drop command for favored treats. It may be best to use a leash and head halter during this training if there is any concern that the dog might resist or become anxious.

While your dog may appear to tolerate or even enjoy handling from people of all ages, you must teach your child how to meet, greet and handle animals. The child will be safest if taught to avoid hugging, tugging on the leash, collar or tail and handling around the eyes, ears and muzzle. Even if the dog is familiar it is best to avoid reaching toward the head or face to face greetings.

Children must also be taught that strange pets may not behave in the same way as their family pet. A simple rule is that the child should NEVER approach another family's pet without being given permission and then to approach slowly and avoid reaching for the head and face. Children should be taught to avoid pets entirely if they are displaying any signs that might indicate fearfulness (shaking, ears back, tail between legs, crouch, trying to escape) or aggression (growling, showing teeth, barking, hair standing on end). Although most children would be tempted to run away from an aggressive dog, they should be taught to stand still like a tree, with the arms against the body, and avoid eye contact and yelling or screaming. If the child is on the ground they should curl up and cover their head and ears with their arms and fists, and remain still until the dog moves away. Any threatening dog or bite should be immediately reported to an adult.

COMPULSIVE, STEREOTYPIC & DISPLACEMENT DISORDERS

What is a displacement behavior?

Displacement behaviors arise from situations of either conflict or frustration. When an animal may be motivated to perform two or more behaviors that are in conflict with each other (e.g. approach-withdrawal, greeting but fear of being punished). The inability to perform both of the strongly motivated behaviors can lead to conflict resulting in the performance of a displacement behavior. Similarly, when an animal is prevented or "frustrated" from performing a highly motivated behavior (e.g. territorial aggression but dog is behind a barricade) a displacement behavior can also be observed. These are usually normal behaviors that are shown at an inappropriate time, appearing out of context for the occasion. Overgrooming in the form of acral lick dermatitis, yawning, circling, and vocalizations may be performed in stressful situations as displacement behaviors.

By comparison, when an animal is placed in a situation of either conflict or frustration, the behavior may be redirected toward an alternative target. This may be the case when a cat is sitting on the windowsill and is aroused by cats on the property. However because access to the stimulus is prevented, the aggression may be directed to a cat or person that approaches. This is known as redirected behavior.

What is a stereotypy?

Stereotypes are repetitive behavior patterns without obvious goal or function. They are usually derived from normal behaviors. Stereotypic behaviors may be performed as components of displacement behaviors or compulsive disorders. They can also be due to physiological changes such as might occur with a neurological disorder (circling, head bobbing). Examples of stereotypic behavior include pacing and excessive grooming.

What is a compulsive disorder?

When an animal is repeatedly placed in a state of conflict, displacement behaviors may begin to be manifested during any state of stress or arousal. Eventually, the behavior may become compulsive as the pet loses control over initiating or terminating it. The compulsive behavior may then occur in situations where the pet is minimally aroused. Compulsive behaviors are often derived from normal behavior patterns but appear to be abnormal because they are excessive, exceedingly intense, or performed out of context. Although some compulsive disorders are repetitive and may therefore be referred to as stereotypic (wool sucking, pacing, tail chasing), other compulsive disorders such as freezing or staring are not truly repetitive.

There may be a genetic predisposition to compulsive behaviors. For example, flank sucking is most commonly seen in Doberman pinschers, spinning in bull terriers, and fly chasing in miniature schnauzers. In cats, wool sucking is observed more commonly in oriental breeds.

Although many compulsive behaviors arise spontaneously as a response to conflict or anxiety, behaviors may become compulsive or stereotypic because they have been conditioned. For example, the owner who gives the young pet attention when it playfully chases its tail or the beam of a flashlight may encourage and reinforce the performance of the behavior. Similarly, owners that offer food or a toy in an effort to disrupt the behavior may also be rewarding the very problem they wish to stop.

In each case it is essential to diagnose, rule out or treat any medical condition that might contribute to the problem. Some compulsive disorders have a component of self-mutilation (e.g. acral lick dermatitis – tail biting) that will require medical treatment. If the problem persists after all medical problems are diagnosed, treated, or ruled out, then behavioral modification, environmental manipulation and drug therapy may also be indicated.

In dogs, compulsive behaviors include acral lick dermatitis, flank sucking, pacing, circling, incessant or rhythmic barking, fly snapping or chasing unseen objects, freezing and staring, polydypsia (excessive drinking), sucking, licking, or chewing on objects (or owners), tonguing or licking the air and other forms of self mutilation. In cats, excessive sucking and chewing, hunting and pouncing at unseen prey, running and chasing, paw shaking, freezing, excessive vocalization, self-directed aggression such as tail chasing or foot chewing, over-grooming or barbering of hair and possibly feline hyperesthesia may all be manifestations of conflict, and may become compulsive disorders in time.

How should compulsive disorders be treated?

Since some stereotypic or compulsive behaviors are initiated by underlying medical problems, a complete medical work-up is always the first step. Behaviors must be evaluated individually since not all require treatment. In fact, treatment may only be necessary if the behavior poses health risks to the animal or seriously annoys the owner. For some pets, the compulsive behavior may be the most practical and acceptable outlet for reducing stress or resolving conflict in their home environment. For example, if flank sucking causes no physical harm, but occupies and calms the dog, then the compulsive behavior may be preferable to the use of calming drugs, or the development of other disorders (acral lick dermatitis, destructiveness, excessive vocalization).

Reducing stress or finding methods of decreasing the sources of arousal and conflict are the first aspect of treatment that should be explored. Inconsistent training may lead to problems in the relationship between pet and owner. The environment should be closely examined to ensure that the pet has sufficient stimulation, particularly when the owners are frequently absent or otherwise occupied. This must include sufficient exercise, play, and social attention, as well as appropriate toys. Obedience training may be helpful and the owner should be cautioned that inappropriate punishment could actually intensify the problem rather than correct it.

Behavioral modification is most appropriate when owners can identify and predict those situations and times when compulsive behaviors are likely to arise. They can then initiate an alternative activity (before the compulsive behavior is overt) that is incompatible with the problem behavior, such as play, training, feeding, or providing a chew toy. Finding the most appealing and durable toys for the pet including toys which require manipulation to release food treats, feeding frozen food and treats, and altering the environment (e.g. hiding treats for the pet to find) may help to keep the pet occupied and distracted at times when the compulsive disorder might otherwise be displayed (see 'destructiveness' and 'behavior management products'). Owners that have been rewarding the problem must remove all attention or rewards. When the behavior is exhibited in the owners presence, inattention can be given by turning or walking away, or you could utilize some form of remote interruption device, to ensure that there is no positive consequence for the behavior. These devices (ultrasonics, water gun, siren, remote citronella collar, or leash and halter) may also allow you the opportunity to direct the pet into a normal acceptable behavior.

Denying the pet access to the focus of its obsession has mixed results. For example, a bandage or an Elizabethan collar may allow acral lick dermatitis or feline psychogenic alopecia to heal, but once the collar is removed, most cases relapse. In many cases, restricting access will worsen the problem by increasing anxiety or arousal. Instead, the underlying cause of the anxiety or conflict should be identified, removed or the animal desensitized to the stimulus.

Drug therapy may be extremely useful for pets with stereotypes just as it is in humans with obsessive-compulsive disorders. Since lowered serotonin and increased dopamine levels may be associated with some compulsive disorders, drugs that bring about a normalization of one or both of these neurotransmitters (e.g. clomipramine, sertraline, paroxetine, fluoxetine) may be effective in the treatment of these disorders. A short course of therapy with anti-anxiety drugs may also be useful when the pet must be exposed to a potentially stressful or anxiety producing situation (new home, dramatic change in schedule, new baby).

What is canine acral lick dermatitis?

Acral lick dermatitis is when dogs repeatedly lick at specific sites on one or more of their limbs, often causing significant damage. Large breeds such as Doberman pinschers, Great Danes, German shepherds, Labrador retrievers, Golden retrievers and Irish setters are most commonly affected. Underlying medical abnormalities (e.g. arthritis, fracture, and skin disorders) may initiate or contribute to the problem. The condition arises when the pet is exposed to chronic stress or recurrent situations of conflict, and this leads to excessive licking. It has also been suggested that self-injurious behaviors such as acral lick dermatitis may arise in situations of understimulation. The area becomes raw and itchy which further stimulates the dog to lick and chew.

With acral lick dermatitis, treatment must be directed at both the behavior disorder and the skin trauma. Therefore even with behavior therapy, treatment of the skin condition is also necessary. Medical therapy might consist of treatment with long term antibiotics, anti-inflammatory agents, and preventing access to the area until the lesion heals. Behavioral management and drug therapy is much the same as for other compulsive disorders.

What is canine flank sucking?
Flank sucking is when the dog takes a section of flank skin into its mouth and holds the position. Since the Doberman pinscher is most commonly affected, a hereditary component is likely. If the sucking does not cause significant lesions and does not interfere with the apparent health or welfare of the pet, flank sucking may be an acceptable "coping" mechanism. When the behavior does cause physical damage or becomes so compulsive as to contribute to other behavior problems (decreased eating, aggressive toward owners when approached during sucking) then treatment is necessary. Behavior management and drug therapy is the same as for other compulsive disorders.

What is tail chasing or spinning in dogs?
Compulsive tail chasing may be a displacement or compulsive disorder in some dogs, but could also be a type of epileptic disorder, or be due to pain or medical illness. Some cases such as those seen in bull terriers may exhibit a more intense spinning or whirling behavior. Other concurrent behavior problems such as aggression have been reported in "spinning" bull terriers. In some cases, the problem may have started as play behavior that was rewarded by the owner. Once underlying medical problems are treated and an epileptic disorder has been ruled out, behavior and drug therapy is much the same as for other compulsive disorders.

What is feline psychogenic alopecia?
Alopecia or hair loss can result when cats over-groom and remove fur. Over-grooming can take the form of excessive licking, or the pulling out of tufts of hair. The diagnosis of psychogenic alopecia as a compulsive disorder is reserved for those cases in which no underlying medical problem is evident. Most cats with alopecia have an underlying skin disorder such as fleas, flea bite hypersensitivity, inhalant allergies, food allergies, parasites, infections or dysfunction of internal organs or the endocrine system. A steroid trial and an 8 week or longer food trial may often be recommended before considering the diagnosis to be purely behavioral. Cats normally are fastidious groomers and as much as 30 – 50% of their time awake is spent performing some type of grooming behavior. As with other compulsive disorders, feline psychogenic alopecia may begin as a displacement behavior arising from situations of conflict, frustration or anxiety, but might in time become compulsive.

Increasing interactive play with owners (chase toys, training) and increasing environmental stimulation (play centers, chew toys, food or catnip packed toys, kitty videos) can all be utilized to help calm and settle the cat. Toys should be kept out of the cat's reach until put out daily by the owner. Then the toys should be rotated every 1 – 3 days to provide different play items. When home, the owner should provide periods of interactive play and perhaps even a short training session to keep the cat occupied and focused. Attention should never be given to the cat when the behavior is exhibited. In fact, inattention or some form of remote punishment device, may be the best way to ensure that no rewards are given. Remote devices such as a water rifle, a can of compressed air, or an ultrasonic or audible alarm may also serve to interrupt or deter the undesirable behavior without causing fear of the owner. As soon as the undesirable behavior ceases, the owner should immediately engage the cat in some alternative acceptable behavior (e.g. play, chew toys). The owner should also try to identify environmental or social changes that may be contributing to anxiety and the behavior.

If behavioral therapy alone is not successful, drug treatment is often initiated, using antihistamines, anti-anxiety drugs, or antidepressants.

What is feline hyperesthesia?

Feline hyperesthesia is a poorly understood condition that has also been referred to as rippling skin syndrome, rolling skin syndrome, or twitchy skin syndrome. It may be a compulsive disorder but it is also possible that there is an underlying medical or neurological cause, behavioral cause or that the problem arises in situations of high arousal or anxiety. The normal response of many cats to having their back scratched can include rippling of the skin, an arched back and varying degrees of vocalization. In hyperesthesia, the affected cat may have a more exaggerated response to touching, rubbing or scratching of the back. This behavior may then become a compulsive disorder as the frequency increases, the response becomes more intense and the signs begin to appear with little or no apparent stimuli. In addition to rolling skin, muscle spasms and vocalization, the cat may have dilated pupils, and may seem to startle, hallucinate and dash away. Some cats will defecate as they run away. There may also be some grooming or biting at the flank, tail, or back displayed along with the above behaviors.

Behavioral management requires the identification and control of the types of handling that lead to the behavior. Avoiding or minimizing these types of handling, or desensitizing and counter-conditioning techniques so that the cat learns to "tolerate" these stimuli, may be successful at reducing the cat's level of arousal. Drugs might include those for seizure disorders, antidepressants for compulsive disorders or anti-anxiety drugs to reduce conflict and anxiety.

What is fear?

Fear is a physiologic, behavioral and emotional reaction to stimuli that an animal encounters. The physiologic reaction results in an increase in heart rate, increased respiratory rate (panting), sweating, trembling, pacing and possibly urination and defecation. Behaviorally an animal will exhibit changes in body posture and activity when afraid. The animal may engage in an avoidance response such as fleeing or hiding. A fearful animal may assume body postures that are protective such as lowering of the body and head, placing the ears closer to the head, widened eyes, and tail tucked under the body. If the animal perceives a threat, the response can also include elements of defensive aggression. Whether an animal fights or flees when fearful or defensive depends on its genetic predisposition and the environment that it

is in. The emotional reaction in animals can be difficult to gauge because animals are non-verbal. However, by observation of body postures and facial expressions it is possible to conclude that an animal is afraid.

Is fear ever an abnormal response in animals?

In many situations it is "acceptable and understandable" for an animal to be afraid. However, there are times when animals exhibit fear when it is maladaptive or dangerous for humans. When animals are frightened they may become aggressive (fight), run away (flight), or stay still (freeze). The response a pet exhibits depends on the pet's personality, the type of stimulus, previous experience with the stimulus, whether it is on its own property (where it is more likely to fight), whether it is in the presence of offspring or family members (where it is more likely to fight), or whether it is cornered or restrained and unable to escape (where it is more likely to fight).

What is a phobia?

This is an intense response to a situation that the animal perceives as fear inducing. The response is out of proportion to the stimulus and is maladaptive. Common phobias in animals involve noises and places. Phobic responses have physiologic, behavioral and emotional responses similar to fear, but they are extremely exaggerated.

What is anxiety?

The human definition of anxiety is a diffuse feeling of impending danger or threat. It appears that animals can exhibit this diffuse type of anxiety, often manifested as generalized anxious behavior in either specific situations (the veterinary hospital, new locations) or in a non-specific way (anything out of the routine schedule or environment). Anxiety is manifested by some of the same physiologic signs as fear, but also may be displayed as displacement or redirected behaviors, destructive behaviors, or excessive vocalization, and may become stereotypic or compulsive over time.

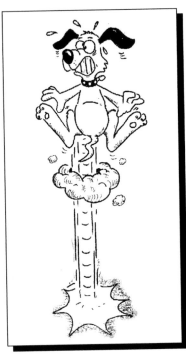

What types of stimuli might trigger fears, phobias or anxieties?

The triggers for these behaviors are as varied as there are breeds of dogs and cats. Animals may be frightened of people, other animals, places or things. Others may only respond with fear or phobia in one particular situation such as toward a thunderstorm.

What causes fearful, phobic or anxious responses?

Sometimes fear is the result of an early experience that was unpleasant or perceived by the animal as unpleasant. If the fearful response was successful at chasing away the stimulus, or if the pet escaped from the stimulus, the behavior has been rewarded. Owners that try to calm their pet by providing treats or affection may be rewarding the fearful behavior. Also, it should be noted that punishment, in close association with exposure to a stimulus might further cause fear and anxiety toward that stimulus.

It does not take an unpleasant experience however for fear to develop. Any stimuli (people, places, sights, sounds, etc.) that a dog or cat has not been exposed to during its sensitive period of development, which is up to 3 months in dogs and 2 months in cats, may become a fear evoking stimulus. For example, the dog or cat that is exposed to adults, but not children during development may become fearful when first exposed to the sights, sounds or odors of young children. The pet's genetics also contributes to its level of fears and phobias to stimuli.

Phobic responses can occur from just one exposure or gradually increase over continued exposure. In many cases of anxiety, neurotransmitter (brain chemical) function and levels may be altered and contribute to the overall behavior. Again, learning or the consequences that follow the phobic response (rewards, escape, punishment) may aggravate the problem.

Illness, pain and the effects of aging may lead to an increase in fear or anxiety in situations where there was previously little or no evidence. These changes may change the way a pet perceives or responds to a stimulus. Age related changes in the brain (cognitive decline) or in the sensory system (hearing, sight), arthritis, diseases that affect the hormonal system such as an increase or decrease in thyroid hormones or an overactive pituitary gland (Cushing's) and organ decline (liver, kidneys) are just a few examples of health and age related problems that might contribute to increasing fear and anxiety.

Is it possible to prevent fears, phobias and anxieties?
A good program of socialization and exposure to many new and novel things while an animal is young can be helpful in preventing fears and phobias. However, in the phenomena of "one trial" learning, an event is so traumatic that only one exposure can create fears, phobias or anxieties.

Owner responses when their pet experiences a new situation that could potentially be frightening are important. Calm reassurances as long as the pet is not acting fearful, happy cheerful tones, and relaxed body postures of owners help pets experience new things without fear. Bringing along treats and play toys and giving them to the pet when it enters new environments (e.g. veterinary clinic, schoolyard) or when it meets new people or other pets can help turn the situation into one that is positive. Conversely, anxiety or apprehension on the part of the owners or fear evoking training techniques such as punishment may serve to increase the pets' fear and anxiety. Knowing your pet and their individual temperament will also determine what situations you can and should expose your pet to.

How can these problems of fears and phobias be treated?
Each time your pet is exposed to an anxiety, fear, or phobia-inducing situation and cannot be made to calm down, the problem is likely to worsen. Finding a way to control, relax, calm, or distract your pet in the presence of the stimulus is needed to correct the problem and to teach your pet that there is nothing to be feared. An owner who is calm and in control reduces

the fear and anxiety associated with new stimuli and situations. For most cases of fear, behavior modification techniques, where the pet is exposed to mild levels of the stimuli and rewarded for non-fearful behavior, are utilized. For low levels of fear or anxiety, especially when the pet is being exposed to new stimuli, many pets will calm down with continued exposure, as long as nothing is done to aggravate the fear. These retraining techniques are discussed in 'behavior modification – reducing fear and anxiety – desensitization, counter-conditioning and flooding'. Consequences that reinforce the fear (inadvertent rewards or retreat of the stimulus) or aggravate the fear (punishment) must be identified and removed. Drug therapy may also be a useful adjunct to behavior therapy techniques and may be necessary in the treatment of some phobias.

REWARDS – LEARNING & REINFORCEMENT

The best way to train your pet is through the proper use of positive reinforcement and rewards while avoiding punishment. The goal of training is to "learn" the proper task and/or behavior. The training sequence is to give a command, to get the desired response and to use a reward to mark and reinforce the correct response. Generally the most difficult aspect of training is to find techniques that immediately get the desired response after each command (see 'basic training' for more details).

How does learning take place?

Learning occurs by establishing the relationship between behavior and consequences. There can be different possible outcomes of behavior. The relationship between behavior and consequences can be positive or negative.

When there is a positive relationship between behavior and consequences, the more your pet performs a certain behavior, the more of the consequence it receives. If there is a negative relationship between behavior and outcome, the more of the behavior the pet does the less of the consequence it receives. When we increase a behavior by removing a stimulus this is known as negative reinforcement. For example, when a dog barks at an intruder (such as the postman) the barking has been reinforced because the stimulus (the postman) was removed. Negative reinforcement can also be used for training when a pull on a head halter or a spray of citronella is terminated as soon as the desirable behavior is observed.

What is positive reinforcement?

Positive reinforcement is anything that increases the likelihood that a behavior will be repeated. There is a positive relationship between behavior and consequence. The more the pet does a behavior, the more consequence it gets and what it gets is good. This makes that behavior increase.

What kinds of things will a dog consider positive reinforcement?

They will differ from dog to dog. For some it may be a pat on the head, a play session, a fun toy, a walk, or a food treat. The key is to select the reward that motivates your pet. It can be useful to feed your dog, depending on its age, at one or two scheduled meal times. Training sessions can then be performed just prior to mealtime when the dog is at its hungriest. Most puppies can then be motivated with pieces of food. In the same way, toys, play sessions

and affection can be withheld until training time so that the dog is "hungrier" for these rewards. Some of the dogs that are hardest to train are those that are difficult to motivate. These dogs may do better with a few special treats that are saved specifically for training sessions (e.g. hot dog slices, small morsels of cheese), or pieces of dog food sprinkled with flavoring such as powdered cheese or garlic. By the way, if there's no good reason to give your dog a treat, don't – it fills him or her up, and accomplishes nothing. Consider these tidbits and biscuits not as treats but as "training rewards". If these rewards are saved exclusively for training they become more motivating and the pet will learn quickly what behavior leads to that reward. Whenever you are giving the dog something of value from food to a walk, first give your dog a command so that each reward can be earned.

How do I properly use positive reinforcement?

The proper use of positive reinforcement is more than just giving a treat or a pat on the head. The timing of the reinforcement is very important. Remember, your pet is behaving all the time. So, you need to be sure to reinforce the behavior that you want and not some other. Therefore, closely associate the reinforcement with the behavior you wish to increase. Reinforcement must immediately follow the behavior. If there is any delay, you run the risk of the pet engaging in another behavior while you are administering the reinforcement. One example is when you teach a dog to sit. You tell your dog to 'sit', and manipulate it into the position. While you are saying 'good dog' and giving a food treat, the dog stands up. What has just happened? You have rewarded 'sit' and 'stand up'. Another example is when you are house-training your dog. You send your dog outdoors to eliminate and as soon as the dog is finished, you call the dog back into the house, dry its feet and give it a reward. What happened this time? You just rewarded your dog for coming back into the house and having the feet dried.

Should I reward my pet every time?

The frequency of reinforcement is important. The rate at which behavior is reinforced is called the "schedule". There are several different schedules of reinforcement.

A. Continuous reinforcement. Every time your pet engages in a behavior it is reinforced with a reward. While this may sound like a good idea, it is actually less than ideal. If you reward a behavior continuously, once you cease rewarding the behavior, it will often stop.

B. Ratio or variable rate of reinforcement. The reinforcement does not come after each performance of the behavior but intermittently. This may mean that instead of a reward every time, the pet gets a reward every third time, then perhaps two in a row, then maybe not until the pet has performed the behavior five more times. What happens if you reward this way? Behavior tends to be stronger and last longer.

C. Start training new commands or tasks with continuous reinforcement but switch to intermittent, variable rates as soon as your pet is responding consistently.

What if my rewards are not working?

First, you may not be reinforcing the correct task. Remember the example of 'sit' and 'stand up'. Be sure that the timing of your reinforcement is immediately after the behavior you wish to increase. Second, you may be phasing out your reinforcement before your pet has adequately learned the new behavior. Go back to basics and be sure your pet understands what to do. Therefore, until your dog consistently responds to the command, it can be valuable to leave a leash attached so that you can immediately show your pet what it is "supposed" to do. It is also possible that you may be repeating commands several times, or in different ways and thus confusing your pet.

What type of rewards should I use?

Rewards do not always have to be food. For many pets, owner attention can be a reward as can a walk in the park or a game of fetch. What is important is that it be appropriate and motivating for your pet. Remember, you need not give a "special" reward such as food each time your pet performs a task, but always acknowledge good behavior if only with praise or affection.

Is there a wrong way to reward my dog?

Yes. We may reinforce behaviors that we do not want. Remember that positive reinforcement makes behavior increase. So, there may be times when you may be inadvertently giving reinforcement when the pet is exhibiting a behavior that is undesirable. Giving any form of attention to a barking dog, a dog that is jumping up, or a dog scratching at the back door only serves to reward the behavior. Sometimes people even give a bit of food, pat the dog, or play with it in an attempt to calm it down. What they are really doing however is reinforcing the problem behavior. Similarly you may think that you are punishing your dog when you are indeed reinforcing behaviors. Examples include scolding your dog with an insufficiently harsh tone of voice, or gently pushing the dog away when it is play biting. What is worse is that when these behaviors are rewarded occasionally or intermittently, the behavior becomes stronger and lasts longer. A reward should never be given unless it is earned.

What are other ways in which rewards can be used?

There are other situations where rewards can be most helpful. For example, it may help a puppy or even an adult dog to learn to accept new people if that greeting is always coupled with a food treat. This will help the pet learn that new people bring something good. In other cases, rewards can be used to encourage desirable behavior. Food enhanced toys may encourage a dog to chew on them instead of the household possessions (see 'destructiveness – chewing' for examples). Removal of a reward as soon as the dog exhibits undesirable behavior is another training tool known as negative punishment (e.g. stopping play when the dog bites too hard). In this example, the reward is used as a punishment since play biting should be reduced or cease since it leads to the reward being removed.

What type of rewards would I use for my cat?

Cats respond to training like dogs, however, they seem to need reinforcement at a higher rate than dogs to maintain performance. Food is often the best reinforcement for cats, but many will enjoy play sessions with favorite toys as well. Like dogs, finding small tidbits of human food, or special cat treats with high appeal, may be more motivating than regular food. Train your cat with these treats before mealtime, not after, and feed your cat on a meal schedule not free choice so that it is hungry at training times. Remember to think of toys and snacks as rewards, not as treats.

What is clicker training and how does it work?

A clicker or an audible tone (found on some remote collars) can be paired with a food reward by consistently sounding it just prior to giving the food until it becomes a conditioned stimulus for food. The value of a clicker is that it can then be used as a reward to immediately mark correct responses in a convenient and precise manner, with the food being given shortly afterwards. While they can become effective enough to reinforce responses without the need for food, regularly giving the food treat following these secondary reinforcers will help continue to maintain their value. Because it is predictive of a reward, the clicker can be used as a bridging stimulus (where the clicker reinforces the correct response and the food is given as soon as it can be given (even if after a short delay). In addition to clickers, favored food rewards can be paired with praise, stroking or petting.

SELECTING A PET – GUIDELINES

Many behavior and health problems in pets can be prevented by seeking guidance before obtaining a new pet. Such a consultation will help you select the best pet for the household, but also provide information on how to prepare in advance for the new arrival. Selection topics to be discussed include the species, breed, age, and sex of the pet, where to obtain the pet and how the kennel, breeder, and pets can best be assessed. Advice on preparing the home will include housing, bedding, feeding, training, exercise, scheduling and health care requirements.

What breed is best for my home and family?

The first decision is whether to obtain a purebred or a mixed breed. By selecting a mixed breed from a pound, an abandoned animal will be re-housed. Some of the genetic problems associated with inbreeding can be avoided and the initial cost to acquire the pet will be considerably lower by obtaining a mixed breed. However, the best way to predict the behavioral and physical attributes of an adult dog or cat is to obtain a purebred from known parentage. This is particularly important when selecting a puppy or kitten. Unless the parents are known it is extremely difficult to predict the size, health, or behavior that is likely to emerge as the dog grows up. In contrast, selecting an adult allows assessment of the physical characteristics, health and behavior of the animal.

If a purebred is chosen, it should be a breed whose physical and behavioral characteristics best suit the family. However, with hundreds of breeds to choose from and such a wide variation of behavior types within a breed, the most consistent selection factor will be the physical characteristics. Therefore first select a few breeds that appeal in physical appearance, including coat type, size and shape. Also consider that the lifespan, since the giant breeds of dogs live considerably shorter lives than smaller breeds.

Before the selection consultation, visit dog shows to observe the appearance of the adult dog of each breed. Do some reading. There are a variety of books, CD ROMs and Internet sites that can help to guide you through the selection process. Some books concentrate on the physical characteristics, history of the breed, or health concerns, while others cover breed behavioral characteristics, and how to select individuals from a breeder, shelter, or litter. Behavioral factors to consider as you try to decide upon a breed of dog include activity level, exercise requirements and any reported behavior problems of the breed. Perhaps the most important factor to consider is the origin of the breed as the traits and behaviors for which the breed has been bred and selected (herding, protection, hunting, etc.) are the most strongly inherited. Once you have narrowed the selection down to a few breeds, your veterinarian can guide you regarding the physical and behavioral problems that you need to be aware of for each breed.

At what age should I obtain a pet?

Puppies are most social from about 3 to 12 weeks of age. For the first seven to eight weeks primary socialization should be directed to other puppies and littermates to aid a puppy to develop healthy social relationships with other dogs. From seven weeks on, well before the socialization period ends, socialization should be directed to people, new environments and other pets. For these reasons, the ideal time to select and obtain a new puppy is at 7 to 8 weeks of age. This allows adequate time to be in its new home, and bond to its new family, well before its primary socialization period ends.

Since the most receptive period for kitten socialization is 3 to 9 weeks of age, a kitten should either be obtained by 7 weeks of age, or the new owners must ensure that the kitten has had adequate human contact prior to 7 weeks of age. Don't obtain a kitten much earlier than 7 weeks since this deprives it of social contact with its mother and littermates.

Acquiring an adult dog or cat can avoid some of the problems of bringing a new puppy or kitten into the home. This is especially true for dogs where the time and commitment required to train a puppy are considerable. Fulfilling the play, feeding, elimination, and exercise needs of a puppy or kitten may be impractical for a family who spends much of the day away from home. On the other hand, an adult dog or cat that has had insufficient or inappropriate training or insufficient socialization may have behavior problems that are difficult to resolve. For owners who are ready and able to meet the demands of a growing puppy or kitten, obtaining a pet during its primary socialization period is strongly recommended.

Should I consider a male or female pet?

In dogs, males tend to be slightly larger in stature than females of the same breed and somewhat more dominant. Castration of male dogs reduces sexually dimorphic behaviors such as mounting, roaming, urine marking, and aggression directed toward other male dogs (see 'neutering' – canine). Castration in cats reduces urine odor and sexually dimorphic behavior traits such as roaming, fighting, and urine marking by about 90% (see 'neutering' – feline for more details).

Where should I obtain my pet?

Perhaps the most important reason to obtain a pet from a breeder or private home is to observe the physical characteristics, health and behavior of the parents. Choose a breeder who is open and willing to answer questions, and who will allow you to tour the kennel and meet the parents. When a puppy or kitten is obtained from a breeder or private home you are also able to observe the early environment and assess the exposure to people that the pet has had. A personal relationship with the breeder may be helpful should later problems arise. Be certain to ask your veterinarian to prepare you with appropriate questions for the breeder including eye examinations, hip dysplasia certification for the parents and any other health or behavioral problems to which the breed may be prone. Dogs or cats acquired from pet stores, puppy mills, or shelters, may have received insufficient early socialization, are at higher risk for contracting disease, and the parents cannot be observed.

How do I decide which pet to choose?

The value and effectiveness of performing assessment tests on young puppies and kittens is highly debatable since many behavior and health problems do not emerge until the pet matures. Perhaps the best approach is a simple, common sense evaluation. Dogs can be observed and handled to determine which ones are the most sociable, playful, or affectionate. Those with undesirable traits such as shyness, or uncontrollable biting may be less suitable. Different puppy temperament tests have been detailed in the literature, but there is no good available evidence that they are predictive of future behavior. What puppy testing can do is identify problem areas that may need attention from an early age. Recent studies have shown that assessment testing may become increasingly more accurate as the dog ages. With the emergence of the fear period, the end of the socialization period, and emerging dominance hierarchies each month, assessment testing becomes increasingly more accurate at predicting adult behavior. In fact, one advantage in selecting an adult pet is that it might be possible for a trained observer to be able to accurately assess the pet's temperament and personality to determine what behavior problems might arise.

For cats, **three personality types** have been identified: 1) **sociable**, 2) **timid and unfriendly**, or 3) **active and aggressive**. Because the socialization period for litters ends earlier than in dogs, early handling is extremely important. Kitten assessment tests can be a valuable tool in determining the effects of genetics, socialization and early handling. If the cat tolerates handling, lifting and petting with little or no fear or resistance it is likely to make a good family pet. Fearful, timid, hard to restrain or aggressive cats should be avoided.

SELECTION RESOURCES

Numerous internet sites are available that contain breed facts and pictures and breed selection guides. In addition, there are often breed fancier sites and breed organizations that provide more detailed advice on individual breeds, but may be somewhat biased in favor of the breed.

Internet sites: (breeds and pet selection) e.g. waltham.com, purina.com, ckc.ca, akc.org, cfainc.org, dogs-in-canada.com

1. Ackerman L. The Genetic Connection. AAHA Press, Lakewood, CO, 1999
2. American Kennel Club Complete Dog Book. NY: Howell House, 1997
3. Baer N, Duno S. Choosing a Dog. Your Guide to Picking the Perfect Breed, NY, Berkley, 1995
4. Benjamin CL, The Chosen Puppy: How to Select and Raise a Puppy from an Arnimal Shelter, Howell Book House, 1990
5. Caras R. The Roger Caras Dog Book. M. Evans and Company, NY, 1996
6. Clark RD, Stainer JR ed. Medical and Genetic Aspects of Purebred Dogs. (2nd edition), St. Simons, GA: Forum Publications, 1994
7. Clark RD. Medical, Genetic, and Behavioral Aspects of Purebred Cats. St. Simons, GA: Forum Publications, 1992
8. Coren S. Why We Love the Dogs We Do: How to Find the Dog that Matches Your Personality, Firefly Books, 2000
9. Hart BL, Hart LA, The Perfect Puppy, W. H. Freeman and Co., New York, 1988
10. Kilcommons B, Wilson S. Paws to Consider. Choosing the Right Dog for you and your family, NY, Warner Books, 1999
11. Lowell M, Your Purebred Puppy-A Buyer's Guide. NY: Henry Holt, 1990
12. Lowell M, Your Purebred Kitten-A Buyer's Guide. NY. Henry Holt, 1995
13. Tortora D. The Right Dog for You. NY: Simon & Schuster, 1983

Canine Behavior

Aggression is the most serious and dangerous behavior problem that dog owners may need to deal with. Since there are many different types of aggression, making a diagnosis, determining the prognosis (the chances of safe and effective correction) and developing an appropriate treatment plan are usually best handled with a veterinary or applied animal behaviorist. In some cases medical conditions can contribute to aggression, therefore before a behavior consultation it is essential that your dog have a complete physical examination and a set of blood tests to rule out organ dysfunction (see 'behavior – causes and diagnosis of problems'). In order to treat the problem effectively, it will first be necessary to determine which type of aggression your dog displays: dominance-related, fear, possessive, protective and territorial, parental, play, redirected, pain induced, pathophysiological or medical and learned. In many cases more than one form of aggression may be exhibited (see 'aggression – introduction to aggressive behavior').

What is dominance aggression and how is it diagnosed?

One of the most common types of aggression seen by veterinary behaviorists is dominance-related aggression. In order to achieve security and cohesiveness within a group or pack, a hierarchy develops. Although the way a dog fits into a human family is not entirely analogous to how it would fit into a pack of dogs, the dog is likely to take a position of control and leadership or deference and compliance in relationship to each family member. This relationship develops from a combination of genetic factors as well as what the owner teaches the dog in its day to day training and interactions. Furthermore, if aggressive displays are successful at causing the owner to retreat, then they are being reinforced, while any anxiety or retaliation on the part of the owner can promote a fearful response. Once a dog develops a position of leadership with a family member (or other dog), any challenge to that dog's leadership may lead to aggression. Dogs use facial expressions and body postures as signals to display dominance, such as standing tall, a high wagging tail, eye contact, or snarling. Aggression towards family members in one or more of the following circumstances along with dominant signaling may indicate dominance aggression:

A. Protecting resting areas or resources (food, toys)

B. Overprotection (possessive) of a more subordinate family member

C. Staring, eye contact

D. Handling by the owner (lifting, petting, hugging, rolling over onto back or side)

E. Restraint, pulling, pushing, discipline, punishment

Dominance aggression must be differentiated from fear-induced and defensive aggression, although multiple forms of aggression can be concurrent. If any of the above situations lead to fear or anxiety on the part of the dog, the dog may respond with defensive aggression, accompanied by fearful facial expressions and body postures (see 'aggression toward family members' for treatment).

What is fear aggression and how is it diagnosed?

Fear aggression arises when a dog is exposed to people or other animals that the dog is unfamiliar with or those that have been previously associated with an unpleasant or fearful experience. Although some dogs may retreat when fearful, those that are on their own territory and those that are prevented from retreating because they are cornered or restrained, are more likely to fight. If the person or animal retreats, acts overly fearful or the pet is harmed or further frightened in any way (e.g. a fight, punishment), the fear is likely to be further aggravated. Fear aggression toward family members might arise out of punishment or some other unpleasant experience associated with the owners. Many cases of fear aggression are seen as combinations or complicating factors of other forms of aggression (dominance, maternal, possessive, etc.). Fearful body postures in conjunction with aggression are diagnostic of fear aggression. Behavior therapy, perhaps in combination with drug therapy can be used to treat most cases of fear aggression (see 'fears and phobias – animals and people').

What is play aggression and how is it diagnosed?

Play aggression is commonly seen in young dogs toward people or other pets in the family. Overly rambunctious play along with grabbing, nipping or biting of people or their clothing are some of the common signs of play aggression. Although it is a normal behavior, it can lead to injuries and, if handled incorrectly could lead to more serious forms of aggression as your dog matures (see 'canine aggression – sibling rivalry'; 'biting', and 'play and exercise in dogs').

What is possessive aggression and how is it treated?

Possessive aggression may be directed to humans or other pets that approach the dog when it is in possession of something that is highly desirable such as a favorite chew toy, food, or treat. While protecting possessions may be necessary if an animal is to survive and thrive in the wild, it is unacceptable when directed toward people or other pets in a household. What can be confusing for some owners is that it is not always food that brings out the most protective displays. Novel and highly desirable objects such as a tissue that has been stolen from a garbage can, a favored toy, human food, or a piece of rawhide are some of the items that dogs may aggressively protect.

Treatment must first be directed at preventing possible injury. At first it may be best to confine your dog so that it cannot gain access to any items that it might pick up and protect. Dogs that protect their food can be given a less palatable diet, and fed in a separate room away from family members. Dogs that protect their treats or toys should have them taken away, and only allowed access to them when alone in the crate or confinement room. When you are available to supervise, a long leash and head collar can be kept attached so that your dog can be prevented from wandering off, and immediately interrupted if it attempts to raid a garbage can or pick up inappropriate objects. Booby-traps (shock mats, Snappy Trainers™, motion detectors,

unpleasant tastes) can also be used to teach your dog to stay away from selected objects. Although prevention can help to ensure safety, if the problem is to be corrected your dog will need to be taught to accept approaches and give up objects on command. The goal is to train the dog that it will receive a favored treat or reward that is even more appealing than the object in its possession. The key to success is to have good control and a well-trained dog. If your dog will not sit and stay, come, or allow approach when it has no object in its possession, then there is little chance of correcting a possessive problem. For details see section on food guarding in 'puppy training – taking charge' and 'controlling stealing and teaching give').

What is territorial aggression and how can it be treated?

Protective aggression may be exhibited toward people or other animals that approach the pet's property (territorial aggression). Generally people and other animals that are least familiar to the dog, or most unlike the members of the household are the most likely "targets" of territorial aggression. While most forms of territorial aggression are likely to occur on the property, some dogs may protect family members regardless of the location. Territorial aggression can be prevented or minimized with early socialization and good control. Young dogs should be taught to sit and receive a reward as each new person comes to the door. To reduce potential fear and anxiety toward visitors, you should ensure that a wide variety of visitors come over to visit the puppy, while the puppy is young and sociable (see 'socializing your new puppy'). In time, most dogs will begin to alert the family by barking when strangers come to the home. However the dog that has been well socialized and under good control can be trained to quickly settle down and relax. For dogs exhibiting territorial aggression, you will need to gain enough control to have your dog sit, stay and when calmed down, take a reward at the front door. Generally a leash and head collar will give the fastest and most effective control. Using a desensitization and counter-conditioning program you can begin retraining with low levels of stimuli (such as people arriving in a car, walking past the front of the house, or perhaps even a family member knocking on the door or ringing the bell). The idea is that each time someone arrives at the house or rings the bell, the dog will come to expect a favored reward (toy, cheese, hot dog slice or play session). Once the dog can be controlled and receives rewards in this environment, gradually more intense stimuli can be used. Sometimes, an anti-bark collar, shake can, or air horn, can be used to disrupt the initial barking, so that the pet can be directed to perform the appropriate behavior and get its reward.

What is predatory aggression and how can it be treated?

Predation is the instinctive desire to chase and hunt prey. Predatory behaviors include stalking, chasing, attacking, and ingestion of prey animals, but may occasionally be directed at people or other pets. Some dogs that have never shown chase or predation, may display the behavior when running together with a group of dogs. Although the desire to chase can be reduced by using a head collar and desensitizing and counter-conditioning in the presence of passing stimuli, this is a very dangerous form of aggression, which must be prevented. Whenever the dog is outdoors it should be confined to an escape proof pen or run, or controlled securely by the owners. A leash and head collar or a leash and muzzle, can help to ensure safety when out for walks (see 'behavior modification – reducing fear and anxiety – desensitization, counter-conditioning and flooding' and 'controlling pulling, lunging, chasing, and jumping up').

What is pain-induced aggression and how can it be treated?

Pain-induced aggression is usually elicited by some form of handling or contact that elicits pain or discomfort. However, even if your dog is not exhibiting pain, certain medical conditions (endocrine imbalances, organ disease, etc.) may make the pet more irritable and perhaps more prone to aggression. Fear and anxiety further compound many of these cases. Once your dog learns that aggression is successful at removing the stimulus, aggression may recur when similar situations arise in the future, whether or not the pain is still present. Treatment first requires that the medical or painful condition is resolved. Next, you will need to identify the types of handling and situations that have led to aggression in the past. With desensitization and counter-conditioning, your dog can slowly and gradually be accustomed to accept and enjoy these situations. Once the dog learns that there is no more discomfort associated with the handling, but that there may be rewards, the problem should be resolved. A muzzle or leash and head collar, may be the safest way to begin the retraining.

What is maternal aggression and how can it be treated?

Maternal aggression is directed toward people or other animals that approach the bitch with her puppies. When bitches go through pseudopregnancy they may also become aggressive and begin to protect nesting areas or stuffed toys at the approximate time when the puppies would have been born. Once the puppies are weaned and the dog is spayed the problem is unlikely to recur. In the interim, the owners can use a leash or leash and head collar, along with the come command and rewards to teach the dog to leave the litter, at which time the puppies can then be handled. With desensitization, counter-conditioning, good control and highly motivating rewards, it may be possible to train your dog to accept approach and handling of the puppies.

What is redirected aggression and how can it be treated?

Aggression that is directed toward a person or pet that did not initially evoke the aggression is classified as redirected. This is likely to occur when the dog is aroused and a person or other pet intervenes or approaches. Dogs that are highly aroused must be avoided. In some cases a water rifle, air horn, or long leash can be used to safely remove the dog from the situation. If the aggression and arousal does not immediately subside, consider locking your dog in a dark, quiet room, until it settles down and will come out for food or play. Since redirected aggression arises out of other forms of aggression, it is important to identify and treat the initial cause of aggression (e.g. fear, territorial, sibling rivalry, etc.), or to prevent the problem. This can be accomplished by avoiding exposure to the stimulus for aggression or by keeping a leash and head collar or leash and muzzle on your dog when exposure is possible.

What are some of the other causes of aggression?

Aggression associated with medical disorders may arise at any age, may have a relatively sudden onset and may not fit any canine species typical behavior. Some medical conditions can, on their own, cause aggression, but in many cases a combination of behavioral factors and medical problems cause the pet to pass a certain threshold at which aggression is displayed. Infectious agents such as rabies, hormonal imbalances such as hypothyroidism, psychomotor epilepsy, hyperkinesis, neoplasia, and a variety of genetic and metabolic disorders can cause or predispose a dog to aggression. Painful conditions such as dental disease, or arthritis, and medical conditions causing fever, fatigue or sensory loss might increase the pet's irritability (see 'behavior – causes and diagnosis of problems' and 'behavior problems of older pets').

In rare circumstances, aggression has no identifiable etiology and no particular stimuli that initiate the aggressive displays. There may be a genetic propensity to aggression in some lines of some breeds, but many of the cases previously labeled as "idiopathic", "rage" or "mental lapse aggression" have been disputed and in some cases subsequently reclassified. Only when there is no identifiable stimulus or cause for the behavior, or when an abnormal EEG is documented, should the diagnosis of idiopathic aggression be considered.

What is learned aggression and how can it be treated?

Although learned aggression can refer to dogs that are intentionally trained to act aggressively on command (or in particular situations), learning and conditioning are also important components of many forms of aggression. Whenever a dog learns that aggression is successful at removing the stimulus, the behavior is further reinforced. Some forms of aggression are inadvertently rewarded by owners who, in an attempt to calm the pet and reduce aggression, actually encourage the behavior with patting or verbal reassurances. Pets that are threatened or punished for aggressive displays may become even more aggressive each time the situation recurs. In addition, if the response of the owner, or the stimulus (person or other pet) is one that evokes anxiety or fear, the aggression is likely to escalate.

Treatment with flooding is intended to teach the pet that the stimulus is not associated with any harm and that aggression will not successfully remove the stimulus. With desensitization and counter-conditioning, the dog is not only taught that the stimulus is safe, but that it is associated with a reward (see 'behavior modification, desensitization, counter-conditioning, differential reinforcement and flooding').

Why is my dog aggressive towards other dogs?

Aggression between dogs can result in injury to dogs and/or to the people trying to separate them. The behavior can consist of growling, snarling, barking, lunging, snapping and biting.

Why would my dog fight with dogs he has never met?

Aggression between unfamiliar dogs can be due to dominance, fear, or protective behavior over territory or owner.

Dominance motivated aggression

This aggression can be elicited by dominant gestures or postures from either dog. These can include placing head or feet, on the back of the other dog, dominant body postures such as eye contact, and high tail and stiff legged approach. Owners may inadvertently reinforce the behavior by leash tightening and vocal cues. These may signal to the dog that the impending approach is problematic. Unfortunately leash restriction does not allow the dog to react with a complete rate and range of responses including body postures, approach and withdrawal. Additionally, this behavior can be elicited by smaller dogs that repeatedly "attack" larger dogs that are attempting to avoid interaction. Dogs of near equal dominance and those of the same sex are most likely to compete for dominance. Some extremely bold or assertive dogs will fight rather than back down when challenged. Although dominance challenges may be a source of aggression when two dogs are meeting each other for the first time, most dominance hierarchies are established with posturing and no fights. It is likely therefore that fear, territorial behavior and learned components, would contribute to an attack. Dominant aggressive dogs may be over-assertive and/or overprotective if the owners do not have good control or have taken a subordinate position in relationship to the dog.

Territorial aggression toward other dogs

This aggression is primarily exhibited when unfamiliar dogs are on the resident dog's property, or what the aggressor considers his territory. Some dogs get highly aroused at the sight of other dogs on their territory and may jump fences, or go through windows or doors to get to the intruder.

Fear based aggression toward unfamiliar dogs

This aggression is very common in aggressive encounters with other dogs. The diagnosis is made based on the body postures and reaction of the dog when faced with another dog. The fearful dog will often have the tail tucked, ears back and may lean against the owner or attempt to get behind them.

They may be barking at the approaching dog and backing up at the same time. Often the dog is avoiding eye contact. This behavior can be precipitated by previous aggressive attacks from which the dog could not escape and sustained injury. Owners that try and calm their aggressive dog may serve to reinforce the aggression, while those that try and punish the dog will only serve to heighten the dog's fear and anxiety in relationship to the stimulus. Good control can help to calm the dog, while owners who have their dogs restrained on a leash (especially with a choke or pinch collar) and have poor control often have highly defensive dogs. Dogs that are restrained on a leash or tied up are more likely to display aggression when frightened, because they cannot escape.

Learned components of aggression

Learning and conditioning aggravate most forms of inter-dog aggression. Should threats or aggression result in the retreat (or removal by the owner)

of the other dog, the behavior has been successful. If the owner tries to calm the aggressive dog or distract it with food treats, this may only serve to reward the aggressive behavior. One of the most common mistakes is to punish the dog that is aggressive toward other dogs. This usually serves to heighten the dog's arousal, and teaches the dog that the stimulus (other dog) is indeed associated with unpleasant consequences. Many owners, in an attempt to gain more control, then increase the level or type of punishment (e.g. prong collars) which further heighten the dog's arousal and in some cases may lead to retaliation and defensive aggression toward the owners. And, if the dog to dog interaction results in pain or injury to one or both dogs, the dogs will quickly learn to become more fearful and aggressive at future meetings. In short, if the owners cannot successfully control the dog and resolve the situation without heightening the dog's anxiety or increasing its fear, the problem will progress with each subsequent exposure.

How can I prevent my dog from becoming aggressive with other dogs?

Prevention starts with puppy training and socialization. Early and frequent association with other dogs will enable your pet to learn proper interactions and reactions to other dogs. This can be very helpful in prevention of aggression to other dogs.

You must have good control of your dog. This means that your dog will take contextual cues from you, and may be calmer and less anxious in the presence of new stimuli. Moreover, the dog should reliably respond to commands to 'sit', 'stay' and 'quiet'. If necessary, the dog may need a head halter to give you additional control. When in situations where the dog may encounter other dogs, a leash is necessary.

For territorial behaviors, what is most important is to prevent the dog from engaging in prolonged and out of control aggressive displays both in the home and yard. Aggressive displays include barking, lunging, fence running, jumping on doors, windows and fences. These types of behaviors should be discouraged and prevented. One important component is teaching your dog a 'quiet' command for barking (see 'barking').

My dog is already aggressive to other dogs. What can I do?

First and foremost, you must have complete control over your pet. This not only serves to calm the dog and reduce its anxiety, but also allows you to successfully deal with each encounter with other dogs. Leashes are essential and the use of head collars and/or muzzles are strongly recommended for dogs that will be in situations with multiple dogs.

Begin by establishing reliable responses to basic obedience commands. If the dog cannot be taught to 'sit', 'stay', 'come' and 'heel', in the absence of potential problems, then there is no chance that the dog will respond obediently in problematic situations. Reward selection can be critical in these cases, since the dog needs to be taught that obedient behavior in the presence of the stimulus (other dog) can earn the dog-favored rewards. The goal is that the dog learns to associate the approach of other dogs with rewards.

Long term treatment consists of desensitization (gradual exposure) and counter-conditioning the dog so that the approach of the other dogs leads to a positive emotional response. In training terms the dog must be taught to display an appropriate, acceptable response when other dogs approach (e.g. 'sit', 'watch', 'relax') which can be reinforced (differential reinforcement or response substitution). This must be done slowly, beginning with situations where the dog can be successfully controlled and rewarded and very slowly progressing to more difficult encounters and environments. The first step is to perform training for its favored rewards, in a situation where there are no dogs present and the owner is guaranteed success. Food or toy prompts can be used at first, but soon the rewards should be hidden and the dog rewarded intermittently. The selection of favored food or toys is essential since the goal is that the dog will learn that receiving these favored rewards is contingent on meeting other dogs.

Once the dog responds quickly and is receiving rewards on an intermittent basis, training should progress to low-level exposure to other dogs. If the owner's training and the rewards are not sufficient to control the dog in the absence of the other dogs, then utilizing a leash and head collar, selection of more motivating rewards, and seeking the assistance and guidance of a behaviorist should be considered. The next steps in desensitization and counter-conditioning rely on a stimulus gradient. In other words your dog needs to be controlled, (preferably with leash and head halter) and respond to commands and rewards in the presence of gradually more intense stimuli.

Begin with a calm, and well-controlled second dog, in an environment where your dog is least anxious or threatened, and at a sufficient distance to get your dog to respond to your commands. Gradually the dog is exposed to dogs at closer distances and in more familiar locations. Using the head halter and a prompt (reward prompt, set of keys) it should be possible to keep the dog focused on the owner and sufficiently distracted. While dogs with fear aggression may improve dramatically, dogs with dominance-related aggression that are trained in this manner usually do not greet other dogs, but should walk calmly with their owners and not initiate fighting behavior.

Dogs that are exhibiting territorial aggression should be retrained in much the same manner, but the gradient of stimuli will need to be adjusted. Begin in the front hall or on the front porch with no other dogs around. Then with the dog controlled in the hall or on the porch, other dogs could be brought to the perimeter of the property. Over subsequent training sessions, the dogs could be brought closer to your dog, or your dog could be moved closer to the other dog (see 'behavior modification – desensitization, counter-conditioning, differential reinforcement and flooding').

Another way to disrupt the undesirable response and get the dog's attention is to use an air horn, shake can or citronella spray collar. In fact, if the dog barks prior to the aggressive display, a citronella spray bark collar will be activated by the dog's barking insuring immediate timing and disruption. Once the inappropriate behavior ceases, and you get your dog's attention, the dog should be redirected to an appropriate behavior such as play. The greeting should be repeated, until no threats or aggression are observed.

Success can be achieved in a number of ways, but head halters are generally the most important tools. Head halters provide enough physical control that the desired behavior can be achieved (sit, heel) since pulling up and forward, turns the head toward the owner and causes the dog to retreat into a sit position. With the dog's head oriented toward the owner and away from the other dog, lunging and aggression can be prevented, and the dog will usually settle down enough to see and respond to the prompt. A second hand can guide the muzzle under the chin to insure eye contact and help to calm the dog. Rewards can and should be given immediately for a proper response (sitting, heeling), by releasing tension on the leash. If the dog remains under control with the leash slack, the reward (toy, food, affection) should be given, but if the problem behavior recurs, the leash should be pulled and then released as many times as is necessary to get and maintain the desired response. The dog's anxiety quickly diminishes as it learns that the other dog is not to be feared, that there is no opportunity to escape, that its responses will not chase away the other dog, that responding to the owner's commands will achieve rewards, and that the owner has sufficient control to achieve the desired behavior (which further calms the dog). Also since there is no punishment or discomfort that might further aggravate the situation and rewards are not being given until the desired behavior appears, fear and anxiety will be further reduced.

Are there drugs that can help the treatment program?

Occasionally, for fear aggressive dogs in particular, anti-anxiety drugs may help to calm the dog enough so that the retraining session is successful. For situations where the problem has become highly conditioned and intense, antidepressants may be useful for regaining control. In most cases however, the best calming influence is a head halter, good owner control and some strong rewards.

AGGRESSION TOWARD FAMILY MEMBERS

What does "dominance hierarchy" mean?

The concept of dominance hierarchy is used when describing social relationships within groups of animals. Animals that live in groups do so because of the advantages. These include cooperative raising of the young, ease of obtaining food and defense against predators. Since group members offer benefits to each other, it is counter-productive to fight among members and risk injury. Therefore, communication and an understanding of how to share resources is essential. Resources are usually allocated to the strongest members first. Those at the top get things such as food, resting-places, mates and favored possessions preferentially over lower ranking individuals. This has been termed "dominance" hierarchy. The rank of an individual is determined by such factors as genetics, which individual was first on the territory, age, results of competitive encounters, and the competition for resources.

In an encounter where one animal acts "dominant" there needs to be another who acts subordinate or fighting will occur. Subordinate or submissive behaviors in dogs include looking away, or lowered head, body, tail and ears. Extreme submission is shown by crouching down and rolling over and exposing the abdomen. Note that a dominance or pack hierarchy will develop in a group of dogs, but that dominance or leadership refers to the relative relationship of two individuals. Dominance is the quality of a relationship, not of an individual. Whether a dog is subordinate to one dog or person, has little bearing on whether that dog is subordinate to another person or dog. Often an alternate view is proposed which uses the premise that hierarchies are maintained by the deference of individuals, not by dominant actions.

How does this apply to dogs in human households?

Dogs have evolved from wolves, which live in social groups, so the domestic dog is evolutionarily prepared to live in a group. Each member of this social group develops a relationship with every other member of the group and is either dominant or subordinate to that individual. You may have little control over which dog in your home becomes leader in regards to the other dogs in the home. Most dogs work things out between themselves (see 'aggression – sibling rivalry' for more information).

However, each human in the family must be a leader in his or her relationship with the dog. Yet humans do not communicate with exactly the same body language, postures, signals and actions as do dogs. Therefore, relationships that develop with humans are not entirely analogous to those that develop between dogs. Human leadership and control must be achieved through actions, training and handling that teach the dog to defer to the owner to receive rewards. A leadership program in dogs teaches the dog that rewards are earned for compliance and obedience, that handling and restraint on the part of the owners are to be tolerated and enjoyed, that rewards cannot be obtained on demand and that the owner initiates favored activities such as play and walks. Confrontational techniques and those that use physical restraint and handling to gain control should be avoided as they may lead to defensive and fearful responses. When a dog has access to all things on demand or when it desires them (food, resting places on furniture and beds, owner attention at any time, territorial displays at doors and windows) the dog may assume it is dominant to the humans due to what it perceives as owner deference. If the dog perceives itself as the "leader" in its relationship with the humans in the home , it may respond with aggressive displays, threats and actions when challenged for control of its access to critical resources (food, toys, personal space). With the responsibility of being leader these dogs may also be more possessive, protective, and anxious than dogs that have the "comfort" of knowing that another (owner or other dog) is in charge and in control of their pack or household. Keep in mind, a dog may assume a dominant role when it perceives that no one else in the group has taken that position rather than it having a strong desire to "control".

In many cases of social status or dominance aggression there are aspects of arousal, conflict and anxiety that are key factors in the aggression. When dogs challenge their owners to maintain a favored resource (e.g. sleeping area, toy, or attention of a family member) the problem may be aggravated by the owner's reaction (e.g. withdrawal that reinforces the behavior or threats, punishment, and anxiety which increases the dog's fear, defensiveness, and anxiety) and over time learns that aggressive behavior results in a successful outcome for the dog.

How can I prevent my dog from becoming in control?

It is important that owners set themselves up as leaders very early in their relationship with their dog. Most dogs readily obey but some require a fair amount of patience and consistency since they may be genetically more likely to challenge and resist (see 'basic training' and 'taking charge'). Becoming the leader does not imply harshness or punishment, but control of resources and behavior. This is accomplished with training and supervision. The individual temperament and genetic predisposition of the puppy will determine the methods needed by the owner to become the leader. Equally important is to recognize deference when it occurs. When your dog looks away, lowers its head or avoids, especially when you are reprimanding it, this is deference. From the dog's perspective the encounter is over and if the human persists, the dog may respond with fear and defensive behaviors. Remember, just because the dog defers once does not mean he will in another setting. Each context is separate and the dogs' desire for the resource in question figures into the response.

How can I determine if my dog is exhibiting social status aggression?

The beginning signs of social status or dominance aggression are usually subtle. Dogs mostly use facial expressions and body postures to signal intent. A low body and wagging tail show friendly approach; a high wagging tail, eye contact and perhaps teeth showing could be an assertive approach. Challenges between owner and pet usually begin with prolonged eye contact and maybe growling and/or snarling (lifting of the lip exposing teeth usually without noise) over resources such as food, resting places, moving the dog and perhaps handling the body. If the owner sometimes acquiesces but at other times continues the "challenge" the relationship may be unclear and the dog may escalate the aggression to snapping, lunging and biting. It will be necessary to determine the context of the aggression such as certain types of petting or handling, approaching when the dog is resting or sleeping, touching the food or toys, discipline or scolding the dog, ability to handle the body, or stepping over the dog. These aggressive displays may not occur in every situation, only those where the dog feels that its authority is being challenged.

Aggressions in these contexts are not the only criteria for determining if a dog is behaving in a dominantly aggressive manner. The body posture of the dog during the encounter is very important. Dominant dogs will usually have eye contact, may be "stiff", or tense and standing tall with their tail usually up. Fearful dogs can show aggression in the same contexts as dominantly aggressive dogs, but their body posture will be more consistent with fear and would include lowered head and body, tail tucked and perhaps averted eyes. It is also possible to have multiple motivations. Many dogs are showing aggression in the above mentioned contexts are anxious and fearful. Not all social status aggressive dogs behave the same and a description of what the dog looks like, how they responded to challenges and where they occur and with whom are important pieces of information to obtain before making a diagnosis. Additionally, a dog may only show aggression in limited contexts, say food guarding only, and in such case is probably not motivated by dominance but food guarding behavior. Within a family a dog may exhibit social status aggressive behavior to some family members and be subordinate and non-aggressive to others.

How the dog looks during these encounters is important but more so is how the dog behaved during the first initial aggressive episodes. It is possible for a dog to growl at their owner because of fear and if the owner backs away the pet learns that aggression works. Over time, with repetition of the same scenario the dog learns that aggression results in a favorable outcome. This may result in a dog that acts confident rather than fearful, but underlying anxiety and fear may be the cause of the aggression. This would result in a different diagnosis, rather than social status aggression this dog may be exhibiting fear or conflict aggression.

What should I do if I believe that my dog is acting in a "dominant" manner and/or exhibiting dominance motivated or social status aggression?

All aggressive challenges should be taken seriously. Dogs are capable of hurting and inflicting a great deal of damage with their bites. Physically confronting a dog that is acting in an aggressive manner can result in the escalation of the aggression and subsequent injury to humans. Dogs who have been controlling their environment and human housemates for some time will not easily relinquish the "leader" role. Physical challenges could also lead to fearful and defensive aggression.

Therefore it is important to be able to accurately determine how the dog will behave. All aggressive and potentially aggressive situations should be identified and avoided. The situations and responses are not always predictable. At no time should family members attempt to "out muscle" the dog and force it to obey. This can result in serious human injury.

First, identify all situations that might lead to aggression and prevent access to these circumstances (by caging or confinement or environmental manipulation) or otherwise control the dog when a confrontational situation might arise. Although the long-term goal would be to reduce or eliminate the potential for aggression in these situations, each new episode could lead to injury and further aggravation of the problem. A head collar and lead is a good way to control the dog inside the home while a muzzle may be even more effective at preventing bites.

Second, identify and correct those situations where the dog may not be aggressive but is asserting its control. Dogs should not be allowed into areas or onto furniture where they might be possessive, protective or unwilling to obey. In principle your dog should not have resting and sleeping areas such as your bed or your furniture since these are places where people are, and therefore a potential location for an encounter and injury. Dogs should sleep on their own mat or in their own area and be under constant supervision when they are out of these areas and around family members. In addition, dogs that lead or pull the owners through doors or on walks, must be taught to heel and follow. During training and when giving commands insure that your dog always obeys. Leave a leash and head halter attached to insure success. Mouthing, play biting and tug of war games should be avoided. While they might not increase aggression they do allow the dog to learn how to use its mouth to control outcomes. .

Third, withdraw all privileges and rewards. Affection, attention, praise, food, treats, play and toys are rewards and must be earned. When rewards are given on demand, the dog is controlling the owner, and the owner is rewarding the domineering or demanding behavior. In order to retrain these dogs and show that the owner is in control the dog needs to learn that these resources will only be given when they are earned for obedient and subordinate actions in the presence of the owners. Rewards also take on their highest degree of motivation when they have been withheld. Just as it would be inappropriate to try and train a dog with a piece of food immediately following a meal, it is of little value to try and use affection or play as a reward for a dog that receives play or attention on demand. Therefore if a dog seeks any form of attention, affection, play, or food, the dog must be ignored so that it cannot achieve control over these resources.

Fourth, reward-based obedience training is essential for all dogs, but especially those that are disobedient or showing social status aggressiveness. Begin in safe and successful environments with rewards given for compliance. Once successful, these commands should be practiced in a variety of environments and with all family members. Again use a leash and head halter to ensure success, while controlling the head and mouth.

Fifth, be in "control". Do this by controlling the resources that the dog wants and then require the dog to "earn" them. Usually this means that before the dog gets what it wants, the dog is asked to come, sit, stay or "go to its mat." For example, the dog can be taught that in order to receive food, petting, play, or walks it must first respond to one of these commands. Because the dog wants something it is more likely to comply. Some dogs will not sit when asked. If they do not obey, they do not get what they want. Should the dog come to you to demand attention, affection, play, or food, ignore it. The rewards must be only given when your dog responds to one of your commands. Commands should be given calmly, but firmly and you should be willing to walk away if the dog does not comply. It is essential to only give the command one time. Repetition of the command allows the dog to decide when to comply. The goal is to demand immediate and prompt compliance or the dog does not receive the resource it desires.

What can be done if my dog refuses to obey my commands?

It is essential that the owner avoid any confrontation or situation that might lead to injury or where the owner may not be able to safely gain control. Each time your dog fails to comply, it reinforces his or her control over you. For these dogs you can gain more immediate control if the dog is fitted with a remote leash and head halter, that can then be used to take the dog for walks and is left attached when the dog is indoors and the owner is at home (except for bedtime). Each time the dog is given a command that is not obeyed the leash and head halter can be used to get the desired response. Although the head halter and remote leash is an excellent means of ensuring success and physical control, you have not succeeded until the dog will respond to the verbal commands, without the need for leash pulls and halter management. In other words if the dog responds to the command it is rewarded, but if it does not obey, you must make it obey using the leash and halter (never punishment), and repeat the exercise until the dog responds to the verbal command alone. Another important advantage of the head halter is that it provides for safe control. By pulling forward and upward with a leash, the mouth can be closed, the dog can be looked in the eyes, and released and rewarded for subordinate or obedient responses. A remote leash and basket muzzle can also be used to ensure safety but they do provide the same degree of head and muzzle control as a long lead and head collar.

For some dogs, these steps will help decrease the aggressive behavior. Many dogs like routine and control and have only assumed control because no one else in the household was in the leader position. However, do not expect a cure because some dogs with social status aggression may continually attempt to control situations and resources and can cause injury if confronted. Social status aggression that is long standing has already resulted in owner injury, and multiple challenges should be discussed with a behavior consultant to determine if and how the problem can be corrected safely. Although there are no drugs that specifically reduce dominance or help the owners to attain leadership, drug therapy may be useful in some cases as an aid to behavior therapy.

AGGRESSION – SIBLING RIVALRY

What is a dominance hierarchy and why is it important to dogs?

Dogs are social animals whose evolutionary history makes them willing and able to live in groups. Group living enabled wolves to work together to obtain food, raise their young and defend their territory. It would be counter-productive for members of a group to fight with each other and risk injury. That would prevent them from working with the group. Although domestic dogs are not wolves, they do have a social structure in which each dog is either dominant (leader) or subordinate in its relationship with each pack member. This is a "dominance hierarchy". The leader or "alpha" dog is the one that has first access to all the "critical" resources. These resources include food, resting places, mates, territory and favored possessions. Assertion of dominance by the alpha is generally communicated through facial expressions, body postures and actions. Fighting is rare, since as soon as the subordinate submits or defers to the alpha animal and the alpha gets its way, he or she gives up the challenge.

My dogs have lived together for some time and now they are fighting. Why?

Fights between dogs in the household are often about dominance or social status. Social status aggression most often occurs when dogs reach social maturity at 12-36 months of age. Fights will be about those resources that are considered important to dogs. Therefore fights may occur over treats, owner attention, greeting the owner upon return, sleeping positions near the owner, entering or exiting the home, high arousal situations such as fence running, or movement through tight spaces. These fights occur most often between dogs of near equal status and often, but not always, dogs of the same sex, and seem to be most severe between female dogs.

I try to treat my dogs equally, but they still fight. What am I doing wrong?

Trying to treat two dogs as equals will only serve to counter the natural tendency toward a hierarchy. The dog that is the more dominant in a relationship needs to be supported in its position and the more subordinate must be taught to accept the relationship. When you support or encourage the subordinate dog as it tries to gain access to resources such as your attention, the dominant dog may begin to challenge and fight, in an effort to keep the lower ranking dog in its " place". If you then discipline the dominant dog, or pull the dominant dog away, you have favored, supported and come to the aid of the subordinate dog.

Both my dogs are the same age, and after a third, older dog died, they began to fight – why?

Conflicts may occur between dogs when the dominance status is ambiguous or when they are particularly close in rank. After the decline, illness or death of an older dog, fighting may begin in the remaining dogs even when one is clearly dominant. This is because the older dog may have been dominant to both dogs, and now they are trying to establish new positions. In any case the fighting can be severe and injurious. Although you should generally attempt to allow dogs to resolve their differences on their own you will need to intervene if there is the potential for injury. Under no circumstances should the dogs be allowed to "fight it out". You could be injured due to redirected aggressive attacks, or when you attempt to break up the fight.

My younger dog always deferred to the older dog, but now they fight.

One scenario that can result in social aggression is when an older, previously dominant dog, is challenged by a younger, more domineering dog. This may happen as the older dog ages, or as the younger dog reaches behavioral maturity at 12 to 36 months. This may be an attempt to alter the existing hierarchy but at other times the dog is being a "bully". Sometimes the older dog will acquiesce and things are fine but at other times the owners do not want the change and intervene. In some situations, the older dog will not relinquish the dominant role even though it cannot physically compete with the younger dog. This can result in severe, injurious fights.

How should I break up fighting if it occurs?

This can be a dangerous situation for people and dogs alike. Owners usually try to reach for the collar of the fighting dogs, or if one is small, pick it up. This can result in severe owner injury if the fighting is very intense. If both are wearing leashes they can usually be pulled apart. If all else fails, you might be able to break up the fight with a water rifle, citronella spray, broom or another distraction (such as pepper spray or a fire extinguisher). Reaching for the dog is usually the worst thing to do, as you could be injured (either accidentally or intentionally).

When people intervene in dog fights, redirected aggression is possible. Aggression (growl, snarl or bite) can be redirected to a person, animal or object other than that which evoked the aggression. If during the course of a dog fight, you pick up one of the dogs, the other may continue to attack and direct it at you.

What should I do when one of my dogs challenges another?

Aggression between household dogs can be difficult to treat. You will need to identify the subordinate dog, and ensure that you are not encouraging the subordinate dog to challenge the more dominant. It is critical that you never come to the aid of the subordinate against the more dominant. If left alone, the dogs will often use posturing and threats to end encounters without injury. If one dog backs down, the problem may be resolved. However, when neither dog is willing to give up the dominant position (as in a young dog challenging an older dog in the home), fighting will usually result.

A common owner error is the desire to make life "fair". This often results in owners allowing subordinate dogs access to resources, such as attention, treats, toys, or entry into territory that they would not normally have. Usually the subordinate dog would not behave in a manner that would challenge the dominant when no one is around to "protect" it. If you encourage or protect the subordinate dog, it may be "tempted" to break the "rules", and the dominant dog may become aggressive to enforce the "rules". If you then punish the dominant dog for aggression, the subordinate dog learns it can engage in prohibited behavior while the owner is present. This is why, in many households, there is no fighting when the owners are gone. The subordinate is aware of the hierarchy, and does nothing to challenge the dominant dog, unless the owners are around to intervene.

Another potential problem may occur when the relationship between individuals is context dependent. In other words, one dog may be dominant about owner attention but may not care who eats first. This is why it is important to understand the entire social relationship between dogs.

How can I treat this problem?

Although the dominance relationship between the two dogs must be dealt with, the first step is for the owner to gain complete control over both dogs. As leader or alpha your presence and commands should be sufficient to prevent all dominance challenges between dogs and to intervene as needed when threats emerge. Control of each dog is achieved through the use of verbal commands, by leaving a leash and head halter attached for immediate control, and by withholding all rewards unless earned. Attention on demand not only encourages situations where one dog may challenge the other, but also allows your dogs to control you. Inattention on demand teaches the dogs that all rewards are provided only when you choose, and reduces or eliminates those situations where challenges might occur. Head halter with leash control and obedience-reward based training of each dog should first be done separately. With a head halter and remote leash on each dog you will have effective control, and a means of controlling and separating the dogs if needed. With control of the head and mouth, aggressive threats can be curtailed and either dog can be placed in a subordinate posture, by pulling up on the leash, closing the mouth, looking the dog in the eyes, or pulling the head sideways so that the dog's gaze is averted. In severe cases muzzles may be needed to keep people and dogs safe while therapy is undertaken.

Next, treatment must be designed to identify and support the dominant dog. Several differing treatment plans exist. One is supporting the dog that has been in the household the longest, usually this is the oldest dog. Another treatment is to identify the dominant dog based on how the dogs interact, in other words, who threatens and who defers. Care must be exercised to watch for bullies who do not allow other dogs any status and are not consistent in the application of threats and response to deference. All dogs must have some status and the ability to respond in an appropriate manner and thus avoid aggression. In some cases the dog that is chosen is the younger, larger, more physically capable dog, if this dog wishes to be the leader. Often, this is also the aggressor. You must allow the dominant dog priority to go outside, to come in, or to receive food or owner attention and affection. If you are petting the dominant dog and the subordinate dog approaches, make it wait. Importantly, you must avoid all circumstances that elicit aggression. If the more dominant dog approaches or challenges the subordinate dog and the subordinate dog assumes a subordinate posture, the owners are not to intervene as long as the dominant dogs stop. If the dogs are likely to fight when you are away or at homecomings, separate the dogs whenever you are out, or are not available to supervise.

On other occasions, neither dog is willing to be subordinate. This could be due to a challenge to the hierarchy as a younger dog matures, as an older dog becomes sick or aged, when a new dog is introduced into the home, or when one dog is not clearly dominant to the other. You should learn how to recognize canine body language and low-level threats such as eye contact, snarls or low growls. Keep records of threats, attacks, or tension-producing situations. An owner must have excellent control over both dogs in order to succeed. To facilitate treatment, decrease the chances of injuries and increase owner control, a remote leash can be left attached to one or both dogs. Often the best form of owner control is to fit and train each dog with a head halter, and to leave a leash and head halter on each dog when they are together (under the owner's supervision). In other cases, basket muzzles may provide more safety and allow owners to work with the dogs.

Once you have gained sufficient control over both dogs, and have identified the more dominant, you will need to deal with the circumstances that might elicit aggression. Greetings should be low key, and both dogs should be ignored. Treats are avoided and rawhides or other delicious things are not given unless the dogs are separated or on leash. Movement through tight spaces is avoided or controlled. You must be present to ensure that the dominant dog gains preferential access to food, resting places, territory, owner attention and treats. Commands and rewards or the leash and halter can be used to ensure that the subordinate does not challenge, and that the dominant does not continue to show aggression once the subordinate submits. Getting the dogs together without incident can best be accomplished when the dogs are otherwise occupied and when a confrontation is unlikely, such as during walks or feeding. It is usually best to have two individuals to walk the dogs (each person controls one dog) and not to allow them to forge in front of one another. During feeding, keep the dogs at a distance, far enough apart that they do not show aggression. Slowly the dishes are moved closer together as long as the dogs do not react. The food serves as a reward in this situation. If the dogs react, the food bowls are moved further apart. When the owner is not home or supervising the dogs, the dogs are separated or crated.

Basket muzzles could be left on each dog to increase safety while the dogs are together. They can also be used to "proof" the training, by putting the dogs together in situations that previously led to aggression. Drug therapy for one or both dogs may also be useful.

Can social aggression always be corrected?
At times aggression may persist despite owner control and intervention. In those cases alternate living arrangements for one of the animals may need to be made.

BARKING

Why do dogs bark?

Barking is one of the most common complaints of dog owners and their neighbors! But barking is natural. It can serve as a territorial warning signal to other dogs and pack members. Dogs may vocalize when separated from their pack or family members. Barking also occurs during times of indecision, anxiety, or frustration. Medical problems can also contribute to vocalization, especially in the older dog.

How can barking problems be prevented?

Socialization and habituation – get puppies used to as many new people, animals, situations and noises as possible. This will minimize the amount or intensity of alarm barking. Barking should only be allowed to alert owners and then be controlled and stopped before the dog becomes agitated and out of control. Owner control, training and leadership are essential (see 'puppy training – taking charge').

How can I stop my dog barking when I leave?

Effective crate training techniques when your dog is first obtained, should decrease the dog's anxiety when it is left alone in its crate (see 'house safety and crate training'). Your dog should gradually be taught to spend longer periods of time away from you. Obtaining two dogs may provide company for each other and may reduce distress vocalization and departure anxiety. If your dog has been barking when you leave for some time, he may be suffering from separation anxiety and you should consult your veterinarian for treatment options.

My dog constantly barks. What does she want?

Attention getting barking can be problematic and is often reinforced by owners giving in to their dog's demands. Allowing a barking dog indoors, or feeding, patting, praising, playing with, giving a toy, or even just going to a barking dog to try and quiet it down, are just a few examples of how an owner may unknowingly reinforce barking. Never reward barking with any type of attention, even occasionally.

How can I train my dog to be 'quiet'?

Training the dog to a 'quiet' command is an invaluable aid for controlling undesirable barking. You must find an effective means of quieting the dog, which should be preceded with a command such as 'quiet'. Just loudly telling your pet to 'be quiet', will probably not be understood, especially if silence does not follow the verbal command. In fact, yelling may just add to the noise and anxiety, thereby encouraging your dog to bark more.

One of the most practical techniques for teaching a dog to cease barking on command, is to first, be able to command the dog to begin barking on cue. Use a stimulus that will cause the dog to bark and pair it with a 'bark' command. Numerous repetitions allow the dog to associate the word 'bark' or 'speak' with the action. Dogs that bark on command can then be taught to turn off the barking by removing the cue or stimulus, and giving a 'hush' or 'quiet' command just before the barking subsides. As soon as your dog is quiet, give a favored treat or reward.

It can be difficult or impractical to teach a dog to be 'quiet' on command if the barking cannot be predicted or 'turned on' or if it is too intense.

Another method to teach a "quiet" command is to wait until your dog is barking, say to a doorbell and while he is barking place a very tasty food treat by his nose. Most dogs will stop barking to sniff the treat. At the same time you must say the word you will use for quiet, such as 'silent', 'hush' etc. When the dog is quiet (as they will be because dogs cannot sniff and bark at the same time) you can praise him, say 'good, quiet' and give the treat. Again, as with all new tasks, numerous repetitions are necessary for lasting learning.

Alternately, distraction or remote punishment devices can be used to disrupt the barking. One of the most effective means of interrupting barking and ensuring quiet is a remote leash and head halter. A pull on the leash disrupts the dog and closes the mouth, which should also coincide with a verbal command such as  'quiet' or 'hush'. Quiet behavior can then be reinforced first by releasing and then giving a reinforcer such as praise or food if the dog remains quiet. Soon the dog should associate the closed mouth and the word prompt with the absence of noise and begin to stop barking when given the verbal prompt alone.

What are my chances of correcting my dog's barking problem?

Chances are good for most barking problems. But the household situation in which the dog resides may make it extremely difficult to correct completely. Even a small amount of barking could disturb a sleeping baby, or upset neighbors, (particularly in apartments or townhouses). When trying to resolve barking problems, the motivation for the barking behavior is an important component. Some stimuli are so strong that it will be difficult to stop the barking behavior. You need sufficient time to implement the correction training.

What can I do to correct my dog's barking problem?

The treatment program must be based on the type of problem, your household, the immediacy of the situation, and the type and level of control that you require. A good behavioral history is important to determine cause, motivation and potential reinforcing stimuli for the barking behavior. Treatment plans need to consider the following:

1) Ensure that your dog is not being rewarded inadvertently. Some owners in an attempt to calm their dog down will actually encourage the barking by giving attention, play, food or affection.

2) Insure that your response is not aggravating the problem. For example yelling at a dog that is barking due to anxiety or as a territorial response is only likely to increase the dog's barking and anxiety.

3) Sometimes the home environment can be modified so that the dog is kept away from the stimuli (sounds and sights) that cause barking. Exposure

might be minimized by confining the dog to a crate, or room away from doors and windows or covering windows so that the dog cannot look outside. Additionally, privacy fencing may be helpful for dogs outdoors. Dogs that bark when left alone outdoors may have to be kept indoors except when the owner is available to supervise. Trigger sounds such as doorbells or telephones that might have become conditioned stimuli for barking should be altered to change their sound.

4) Until effective control and leadership is established, training programs are unlikely to be successful. Increasing interactive play periods and exercise, crate and confinement training, halter training and obedience classes may need to be implemented before bark control training can begin.

5) Once you have sufficient control and the dog responds to obedience commands and handling, it should be possible to train your dog to cease barking on command. Training the dog to cease barking on command can be accomplished with lure reward techniques, distraction techniques, or halter and leash training. Regardless of the technique, rewards should be given as soon as the barking stops, so that the dog learns that quiet behavior earns rewards. It is most important to associate SILENCE with the command used. Over time the behavior should be shaped so that the dog is required to stay quiet for progressively longer times, before a reward is given.

6) Once the owner has sufficient control with training and the quiet command, it may then be possible to begin a retraining program in the presence of the stimuli (people, other dogs) that lead to barking. Training with a head halter and leash often provides a tool for implementing the techniques safely and effectively especially indoors or when the owner is nearby. The stimulus should first be presented to the dog from a distance (e.g. children riding bicycles on the street while the dog stands on its porch), and the dog given a quiet or sit-stay command. Although the halter and leash is generally all that is required to control the dog and achieve the appropriate response, the dog could also be disrupted using a device such as an ultrasonic trainer or shake can. Training sessions are then repeated with progressively more intense stimuli. This type of training can be effective, but progress can be slow and time consuming.

7) Pets that are barking for other reasons (fear, separation anxiety, or compulsive disorders) will require treatment for the underlying problem.

Should I punish my dog when she keeps barking?
Punishment is seldom effective in the control and correction of barking problems. Excessive levels of punishment can increase anxiety and further aggravate many forms of barking, while mild punishment merely rewards the behavior by providing attention.

What anti-barking devices are there and are they effective?
Owner-Activated Products: These products are most useful for getting the pet's attention (disruption) during quiet command training. Ultrasonic devices (Pet Agree™, Easy Trainer™), audible devices (Barker Breaker™, rape alarms), water sprayers, or a shake can (an empty peanut or soda can with a few coins or pebbles sealed inside) are often successful. Without concurrent retraining techniques and an owner with good control, many dogs will soon begin to ignore the devices. However, if the device is used to interrupt the barking and the quiet behavior is then reinforced, the pet may become less anxious and less likely to bark in the presence of the stimulus, or at the very least will quiet much faster on command.

Bark-Activated Products: When barking occurs in the owner's absence, bark activated products (in conjunction with environmental modification and retraining) are often the most practical means of deterring inappropriate barking. Bark-activated products may also be a better choice than owner-activated devices, since they ensure immediate and accurate timing. Off-collar devices are useful for training the dog to cease barking in selected areas, such as near doorways or windows, (or for dogs that bark in their crate or pen). The Super Barker Breaker emits an audible alarm while the Yapper Zapper™ sprays a stream of water each time the dog barks.

Bark-activated collars are useful when barking does not occur in a predictable location. Audible and ultrasonic training collars are occasionally effective but they are neither sufficiently unpleasant nor consistent enough to be a reliable deterrent. The Aboistop™ or Gentle Spray™ collar emits a spray of citronella each time the dog barks and is sufficiently unpleasant to deter most dogs. Although these may be effective in the owner's absence, they have their most lasting effects when the owner is present to supervise and retrain. As soon as the barking ceases, the owner should direct the dog into an enjoyable pastime (e.g. play, tummy rub, favorite treat) as long as the dog remains quiet. Soon the dog may associate the stimulus (people coming to the door, people coming to the yard) with something positive.

Most importantly, bark collars only work when they are on the dog. Most dogs will learn to distinguish when the collar is on and when it is off. When they are not wearing the collar, most dogs will bark.

Is debarking surgery effective?

Surgical debarking is a drastic and often permanent method of eliminating barking. Varying degrees of vocalization may return as the surgical site heals and scars. Devocalization may need to be considered when owners are confronted with the option of immediately resolving a barking problem or having to give up their pet. However, all attempts at behavior modification should be continued to try and address the underlying motivation for barking and perhaps effect a permanent solution.

BITING – PUPPIES

Why is my puppy nipping and biting family members?

Although often thought to be a teething behavior, nipping, mouthing and biting in young dogs is generally a form of social play. Teething is more likely to involve gnawing or chewing on household objects. The first thing you must do is provide ample opportunity for play, without biting. Social play with people could involve controlled chase and retrieve games, as well as long walks or jogging. Although wrestling and tug-of-war games can be fun, they may lead to play that is too rough or rambunctious. Puppies need to learn to inhibit the force of their bite, commonly known as bite inhibition. This is something they start to learn while with their littermates. It is one reason that puppies should not go to new homes until 7 – 8 weeks of age and they have had time to practice social skills with other dogs. It can therefore be extremely beneficial for the puppy to have regular interactive social play periods with other dogs or puppies in the home or in the neighborhood (see 'play and exercise in dogs' for additional information).

How can I stop play biting?

Provided the dog is receiving adequate play, attention and exercise, you can turn the training to bite inhibition. One of the things that they need to learn is how much pressure from their jaws causes pain. Without this feedback, a puppy does not learn to inhibit the force of its bite. Because all dogs can and will bite at some time, this lesson is vital for human safety.

How is this lesson taught? When puppies play with each other, if one puppy bites another too hard, the bitten puppy will yelp, and may also stop playing and leave. This sends the message to the puppy that its' bites were too hard and if it wishes to continue to play, it needs to be gentle. However, people often do not send this message to their puppy. In the beginning, they often allow the puppy to chew on them without reprimands and the puppy assumes that the behavior is acceptable. Children appear to be most vulnerable because their attempts at stopping the biting may not be properly timed or sufficiently abrupt to stop the puppy from biting. In fact a child's response is often seen by the puppy as an invitation to increase its level of chase and play. Adult supervision or a head halter for training should help to insure more immediate success.

The message people should send is that mouthing and chewing on hands is painful. To do this, often all that is necessary is for all family members to emit a sharp 'yip' so that the puppy backs off and cease all play and attention immediately. This sends the message to the puppy that the bites are painful and that biting will cause play to be terminated. When consistently administered this will often stop playful biting. Another option is to use a sharp 'off' command while briefly pushing forward with the hand to back the puppy away (no hitting). The command 'off' followed by the immediate removal of play can act as a form of punishment with the word 'off' soon teaching the dog that if it continues to bite, play will be withdrawn. This training often works for those family members that are a little more forceful and assertive and who are immediate and consistent in their training. If the puppy persists, chases or immediately repeats the behavior, closing a door and walking out of the room can help to teach the puppy that nipping leads to immediate inattention.

What if yelping does not help?

Other techniques are often suggested for play biting. Some involve harsh discipline, like slapping the puppy under the chin or forcefully holding the mouth closed. Remember, pain can cause aggression and cause the puppy to become anxious, fearful or perhaps more excited. These techniques also require that you grab an excited puppy; not an easy thing to do. Some puppies may even misinterpret the owner's attempts at punishment as rough play, which in turn might lead to an increase in the behavior. Physical methods are therefore not recommended. Owners who cannot inhibit the puppy with a yelp, could consider a shake can, electronic alarm, air horn, or ultrasonic device, as soon as the biting becomes excessive.

The use of a head halter with a remote leash attached allows the puppy to play and chew, but a quick pull on the leash can immediately and successfully close the mouth and stop biting without any physical force. By simultaneously saying "no biting", most puppies will quickly learn the meaning of the command. As soon as the puppy stops and calms down, the owner can allow play to resume, as long as biting does not begin again. This is one of the quickest and most effective approaches to stop the biting and get immediate control of the muzzle and mouth, for owners that are not gaining sufficient verbal control.

Remember that play biting is a component of play behavior in puppies. Play is a form of social interaction. Realize that your puppy is trying to play with you even though the behavior is rough. To ensure that you are in control, be certain that each play session is initiated by you and not the puppy, and that you can end each session whenever you choose. One effective strategy when the play gets too rough is to immediately end the play session and leave. Social withdrawal can be a very powerful tool. Leave the puppy alone long enough to calm down. If upon your return the wild playing begins again, leave again. Although it is tempting to pick the puppy up and take it out of the room, this interaction may be interpreted by your puppy as additional play and the biting may continue as you carry the puppy to a confinement location.

Why do dogs tend to pull, chase and forge ahead?

Dogs tend to pull ahead and lunge forward for a number of reasons. The primary reason for most dogs (at least initially) is that they are exploratory, playful and social, and they are motivated to investigate new areas, new odors and new people or new dogs as well as areas where exciting things have been found in the past. The more they pull, the faster they get where they are going. As you pull backwards in an attempt to restrain your dog, he/she is likely to resist by pulling forward even harder, since most dogs tend to pull against pressure. Although perhaps not a scientifically accurate term this is often referred to as an opposition reflex. Dogs that are aggressive to stimuli (e.g. children, other dogs), and those that have the urge to chase or heel (e.g. joggers, cyclists) may pull ahead in an attempt to chase. Dogs that are fearful or defensive may be more aggressive when restrained by a leash since they are unable to escape and more likely to defend their personal space or their family members (defensive or protective aggression). Those dogs that are fearful or otherwise reluctant to leave home may be pulling and forging ahead on their way back home.

How can pulling and forging ahead be controlled?

It is a shame when owners are unable to engage in the simple joy of walking their dog due to extreme leash pulling. The dog should be taught through obedience training, lures and rewards to respond to the 'heel' command. Training should begin in an environment where success can be ensured. Using a control mechanism (leash and collar, leash and head halter), and highly motivating rewards, the dog should first be taught to walk at the owner's side. During the first few training sessions distractions should be avoided so that the rewards and motivation keep the dog's interest and attention. If the dog begins to pull ahead, pulling backwards on the leash and a neck collar, leads to resistance from the dog, causing the dog to lunge forward more intensely. It is best to take 1-2 steps at a time and keep your dog in the correct position, rather than trying to accomplish a long walk. If the dog pulls the leash taut, stop and wait till the dog returns to a slack leash position before rewarding and continuing. As the dog learns where to be in relation to the owner, gradually walk a few more steps. Set the dog up to succeed. This can often be accomplished using a food reward held at thigh level to keep the dog's nose in position.

The head halter is one of the best means of gaining immediate control (see 'management devices in dog training' and 'excitable and disobedient dogs'). When the dog is wearing a head halter and pulls ahead, a pull on the leash will cause your dog's head to turn toward you. Then as you pull upwards and forward, the dog will pull backwards into a sit. Quickly release tension and reward. Continue along your walk and anytime the dog begins to pass you pull forward and upward and your dog should begin to back up. It is not necessary to get a 'sit' with each pull, only a dog who stays beside or just behind you with a slack leash as you walk.

In order to teach the dog to walk by your side, this should start from the time you exit your front door. Have your dog 'sit' and 'stay' and then open the front door. If the dog begins to run out pull up and forward so that the dog returns to the 'sit', and release. Walk slowly forward so that you are between the dog and the door, slowly lengthening the leash while the dog remains in place but leaving no more than an inch or two of slack. Provided the dog does not forge ahead, step through the door and then allow the dog to follow up to (but not past) you. Proceed onto the porch and down onto the yard with the dog following. Any time the dog begins to step or forge past, the leash can be pulled up and forward so that the dog backs up, and released immediately when the dog is in place. Although the dog could be made to sit each time it pulls forward, the goal is to have the dog back up just far enough that it remains at your side. The tension on the leash is then released and the dog is encouraged to walk forward. In short, pulling tends to lead to tension, while walking at your side earns release (i.e. a slack leash). If the dog "puts on the brakes" and will not follow, a tendency is to pull ahead, but, as mentioned, dogs tend to resist by pulling in the opposite direction. To get the dog up and following, loosen the slack on the lead and encourage the dog to follow verbally or with food prompts. Once you have the dog successfully heeling in the yard with no distractions, you can proceed to the front yard and the street while there are still no distractions. With practice, strong motivators and the use of the head halter, the dog can then gradually be walked in the presence of stimuli that might otherwise cause lunging and forging, such as other dogs, cyclists, or children playing.

Another solution is to use "no pull harnesses" (see 'behavior management products'). These devices fit around the dog's body and around the forelegs so that when the dog forges ahead the forelegs and body can be controlled. Although these harnesses do not provide the level of control afforded by the head halter, compared to head halters, they require little or no training and do provide immediate control of pulling.

My dog chases and I am worried he will get hurt. What can I do?

Chasing and running after prey, nipping at heels and herding are normal dog behaviors. These behaviors are more strongly motivated in some breeds of dogs than others. In addition, some dogs may be motivated to chase intruders (people, other dogs) from their property and, when the intruders leave, the behavior may appear to the dog to have been successful. This usually results in the dog continuing in the "chase" behaviors. In order to control chase behaviors, it is necessary to train the dog to do something different than it was doing before. It is not enough to yell "no" and punish the dog. This alone will not stop a behavior that has a strong motivation, but may cause the dog to be more anxious or fearful about the "stimulus" which would INCREASE the problem.

First, let's talk about prevention of chasing behaviors. Once you have witnessed the young dog engaging in an inappropriate chase, now is the time to start training. Get a leash on the dog and teach it to sit and stay. Then present the dog with the distraction that it would normally chase and reward the dog for good behavior. Remember, when off the leash the dog may revert to its old habits. Therefore, try to avoid those situations until you feel confident that the dog will behave.

Once the dog has been engaging in chase behaviors for some time, it will be more difficult to stop the behavior. The very fact that the object the dog chases runs, is reinforcement enough. A program of differential reinforcement or response substitution is necessary to teach the dog the desired and acceptable response when exposed to the stimulus. If there is fear or anxiety when exposed to the stimulus desensitization and counter-conditioning is needed to change the dog's attitude and emotions to ones that are positive (see 'behavior modification, desensitization, counter-conditioning, differential reinforcement and flooding' for terms).

Treatment by differential reinforcement involves teaching the dog to 'sit' and 'stay' for rewards and then gradually introducing objects that the dog chases. It will be necessary to first start with objects the dog is least likely to chase and progress to more tempting items. If the problem is severe, a consultation with a behaviorist may be necessary. Control with a head halter and leash often is the most practical and most successful at ensuring that the dog will 'sit' and 'stay' in the presence of the stimulus. The use of highly motivating rewards (favored food treats, favored toys) can also be used to lure the dog into a 'sit' and given as a reward for staying.

My dog charges the door and jumps on people who enter my home. What can I do?

Another behavior that causes problems for owners is door charging. Door charging is the behavior of the dog speeding to the door whenever anyone knocks or rings the bell. To deal with this problem start by teaching the dog to 'sit' and 'stay' for a food reward in the entry area. This is best done with the dog wearing a headcollar and on a leash. Gradually phase out food treats when the behavior is learned and can be reliably repeated. Next you may need to practice with family members entering the home. Finally, when the dog has mastered the task with people he knows, practice with visitors, keeping the dog on a leash and making it 'sit' and 'stay'. Always require your dog to 'sit' before it gets petted and you can go along way to eliminating jumping behavior. If the dog has never even practiced the task without distractions, how can you expect the dog to perform the task when visitors come over? If door-charging behavior is coupled with aggression, you should seek the help of a behaviorist.

How can I prevent my dog from jumping up on others and me?

For many dogs, jumping up on people is part of their greeting routine. Often, owners have tried to discourage this behavior using methods such as squeezing the front feet, stepping on the dog's toes, or kneeing the dog in the chest. Yet the behavior continues. For some dogs these techniques provide an uncomfortable but acceptable form of attention. For others, the technique leads to increasing anxiety as people arrive at the door. Therefore in both cases the problem is gradually being further aggravated. If that is the case with your dog, then it is important to think about what might be motivating the dog to jump up and what is the reinforcement for the behavior continuing.

Usually the motivation for the jumping up behavior is to greet people. Many dogs like to greet "face to face", like they do with their canine counterparts. Some people, however, find this objectionable. Correction therefore must not be directed at punishing the problem, but rather finding a means of teaching the dog an appropriate greeting posture. This usually is a sit/stay, which can then be rewarded with food and attention. Once the dog has perfected this at the doorway, when there are no people coming or going, its time to begin practicing with family members, before progressing to visitors. Make the dog sit and stay while people come and hand the dog a treat. If the dog gets up, then put him back in the sit and try again until the dog remains sitting through the arrival. Often placing a "treat jar" by the front door with a bell on it will help. Once the dog associates the bell on the jar with a treat, and a treat with a sit/stay, the dog will be more likely to perform the task.

Another way to train this behavior is to set up visitors to come to your home. You will have better control of your dog if you use a head collar and a leash for this exercise. Have the first person come to the door and instruct your dog to 'sit' and 'stay'. Then, let them in. Hopefully with some effort you will get your dog to continue to sit. Have the person enter, give a treat and sit down. After five minutes, have them leave by the back door, come to the front and enter again. This second entry should go easier as your dog will have just seen the person. If you can repeat this 4-6 times for each visitor, the dog will have plenty of opportunity to learn the new task.

Once you understand the motivation, and have trained a new task, you need to be sure you have identified all the reinforcement for the behavior. If the dog succeeds in getting any attention for the jumping behavior, then the dog will continue to jump. Attention may be petting, pushing away, (which resembles play behavior), and even mild reprimands can be reinforcing for a dog that really wants attention. To change this behavior you need to remove ALL reinforcement. This may mean that you do not look, speak, touch or interact with the dog IN ANY WAY when it jumps on you. Walk by the dog, give a command such as 'sit', but do not interact with the dog. Alternately, you could try punishment to see if you can disrupt the behavior just as it begins.

To use punishment for jumping up, you need to be able to QUICKLY AND HUMANELY interrupt the behavior. This is often best done with some type of device that makes a loud noise. Shake cans, ultrasonic trainers, rape alarms, and air horns, all make loud noises that will often startle the dog. As soon as the dog hesitates, you need to give the dog an alternative command so that the dog can do the proper thing and then reward the dog with praise. So, as you administer the noise, you say "SIT" and when the dog sits you reward it with praise and food treats if available. Many dogs soon learn that to avoid the noise, they need to sit and will do so to greet you. Then have the person leave, and re-enter the home. Use the device and command if the dog does not immediately sit, and a good sit and reward as soon as the dog does sit. Continue to have the person leave and re-enter until the dog sits for its reward without hesitating. Another efficient but costly means of immediate interruption is to use a citronella spray collar. Bark activated collars are useful if the dog barks as people arrive at the door. Alternately a remote collar can be used to interrupt the jumping and the desirable response reinforced e.g. sitting.

Another method that is consistently successful at deterring and preventing the jumping up, is to leave a leash and head halter on the dog during greeting. All it takes is stepping on the leash or a quick sharp pull to prevent or disrupt the jumping up. Again, be certain to reward non-jumping behavior.

Some people like to allow the dog to jump up on them at certain times. You must never allow the dog to choose the time. Ideally you should teach your dog to jump up on command such as "give me a hug" or "come up here". This way, you have the behavior under verbal control and you decide when the dog will be allowed to jump up.

CONTROLLING STEALING & TEACHING THE 'GIVE' COMMAND

What is the best way to deal with "stealing" in my puppy?

Most puppies love to explore and chew, so it's no surprise when a young puppy steals household objects. When you try to get these items back from your dog, a chase ensues because either the game is fun and the dog enjoys the attention or because the dog is reluctant to give up its new found "treasure". Pups may raid garbage, steal food off tables and countertops and enter cupboards or refrigerators, where they help themselves to snacks. Despite owner attempts at punishment, these behaviors continue. Why?

When dealing with an unwanted behavior, look for the motivation. Food items are appealing on their own. Some puppies steal objects when they are left unsupervised, because they have not been directed to an acceptable activity. Puppies may continue to steal because the game of chase is so much fun. Each of these motivations has a different treatment.

If left to their own devices, most puppies will get into what we would refer to as "trouble". It is important to supervise your puppy at all times. Keep the puppy with you and in sight. Be sure that you schedule adequate play times daily so that you are helping your puppy engage in the proper behavior. Arrange the environment so that the puppy cannot get to items. For example, close doors, use barrier gates, crate training or motion sensor devices to monitor where your pet can go. It might be helpful to booby-trap objects with taste aversives or motion detector alarms (see 'behavior management products'), to teach the puppy to 'stay away'. At the same time, non booby-trapped items should be located nearby so that the pet learns the safe and acceptable alternatives that it is allowed to chew and play with.

If your puppy continues to steal in your presence, the best means of monitoring and prevention is to leave a long leash attached, preferably to a head halter. Then as the puppy begins to wander, or puts its nose into "out of bounds" areas, a quick pull on the leash coupled with a "leave it" command will teach it to stay away. Bitter sprays on these objects will prove to the puppy that these items are distasteful if it accidentally gets close enough to put its mouth on the object. Then, when there are items that the puppy is allowed to pick up, use the command, 'take it'. This 'take it' command can even be extended to the food bowl or when giving treats or toys to your dog. Before offering the toy, treat or food, first have the puppy sit, and then give the 'take it' command when its time for the reward. The goal is not only that the puppy learn the 'leave it' command, but also that the dog learn only to pick up objects when it has permission to do so.

If your puppy is stealing things because the game is so much fun, then don't play. Instead of chasing your puppy all over the house, try crouching down and in a happy voice, with open arms call your puppy to you. When the puppy looks toward you, say "good puppy, come show me!" Keep up the praise as the puppy approaches. With a treat, entice the puppy to come, show the treat and when the puppy drops the stolen object, say 'good dog'. Make it come closer, sit, and then give the reward. Of course once the dog has learned the 'give' command (below), then this command should be used instead.

Most importantly, never reach for your puppy in anger after it has taken something. Remember, the behavior you want to change is the stealing, not the cowering under the table. When you threaten your puppy in that way, you risk fear and later aggressive behavior.

In addition, you are reducing not improving the chance that your puppy will give up the item voluntarily. For some puppies, if you ignore them when they steal things and try to engage them in something else instead, they may "give up" the object voluntarily.

How can I stop food stealing in my absence?

This usually requires preventing access to problem areas or using "booby-traps". Booby-traps give punishment from the object while the act is occurring and are more helpful in correcting problem behavior. Examples of

these devices are shaker cans®, Snappy Trainers®, Scat Mats®, bitter or hot tasting sprays or electronic avoidance devices such as motion detectors (audible or citronella spray) and citronella spray avoidance units (where the dog wears the collar and a transmitter dish activates the spray if the dog gets too close (see 'behavior management products' for more details). Shaker cans are empty soda cans that have pennies in them. By rigging them to fall easily, they will startle a dog when disturbed. If the dog is stealing food items, they must be made inaccessible. No amount of punishment will be sufficient to deter a dog that has access to a highly motivating food item.

How do I teach the "give it" command?

It is very useful if you can teach your puppy how to give up items with a command but this is not always easy to train. First, you need to have the puppy take something in its mouth (use the take command). Remember, if it is something very desirable, you may have a difficult time getting the puppy to let it go. A rawhide chew or rubber toy may work well. Keep your hand on the object at first and once the puppy has grasped the toy, say 'give', take it away and offer a special food treat. The purpose of this exercise is to get the puppy to open its mouth and release the item. At the same time you need to say, 'give it' so that the action becomes associated with the phrase. By repeated pairing of the words "give it" with the release of objects, the dog will learn the meaning of the words. Continue to practice until the puppy expects to give up the toy for the food treat and then gradually allow the puppy to have the object a little longer before using the 'give' command and offering the treat. Over time you can progress to more difficult items and allow the puppy to hold onto them a little longer before giving the command and offering the treat. At the end of the session you can even give the puppy a special toy such as a food filled Kong® rather than a treat as a substitute for the one you are taking away.

If you are having difficulty getting the toy away at even the most simple step in the program, then you should a) use a toy of less value nylon) b) allow your dog to grasp onto the toy and then give and begin to take it away almost immediately c) prompt the the toy with its favored treat and d) consider a head halte controlling the head and mouth during training.

Whenever you train a new command, repetition and patience a . important. It is not enough to try and teach 'give it' for 1-2 minutes one day and expect your dog to know it the next. It is only through repetition and practice that the behavior will become solidified.

How can I stop my dog from getting on the furniture?

This is another "owner absent" behavior. In order to control it, you first need to teach your pet that going onto the furniture is not allowed and that any attempt to go on the furniture when the owner is present must be prevented. (A leash left attached or a remote citronella collar can be used to immediately deter or interrupt jumping on the furniture). If you cannot supervise, prevent access by closing doors or baby gates, or deter the pet from entering a room or jumping onto a table using motion detectors, Snappy Trainers, Scat Mats, or alarm mats (see 'behavior management products' and 'canine punishment').

COPROPHAGIA

Why do dogs eat stools?

While most cases of coprophagia appear to be purely behavioral, there are indeed numerous medical problems that can cause or contribute to coprophagia. These problems must first be ruled out before a purely behavioral diagnosis can be made.

What are some of the medical causes?

Any medical problem that leads to a decrease in absorption of nutrients, causes gastrointestinal upset or causes an increase in the appeal of the dog's stool, could lead to coprophagia. In addition to a complete physical examination, the puppy's diet and its stool frequency and consistency should be evaluated. Stool testing for parasites would be the minimum level of testing. If the stool is unusually soft or appears to be poorly digested, additional stool or blood tests may be warranted. Feeding a poorly digestible diet, underfeeding, and medical conditions that decrease absorption such as digestive enzyme deficiencies or parasites, could lead to malnutrition, vitamin and mineral deficiencies and therefore an increased

.ppetite and possibly stool eating. In addition, if the stools contain large amounts of undigested food material, there is an increased likelihood that the puppy would eat the stools.

When adult dogs begin to eat stools, it may also be due to malabsorption of nutrients or nutritional deficiencies. In addition, any condition that might cause an increase in appetite or an unusual appetite, such as diabetes, Cushing's disease, thyroid disease, or treatment with certain drugs such as steroids, may lead to an increase in stool eating. Some dogs that have been placed on a highly restrictive or poorly balanced diet may also begin to eat their stools. It should also be noted that if a dog develops a taste for a particular dog's stool, that dog should be tested for any type of condition that might lead to poor digestion of the food (and therefore excessive food elements remaining in the stool).

What are some of the behavior reasons that a dog or cat might eat its own stools?

Coprophagia is a common problem in some puppies, which usually clears up by adulthood. There have been many explanations suggested for this behavior. When left unsupervised, puppies may simply begin to investigate, play with, and even eat stools as a playful or investigative activity. Since coprophagia may attract a great deal of owner attention, the behavior may be further reinforced. There may also be an observational component (copy behavior) since the bitch cleans and ingests the puppy's excrement in the nest, and puppies may learn to mimic the behavior of their mother or playmates who perform this behavior. The owner that uses the outmoded, inhumane and useless training technique of "sticking the dog's nose" in its stool when it has soiled the home, may be further encouraging coprophagia. In adult dogs the innate behavior of grooming and cleaning newborn puppies and eating their excrement, along with the well documented fact that dogs tend to be attracted to sniff and lick infection or discharge of their pack-mates, may explain some of the motivation for coprophagia. Early intervention can help reduce the possibility that the behavior will become a long-term habit.

Why do dogs eat the stools of other animals?

This behavior is akin to scavenging. It is not unusual for dogs to steal food items, raid garbage cans, and chew on, or eat non-food items that most humans would consider unusual or even disgusting. Cat feces and those of some other animals often have enough appealing attributes (odor, texture, and taste), to overcome the fact that they are stools. In fact, stools themselves are seldom unpleasant to dogs. It is one of the odors that they are constantly attracted to when investigating their environment.

How can coprophagia be treated?

Coprophagia can best be corrected by preventing access to stools, by thorough cleaning of the pet's property, and by constant supervision when the pet is outdoors. At the first indication of stool sniffing or investigation the dog should be interrupted with a firm command, punishment device or a quick pull on the leash (this is particularly effective for dogs wearing head halters). If the dog is taught to come to the owners and sit for a special food treat immediately following each elimination, the new behavior may become a permanent habit. Remote punishment and disruption devices may also be useful in that they can interrupt the dog as it approaches the stool without any direct association with the owner. A remote citronella collar may therefore be effective if the owner supervises the dog from a distance (or by watching through a window to the backyard) and immediately and consistently interrupts the dog every time it begins to mouth stools.

Dogs with medical problems should be treated to try and correct the underlying cause. A change in diet to one that is more digestible, or one with different protein sources may be useful. Dogs on restricted calorie diets may do better on a high bulk or high fiber formula. Some dogs may be improved by adding enzyme supplements to improve nutrient digestion or absorption. Specifically, the digestive enzymes in the form of meat tenderizers or food additives, may help increase protein digestion, resulting in a less palatable stool. Other published remedies that have never been proven to be effective are to add papaya, yogurt, cottage cheese or certs to the dog's food, which in some way are supposed to impart a less pleasant taste in the stools. When adding some items to dry dog food, it may be necessary to moisten the food first and allow the product to sit on the food for 10 – 15 minutes to increase effectiveness.

Unpleasant tastes are unlikely to be successful unless the product is suitably noxious as well as odorless (so that the pet cannot detect its presence in the stool). While the dog is out of sight, the stool should be opened with a plastic utensil, the taste deterrent inserted into the center and the stool closed and replaced for the dog to find. Most dogs however, either develop a tolerance to the taste, or learn to avoid those stools that are pretreated. Experimentally, the only form of taste aversion that is consistently effective is when a food type is associated with nauseousness. Since most dogs seem to prefer a well-formed stool, adding sufficient quantities of stool softeners or bulk laxatives will usually deter most dogs.

Why do dogs chew?

Dogs, especially puppies are extremely playful and investigative. While play with people and other dogs is an important part of socialization and social development, exploration and object play are important ways for dogs to learn about their environment. Therefore it is a normal behavior for puppies to investigate their environment by sniffing, tasting and perhaps chewing on objects throughout the home. Dogs that chew may also be scavenging for food (as in garbage raiding), playing (as in the dog that chews apart a book or couch), teething (dogs 3 to 6 months of age that chew on household objects), or satisfying a natural urge to chew and gnaw (which may serve to help keep teeth and gums healthy). Some dogs may chew because they receive attention (even if it is negative) or treats from the owners each time they chew, but the owners are inadvertently rewarding the behavior. Chewing and destructive behaviors may also be a response to anxiety. Dogs that are confined in areas where they are insecure may dig and chew in an attempt to escape. Dogs that are in a state of conflict, arousal or anxiety, such as separation anxiety, may turn to chewing and other forms of destructiveness as an outlet (see 'separation anxiety' for this specific problem).

How can chewing be treated?

First, determine why the dog is chewing. If the dog is a puppy or young adult dog that is chewing at a variety of objects in the household, it is likely that play and investigation (and perhaps teething) is the motive. Dogs that raid garbage and steal food off counters are obviously motivated by the presence and odor of food. Some dogs are attempting to escape confinement while in others chewing may be an outlet for anxiety. Determining the cause and motivation for chewing is therefore essential in developing a treatment strategy. Directing the chewing into appealing alternatives, sufficient play and exercise, and prevention of inappropriate chewing are needed for the exploratory dog. You must ensure that you are not inadvertently rewarding the behavior. Inattention or disruption devices may be useful for these dogs. If the dog is a puppy this behavior may decrease in time, provided you direct the chewing to proper outlets. Dogs that are garbage raiding or food stealing need to be treated by supervision, prevention and booby-traps, since the behavior itself is self-rewarding. Dogs that are destructive to escape confinement must learn to become comfortable and secure with the cage or room where they are to be confined. Alternatively a new confinement area may have to be chosen. Dogs that are destructive as an outlet for anxiety, will need to have the cause of the anxiety diagnosed, and the problem appropriately treated (see 'separation anxiety').

How can proper chewing be encouraged?

Before considering how inappropriate chewing might be discouraged the real key is to provide some appropriate outlets for your dog's chewing "needs." Begin with a few toys with a variety of tastes, odors, and textures to determine what appeals most to the pet. Although plastic, nylon or rubber toys may be the most durable, products that can be torn apart such as rawhide or pigs ears may be more like the natural prey and wood products that attract most dogs. Coating toys with liver or cheese spread or peanut butter may also increase their desirability. The Kong™ is a durable chew toy, but its appeal can be greatly enhanced by placing a piece of cheese or liver inside and then filling it tight with biscuits. Placing soup items or food into the Kong and freezing it, or freezing food items in "Popsicle" makers and placing them in the dogs food bowl may provide a little longer durability to the treats. Since the development of the Kong there are now a wide variety of durable toys that can have food stuffed or frozen inside or placed into small grooves in the toy, so that the dog needs to "work" to get its reward (see 'behavior management products'). Another group of dog toys have compartments that can be filled with food. The dog needs to manipulate the toy by  rolling, chewing or shaking to get the food treats to fall out. To ensure that your puppy is encouraged and rewarded for chewing on its toys, and discouraged from chewing on all other objects, it must be supervised at all times. Whenever supervision is not possible, you must prevent access to any object or area that might be chewed. Although play periods and chew toys may be sufficient for most pets, additional activities such as self-feeders, other pets, interactive toys, and even videos may help to keep pets occupied.

How else can my dog's activity be reduced?

The needs of most working dogs are usually satisfied with daily work sessions (retrieving, herding, sledding, etc), while non-working house-pets will require alternative forms of activity to meet their requirements for work and play. Games such as tug-of-war, retrieving, catching a ball or Frisbee, jogging, or even long walks are often an acceptable alternative to work, allow the dog an opportunity to expend unused energy, and provide regular attention periods. Obedience training, agility classes and simply teaching your dog a few tricks are not only pleasant interactive activities for you and your dog, but they also provide some stimulation and "work" to the dog's daily schedule.

How can I stop the chewing on household objects?

Access to all areas that the dog might chew must be prevented unless the owner is present to supervise, or the area is effectively booby-trapped. Your dog can only be punished for chewing if it is caught in the act. Even then, punishment must be humane, immediate and effective. A shake can, verbal reprimand, or alarm (audible or ultrasonic) can deter the pet in your presence, but the behavior will continue in your absence. Remote punishment (where the owner is out of sight while administering punishment) may teach the dog that the behavior itself is inappropriate (see 'canine punishment'). A head halter and long remote leash pulled each time the dog chews, a water rifle, remote citronella collar or one of the audible or ultrasonic alarms may be effective. However, none of these products are practical when the owner is absent or cannot supervise. Arriving home and punishing a pet for an act that is already completed will only serve to increase the pet's anxiety.

The only way that chewing might be deterred when your dog cannot be supervised, is to booby-trap the areas where the dog might chew. To be successful the punishment must be noxious enough to immediately deter the pet. Taste or odor aversion is often the simplest and most practical type of booby-trap but many pets will have to be conditioned in advance to detest the smell or taste by squirting anti-chew spray (eg. bitter apple, Ropel™) into the pet's mouth or across its nose. A small amount of cayenne pepper mixed with water, oil of citronella or commercial anti-chew sprays may also be successful as deterrents. Alternatively, the spray could be placed on any object that the dog might chew and a fishing line can be attached from the object to a stack of empty cans on a nearby table or counter. At the instant chewing begins the stack will come crashing down. Most dogs are then conditioned after a few events to avoid the particular taste or odor for fear of another "can attack". A shock or alarm mat, mousetrap trainers, indoor invisible fencing (citronella spray or "shock"), or motion detectors are a few other examples of environmental punishment (see 'behavior management products' and 'canine punishment').

What if the dog continues to chew household objects?

Whenever you cannot supervise or monitor your dog's behavior, he or she should be confined to a cage or dog-proof room with any potential chewing sites effectively booby-trapped. Alternatively, a basket type muzzle can be used for short departures.

Why do dogs dig?

Digging behavior in dogs can have many motivations. Some breeds, such as the Northern breeds (Huskies, Malamutes) dig cooling holes and lie in them. On a very hot summer day any dog may dig a hole to cool off. Breeds such as the terriers have been bred to flush out prey or dig for rodents. With their ability to hear high frequency sounds, and their highly acute sense of smell, some dogs dig as a direct result of odors or sounds such as voles and moles that attract the pet from beneath the ground. Pregnant bitches dig when nesting. Dogs dig to bury or retrieve bones. Dogs also dig to escape from confinement. Digging may also be an activity similar to destructive chewing that occurs when pets are left alone with insufficient stimulation or attention. This is particularly so in puppies and in highly energetic dogs.

How can I determine why my dog is digging?

The first step in treating inappropriate digging behavior is to determine the reason for digging. Prevention, remote punishment, and booby-traps may also be needed, but reducing your dog's motivation to dig, and providing for all of its needs are essential so that digging is not merely redirected to a new location. Inhibiting or preventing all digging, without understanding and dealing with the dog's motivation could result in new behavior problems such as chewing, excessive vocalization, or escape behaviors.

Dogs that dig because they are pursuing prey will continue unless you can get rid of the prey. Dogs that dig in an attempt to get cool should be provided with a cool resting area with plenty of shade and water. On very hot days, it may be best to bring your dog inside.

One of the most common reasons for digging is as a form of play, activity and exploration. Additional play, training and exercise sessions may be needed to keep digging behaviors under control, especially if your dog is young and very active. Dogs that continue to dig may require additional stimulation to keep them occupied when the owners are not around. Treatment for this type of digging can be found in 'destructiveness – chewing'. If your dog is outside all day and digging is taking place, you do need to ask yourself if keeping the dog inside may be a better answer. This is particularly true for the dog that digs to escape from the yard or confinement area. If you are unable to keep the dog inside because of house-soiling, destruction, or separation anxiety then you may need to address those problems first.

How can I stop inappropriate digging?

a) PROVIDE A DIGGING AREA

For some dogs it may be useful for you to create an area where the dog is allowed to dig. This could be a spot in the backyard where you have placed soft dirt and perhaps railroad ties around the area to delineate the location. Next, make this place somewhere that your dog would like to dig in. Bury things there that your pet would like to dig up. This might be food, lightly covered. Then put things deeper into the ground. If you do that (naturally when your dog is not watching!) at irregular intervals, your dog should be more likely to dig there, than other locations in your yard. Another option is to allow the dog to dig in a spot where it has already chosen, and to prevent digging in other locations by supervision, confinement (prevention), or booby-traps.

b) SUPERVISION AND PUNISHMENT

Supervision and direct intervention (shaker can, verbal reprimand, and water rifle) can be used to prevent inappropriate digging in the owner's presence but the behavior will likely continue in the owner's absence. Remote punishment (turning on a sprinkler, pulling on an extended leash, a remote collar), booby-traps (placing chicken wire, rocks or water in the area where the pet digs), or covering the surface with one that is impervious (asphalt/patio stones) might teach the pet to avoid the digging site even in the owner's absence. These techniques do not however prevent the pet from digging in other locations.

What else can be done if inappropriate digging continues when I am not around to supervise?

When you are unavailable to supervise your dog, housing the dog indoors is the most practical solution until he or she has learned to stay outdoors without digging. If you would like to continue to leave it outdoors, it is best to confine the dog to an area such as a pen or run, so that it has no access to the digging areas. The run should be inescapable, and could be covered with gravel, patio tiles or have an asphalt or concrete floor so that it cannot escape or do damage. Of course it will be necessary to provide sufficient exercise and stimulation before confining the dog and an adequate number of treats and play toys in the run to keep the dog occupied. Another alternative is to provide an area within the pen or run where digging is allowed.

EXCITABLE & DISOBEDIENT DOGS

How can I determine if my dog is just acting like a "puppy" or is too excitable or disobedient?

Many excitable and rowdy behaviors that we see in puppies will diminish with time and proper early training. The unruly dog is one that continues to be difficult for the owner to manage past puppyhood or 6 – 9 months. This is a dog that does not respond to commands, will not walk on a leash, jumps on people, continually barks for attention, steals things or generally wreaks havoc on the household. The problem is compounded in large dogs because of their size.

Do dogs get "attention deficit disorder" or can they be "hyperactive"?

While hyperactivity disorder does exist in dogs, it is rare. Dogs that are hyperactive, a condition also known as hyperkinesis or attention deficit hyperactivity disorder (ADHD), can be diagnosed by veterinary examination and testing. Dogs with hyperactivity disorder are difficult to train, respond poorly to tranquilization, may exhibit repetitive behaviors such as incessant barking or circling, may have gastrointestinal disorders, and can be extremely resistant to restraint. If these dogs do have attention deficit disorder they may respond paradoxically to amphetamines. This means that instead of getting more excitable when given amphetamines, these dogs tend to calm down. Most cases however, are simply overly energetic dogs that may not be getting sufficient exercise, or who are being accidentally rewarded when they act excitedly (see 'play and exercise in dogs').

Can I identify this type of dog as a puppy?

Excitable and disobedient dogs can often be identified in early puppyhood. These puppies continually mouth owner's hands and resist attempts to control them for even the most minor procedures. Many people do not realize why puppies chew on them and so give the incorrect feedback to control the behavior (see 'biting').

How can I prevent my puppy from becoming a disobedient dog?

Vigorous and frequent exercise sessions and an early start to training are necessary to prevent puppies from becoming too rowdy. Waiting to train your puppy until it is 6 months of age can often let these disobedient behaviors take hold. Then we have to undo behaviors we don't like in order to get the ones we want. Puppies have very short attention spans. You must motivate the puppy to perform using positive reinforcement. With early training, excitable puppies can often have their behavior channeled in the correct direction. Remember that in order for the new behaviors to be long lasting, they must be practiced daily with all family members participating (see 'play and exercise in dogs'; 'puppy – getting started and house training guide'; 'puppy training: basics'; 'teaching – sit, down, stand and stay'; and 'teaching – come, wait, and follow').

I have tried training my dog without success. What went wrong?

Many owners may have tried traditional obedience training without success. The dog still jumps on people, barks incessantly and defies commands. Often times owners are inadvertently making training and reinforcement errors. Perhaps you have tried yelling at your dog, pulling on choke collars and resorted to isolation to avoid the problem, all without success. Let's address these training and correction techniques to see what works, what is ineffective, and why.

When dogs misbehave, isolation or confinement is often used. However, this can make the problem worse. Dogs are social and want to be with people. The more they are isolated, the more unruly they will be when they are let out. Pawing, barking, licking, and jumping-up are attention-getting, greeting and play-soliciting behaviors in dogs. So, the longer the pet is isolated, the harder they will try to engage in friendly activities. Confinement may be necessary when you are not available to supervise your dog, but he or she must first be provided with sufficient exercise, play and attention, and the opportunity to eliminate. When you arrive home and release the dog from confinement, it must be taught to greet you properly. Quiet, calm, and non-demanding behaviors should be rewarded with play, affection and attention, while demanding, jumping-up, or excitable behaviors should be met with inattention.

Another common training error involves actually reinforcing the behaviors that you do not want. For example, when a dog is outside barking to come in and you ignore the dog for 10 minutes but finally let the dog in, what have you accomplished? The dog has just learned that 10 minutes of incessant barking gains access to the indoors. If your dog is extremely rowdy, jumps up or is constantly demanding attention, these are also behaviors that you may be inadvertently rewarding. Instead of patting, giving attention, or perhaps even a treat to try and stop the behavior, it is essential that these behaviors be met with inattention. If you do attend to the dog for unruly behaviors, but ignore the dog when it is quiet, you have set up a situation (from the dog's perspective) where rowdy behaviors get attention and calm ones do not. Therefore, rowdy behaviors continue.

Another common problem is giving your dog a command, and if there is no response, you repeat the command. This sends the message that 2 – 3 repetitions of the command are needed to get the desired behavior. When you ask your dog to do something, be sure that you can get the dog to perform the behavior. Do not ask for a behavior unless you know that the dog can perform it on command. If the pet cannot perform the command, then he does not know what the word means and you need to continue training.

Reprimands and punishment are also often unsuccessful. Punishment for an unruly or overly excitable dog generally just rewards the behavior by providing attention. On the other hand, punishment that is too harsh may lead to anxiety, fear of the owner and problems such as aggression or submissive urination. Disruption devices such as a shake can (small stones in a tin can), an air horn, or an ultrasonic device may deter undesirable behavior without causing fear of the owner. They do not serve as a punishment but do provide a window of opportunity for retraining. In general, punishment is seldom effective at correcting undesirable behavior, and should be discontinued if it is not immediately successful.

In summary, let's look at the excitable and unruly dog. Many owners shout at or physically discipline these dogs, but, as discussed, this may further reward the unruly behavior. Then when these dogs are relaxed or tired out, owners (perhaps thankful for the peace and quiet) ignore them. Demanding behavior is rewarded while quiet behavior is ignored. If this is what is happening in your home, deal with it by treating all demanding behavior with inattention (or disruption techniques) and reward calm, non-demanding behavior with play and attention.

How should I start to regain control?
Retraining begins with good control, and a good understanding of the proper use, timing and selection of rewards. An obedience training class that uses rewards and non-disciplinary techniques for control (such as head halters) is a good start. The goal is to get the desired response, reward the

desired response and gradually shape longer and more successful responses. Clickers can be an excellent way to mark and reward success. The dog should be well exercised and as calm and focused as possible when training first begins. Insure that you are in an environment where there are minimal distractions and that you have enough control so that a successful response to the command can be guaranteed (see 'rewards – learning and reinforcement'). One important concept will be reinforced here. Unless you provide rewards within 5 seconds of the desired behavior, or interrupt the undesirable behavior as it is occurring, dogs may know that you are happy or angry, but they do not know about what! Punishment after the act does no good, confuses the dog, and can even lead to the kinds of disobedient behaviors that owners find objectionable. Remember, you want to **punish** the **BEHAVIOR, not** the **PET**.

What do I do if disobedience and unruliness persists?

Most traditional training techniques and devices use punishment to interrupt and deter misbehavior. Punishment may teach a dog what not to do but it does not teach the dog to perform the desired response. Many of the devices that have been designed to control and train dogs are attached around the dog's neck to "choke" or correct.

The head halter has been designed to gain control over the dog's head and muzzle so that the handler is able to train the dog to perform the desired response. The goal of training is to encourage and reward correct responses rather than punish incorrect responses. A head halter uses a dog's natural instinct to follow a leader using pressure sites that cause the dog to respond in a behaviorally appropriate way. The neck strap simulates the pressure control that a mother dog uses on her puppies. A second strap encircles the dog's nose and simulates how the leader dog would put his mouth over the muzzle of a subordinate dog. The head halter also communicates leadership in a number of other ways. Since dogs have a natural instinct to pull against pressure, a forward and upward pull on the leash will close the mouth and the dog will pull backwards and down into a sit. Therefore, whenever the sit command is given and the dog does not immediately respond, the owner can pull the leash up and forward, look the dog in the eyes, and get the desired response. As soon as the dog is sitting or even begins to sit, the restraint is released and the dog praised. It is important to remember this fact; the natural response of a mother or leader dog is to release the restraint or grasp as soon as the dog submits. Therefore, the release not only serves to reinforce the desired response, but is also consistent with natural canine communication. The command, pull, and release should be immediately repeated if the "problem behavior" is repeated, and positive reinforcement (treat, patting, play) should be provided if the dog continues to "behave". Once the dog is behaving appropriately, yelling, jerking or pulling on the leash and physical punishment are illogical, and will lead to increased resistance, fear and perhaps aggression. Using a leash and head halter, an upward and forward pull can be used to immediately and effectively control barking, jumping up, play biting, stealing objects, or pulling and lunging. Lastly, and equally important, the head halter does not encircle and tighten around the lower neck, so that the dog is not choking while the owner is trying to train.

Some brands of head halters are designed so that they can be left on the dog, just like neck collars, all the time when owners are home. A long indoor lead can be left attached for control from a distance. As soon as the dog begins to engage in unacceptable behavior, it can be interrupted and directed into performing the desirable behavior ('sit', 'down', 'quiet'). By the same token, if you give the dog a command and he does not obey, you can always get the compliance that you require if the halter and leash is attached.

Now that I have more control, what else do I need to do?

Often the key to turning an unruly dog into an acceptable pet is continuous control until you reliably can get the behaviors that you want. This is most easily accomplished by having the dog on a leash (attached to a body harness, non-choke neck collar or head halter). This allows you to immediately interrupt undesirable behavior and teach your dog the correct lesson. Only after the dog no longer engages in the undesirable behavior, and responds to verbal commands, should the leash be removed. An integral component of controlling an unruly dog entails restructuring the situations so that the unruly behavior is not able to take place, or that interruption is immediate. This can take various forms such as keeping the dog on a leash so that it cannot run through the house; closing doors to other rooms and limiting the access of the dog to areas where he is unsupervised. Only interact with the dog in a positive manner and set up situations so that the dog will do as the owner asks.

This brings up another vital issue in controlling excitable and disobedient dogs. Many owners are so frustrated that the only interaction that they have with the dog is negative. They have lost the joy of pet ownership. Worse than that, they do not reward the behaviors that they do want. It is just as important to tell the dog when it is doing the correct behavior as it is to discipline the bad. It is also important to practice the training that you may ultimately need. An example of this is training the dog to 'sit' and 'stay' in the front hall. How will the dog know to 'sit' and not run out the door when people come to visit, (a highly excitable event), if the dog never practiced doing so when things were calm?

TEACH THE DOG
WHAT YOU WANT IT TO KNOW
BEFORE YOU NEED IT

FEARS & PHOBIAS – ANIMALS & PEOPLE

Why is my dog afraid of people and/or other animals?

There are many reasons that dogs can develop a fear of people or the other animals. Firstly, there may have been limited or minimal exposure to people and/or other animals when the dog was young. Socialization is an important aspect of raising a puppy. Without adequate, constant and positive interactions with people and other animals dogs may develop fears. In fact, fears may be very specific so that a dog that has been adequately socialized to a particular "type" of person such as adult males, may show fear toward children, men, women, teenagers, or people of other races. Similarly, dogs that are well socialized to other dogs may show fear toward other animals. Secondly, dogs are impressionable and through the effect of "one trial learning" may take one experience that was intense or traumatic and generalize to many similar situations. This can occur, for example, with a bad experience with a small child which then makes the dog fearful of all small children, or a fight and subsequent injury from other dogs. Sometimes a number of unpleasant events "paired" or associated with a person or animal can lead to increasing fear. For example, if a pet is punished (especially with a painful device such as a pinch or shock collar) when it is exposed to a person or other animal, it may begin to pair the stimulus (the person or other animal) with the unpleasant consequence (punishment). This is especially true with the use of a painful device such as a pinch or shock collar.

Can I prevent fears from developing?

As mentioned above, socialization is the cornerstone to raising a dog that is comfortable with people. Early, frequent and pleasant encounters with people of all ages and types can help prevent fears later. This exposure should begin before 3 months of age and continue throughout the first year. In addition, the dog should be exposed to as many different environments, sights and sounds as possible so that they become accustomed early, before fears emerge.

What signs might my dog show when she is afraid?

When frightened, a dog may cower, look away, tuck its tail and perhaps tremble or pant. At other times the signs may be subtler. A dog may only duck its head and look away, and tolerate petting at first, but then snap. It is important to watch your dog for signs of uneasiness such as backing up, hiding behind you and licking of the lips. Naturally growling, or snarling would indicate aggression, but may also indicate fear (see 'fears, phobias and anxieties').

What information do I need to identify and treat my fearful pet?

Usually a behavioral consultation is needed for dogs that are showing extreme fears and/or aggression. If the fears are mild, then owner intervention may help to improve the problem or at the very least prevent them from progressing. First, it is important to identify what is the fearful stimulus. This is not always easy and needs to be very exact. What persons or animals is the dog afraid of and where does the fearful behavior occur? Often there are certain situations, people, and places, that provoke the behavior more than others.

For treatment to be most successful, it is important to be able to place the fearful stimuli along a gradient from low to high. In other words, you want to identify those situations, people, places and animals that are likely to cause minimal fear as well as those situations, people, places and animals that are most likely to cause the fearful behaviors.

Next, you need to also examine what factors may be reinforcing the behavior. Some owners actually reward the manifestations of fear such as trembling or growling by reassuring their pets with vocal intonations or body contact. Aggressive displays are a successful way of getting the fearful stimulus to leave and thus also reinforce the behaviors. Any ongoing interactions that are fear provoking need to be identified. This could be teasing behaviors, anxiety or aggression on the part of the stimulus (people or other animal), anxiety on the part of the owner/handler, painful interactions including the use of punishment (discussed previously), or overwhelming stimuli.

After I have identified the stimuli, what do I do next?

Before a behavior modification program can begin, you need to be able to control and communicate with your dog. This will require some training. Often in addition, a head collar will be needed. Head collars allow control of the dog's head and neck to ensure that the dog responds to the given command (sit, quiet, and heel). To make the dog feel more secure by knowing who is the "leader", orient the dog away from the stimulus, and prevent the dog from either causing injury or escaping.

Next, teach your dog that when it sits and stays it will receive a delicious food reward. The goal of this training is to allow the dog to assume a relaxed and happy body posture and facial expression on command. Once this is established, then food rewards are phased out (see 'puppy – training basics').

Lastly, begin counter-conditioning and desensitization to acclimate the dog to the stimuli that usually cause the fearful response. This needs to be done slowly and cannot begin until your dog can reliably relax on command in the absence of the stimulus. This is where the gradient that you established earlier becomes helpful and can be the most difficult part of the program since it is generally necessary to set up situations where you can control the dog and the stimulus. Therefore, inviting people to the house, or having some neighborhood children ride their bikes back and forth along the street, may be necessary so that you can insure that the stimuli are predictable and well controlled (see the example of delivery people below). Start by exposing the dog to very low levels of the stimulus, in fact ones that do not evoke fear. The dog is then rewarded for sitting quietly and calmly. Gradually, if the dog exhibits no fear, the stimulus intensity is increased (see 'behavior modification – desensitization, counter-conditioning, differential reinforcement and flooding'). It is extremely important that this is done slowly. The goal is to associate a calm, positive outcome with the once fearful stimulus by only rewarding the desirable response. If the dog begins to show fear during training, it is progressing too fast and could be making the problem worse.

Always set up the dog to succeed. The use of the leash and head collar can greatly improve the chances of success and because of the additional control, will often help the owner to succeed in getting the dogs attention and calming it down; faster than with commands and rewards alone.

But my dog may still encounter the fearful stimulus when we are not in a training exercise. What should I do then?

Each time the dog experiences the fearful stimulus and reacts with fear, the behavior is further aggravated. If possible, it is helpful to try and avoid the fear-producing stimulus. This may mean confining the dog when children visit, or the house is full of strangers. Alternately, walks may need to be curtailed or scheduled at times when encounters with other people and animals can be minimized.

If you do find yourself in a situation where the dog is responding fearfully, do not raise your voice or punish your dog as this will further increase his or her anxiety. If your dog is wearing a head halter it may be possible to reorient the dog so that you can get eye contact and to pull up and settle the dog so that the dog learns to ignore or accept the approaching stimulus. Another option is to use a "happy" tone of voice and walk just far enough away that the dog can be successfully distracted and settled.

How might these techniques be used in a training situation?

Take the example of fear toward a delivery person. Begin by training the dog to sit and stay quietly throughout the house and then by the window and doorway in the absence of anyone approaching. Use only reward based training techniques along with perhaps a head halter to ensure success. Use clicker training or a favored reward such as a toy or treat to mark and reward acceptable responses. As the dog begins to anticipate that a favored reward is imminent the dog's attitude or "mood" should be positive rather than anxious and aggressive. The relaxed sit stay and expectation of rewards are incompatible with the behavior you wish to change, in this case lunging at the window at a delivery person. Once the dog learns to quickly settle and anticipate food at each location on command, training with varying forms of the stimulus can begin. It may take days or weeks for the dog to learn how to perform this task reliably on command. During that time phase out food rewards so that the dog does the task equally well with or without food.

Next, train the pet to perform the desired behavior in the presence of a variety of stimuli that are similar to the actual problem stimulus (e.g. strangers walking across the property). Using desensitization, the stimulus is presented at a muted or low enough level so that the dog can be kept settled and shows no fear or anxiety. Training could begin by having a family member stand by or walk by the window, and then progress to a stranger at the edge of the property. The owner then practices the training to ensure that a calm settle response is achieved and rewarded. Again favored rewards, toys or clicker training should be used for each new step in the program. Again a head halter can be used to ensure a quick and successful response. Repeat this many times so that the dog does it reliably and gradually have the person move closer to the window until the person can walk by while the dog relaxes or plays and gets its reward. Rewards are faded out once each new level is achieved and reintroduced for each new step along the way. The dog is learning the new acceptable response that earns the reward (response substitution) and is acquiring a positive association with the stimulus. Proceed slowly, so that the dog learns to perform the desired behavior over and over before being challenged with the real thing,

Finally, progress to stimuli that more closely resemble the real life situation. Perhaps have the dog sit by the window when a friend or family member dressed as a delivery person walks by the property and finally progress to sessions with delivery people. Some dogs may progress faster if the training is done outside with stimuli across the street or walking across the property.

FEARS & PHOBIAS – NOISES & PLACES

Why is my dog so frightened of loud noises such as thunder, firecrackers and loud vehicles?

Phobias can develop from a single experience (one event learning) or from continued exposure to the fearful stimulus. Although some dogs react with a mild fear response of panting and pacing, others get extremely agitated and may become destructive or panicked. These dogs are experiencing a phobic response to the stimulus. These phobias may develop because of an inherent sensitivity to the stimulus (i.e. a genetic predisposition) or exposure to a highly traumatic experience associated with the stimulus (e.g. a carport collapsing on the pet in a windstorm). With multiple exposure to a fearful event a dog may become more intensely reactive if it is reinforced by receiving attention or affection by well meaning owners who are merely trying to calm the pet down.

What can I do if my dog is phobic in those situations?

Dogs that experience phobias often need professional intervention by a veterinary or applied animal behaviorist. These pets are usually at risk of harming themselves or property when faced with the stimulus especially if their owners are not home. If the dog will be left alone in a situation where it may encounter the phobic stimulus, drug therapy may be needed to prevent injury and destruction.

Is there any way I can treat my dog myself?

Identify the stimuli that evoke the behavior. For gunshots, fireworks or a car backfiring the stimulus might be quite obvious. However, for thunderstorms, it may be the darkening of the sky, a drop in the barometric pressure, or high winds, all of which occur prior to the storm. Naturally, the storm itself and the rain, wind, lightening, and thunder can be the stimulus for the behavior. Some dogs even become phobic of going outdoors because of certain sights or sounds that you will need to identify.

In order to set up an effective retraining program you will need to be able to reproduce the noise. Finding a means of reproducing and controlling the stimulus is one of the most difficult aspects of the retraining program. A recording or video might work for thunderstorms. Unfortunately, as discussed, many dogs are afraid of other components of a storm that are difficult to recreate. Therefore it may be possible to treat some, but not all aspects of the phobic response. Recordings may be useful for desensitizing dogs to the sound of fireworks, and the visual stimuli can be minimized by confining the dog to a brightly lit room with light proof shutters or shades. For gunshots, recordings or a starter pistol set inside 4 or 5 nested cardboard boxes, might be a way to reduce and control the stimulus. Sometimes, increasing the distance from the stimulus or finding some relatively sound-proofed room to do the training might work.

If a recording is used, you will first need to ensure that it does indeed reproduce the fear. Then, to begin to desensitize the pet you will need to begin retraining with the recording at a low enough level that it does not evoke the response and the dog is rewarded lavishly for good (non-fearful) behavior. Retraining should focus on the use of rewards and training the dog to lie quietly in a favorite resting area to receive these rewards even before the stimulus (e.g. recording) is first used. The resting area should help to comfort and provide security for the dog, and the rewards are intended to teach the dog to associate nothing but positives with the low levels of the stimulus. Gradually, the volume is increased so that the dog learns to tolerate the "storm".

Another reason why it is extremely difficult to overcome fears and phobias, is that while you are attempting to desensitize and counter-condition the dog to the noises, the dog is likely to be exposed to a recurrence of the actual event (e.g. a thunderstorm). During these times, do not reinforce the fearful and phobic responses with petting and reassuring vocal intonation. This would serve as reinforcement for the behavior and make it continue. For some dogs, placing them in their favored resting area in a room or area that has been sound-proofed and playing some calming music may help to decrease the dog's reaction. Drug therapy may also be useful in some cases.

Why would my dog become frightened of certain places?

Lack of early exposure to the sights, sounds or perhaps odors of a particular location, or one or more traumatic experiences associated with that location could lead to fear. The fear is aggravated by an owner who tries to calm the dog down with affection or verbal intonations. This only reinforces the fearful behavior. For example, dogs may be frightened of travelling in the car because they become car sick or because the car ride is always followed by an unpleasant experience (such as boarding or a veterinary visit). Your dog may also become fearful of the veterinary hospital if it is always associated with unpleasant experiences, or of a particular room or area of the house (such as a basement or a cage) if an unpleasant event has occurred in that area. Some dogs even become frightened of the outdoors, because of unpleasant experiences that have occurred there.

How can I treat my dog's fear of places?

It is necessary to place the stimuli along a gradient, as well as carefully observing what the dog does. For example, the dog may walk into the garage okay, but begins to get agitated when approaching the car. Or, the dog may be okay approaching the car and only upset when forced to get in.

Desensitization and counter-conditioning are used to retrain the dog. Begin with good responses to obedience commands such as 'sit' and 'stay' for favored rewards. The goal, before beginning the exposure is that a calm, positive state can be achieved consistently on command. Then train and reward the dog in situations where the fear is very mild. With a fear of car rides, the dog might first be rewarded for not showing fear when it is 8 feet from the car, then 7 feet and so on until the dog can approach the car without showing signs of fear. Eventually the dog should learn to take rewards when it enters the car, and at further sessions the dog should learn to relax in the car with the door closed, and then when the motor is turned on. In much the same way it could take a few more sessions until the dog learns to take rewards in a moving car. For the dog that is fearful of the veterinary office you might begin by taking the dog to the veterinarian's parking lot and doing some training exercises for food rewards, and progressing to the front walkway or into the waiting room. It may take many visits to train the dog to enter the examining room for rewards, be greeted by the staff or sit on the examining table. Similarly a dog that is fearful of a cage or particular room, may need to be taught to lie in the doorway for food and rewards. Then proceed a step or two into the room or a little farther into the cage, to receive the reward at each subsequent training session.

In treating fears you must have sufficient control of the pet so that there is no chance of injury and the pet cannot run away or escape from the stimulus. Eventually, the pet will calm down and accept that the stimulus will cause no harm. Obedience training for rewards is a positive way to ensure that you gain control. Begin in situations where the stimulus is not present, because if your dog will not respect your control and take rewards in non-threatening situations, you will not be able to control and settle your dog in problem situations. Often a leash and head collar is the best way to maintain control and ensure that your dog will perform the desired behavior in the presence of the stimulus. The leash and halter prevents escape from the stimulus; helps build the dog's confidence; controls the head and nose in order to get the desired behavior (e.g. sit, heel); allows the owner to redirect the head away from the stimulus and toward the owner; prevents the possibility of a bite or injury; and provides a reward or release for each proper response. It is also necessary to control the stimulus because it must not be removed until your dog calms down and realizes that it will cause no harm. Always end each session on a positive note!

FIREWORK & THUNDERSTORM FEARS & PHOBIAS – TREATMENT

How is this problem treated?
It has been found that the best approach to this problem is to treat the dog by systematic desensitization and counter-conditioning (see 'fears and phobias – noises and places' for more information).

When is the best time to start treatment?
This should be done at a time of year when fireworks or thunderstorms are not likely to be used so that you have control over the situation.

How do I start this systematic desensitization and counter-conditioning program?

The dog is trained to 'sit' and 'relax' on command with gentle reassuring tones. A good walk or exercise first will make relaxation easier. When this has become established the training can be tested in the face of some distraction. Remember to always reward the dog when the task is successfully accomplished. Initially food rewards may be used, but later soothing praise is the best reward. Once sitting and relaxation has been achieved the training should be tested in the face of some distraction. Some owners and handlers find that success can be achieved faster and more consistently throughout the program by using a restraint and control device such as a head halter.

How do I organize the distraction?

Once you have your dog sitting and obviously relaxed and this has been repeated several times, try simple distractions such as having another member of the family approach or even another pet, if available. Once you are confident that your dog will remain sitting then desensitization may begin.

How do I organize desensitization?

For fireworks either a variety of audio and video recordings of the noise or a cap gun can be used, whichever is capable of reproducing the fear response. It is important to start off with a noise at a volume that does not elicit any distress. The starting sound sometimes may be barely audible. For this reason it is probably better to have a record of a firework display rather than using a cap gun. If a cap gun has to be used, this can be recorded and then played at minimal volume. Alternatively, the gun can be muffled using cardboard boxes and towels. Using a stereo "surround-sound" recording system is more likely to produce a sound that is most similar to the actual stimulus (fireworks). This same technique can also be used for thunderstorm phobias, using a video or audio recording of an actual storm. It is much harder to reproduce the actual event for retraining since the noise is not the only element of a thunderstorm and changes in barometric pressure, rain on the windows, darkening skies and flashes and bolts of lightening cannot be reproduced for retraining purposes.

Put your dog on the 'relax' command and then employ another member of the family or assistant to praise and reassure it for staying calm. If the correct response is not achieved, the behavior should be ignored and then go back several steps until you are sure that your assistant is able to achieve a 'sit' and 'relax' which is the first part of the program.

Initiate the stimulus at the lowest volume possible. If there is a reaction the behavior should be ignored until your pet is settled after which it can again be given a treat. Then, once settled, try again to distract the dog at the same time with a much lower volume of the stimulus. Again the head halter might be a better way to gain control and insure that it focuses on the owner.

For how long do I repeat this part of the program?

It is important that you do not overdo it. After every few bangs give a special treat, play with the dog or initiate some particularly pleasurable activity. Make this the end of your first session. It is important you always end a session on a high note with a good response, even if that means turning the volume right down again.

When do I restart training?

This depends very much on the individual dog. It can be as short a time as an hour or as long as the next day. It is important, however, not to leave too long a gap between training sessions.

What happens in the new session?

The new session is started with the same level of noise but this is soon increased slightly, bearing in mind that it is important not to go beyond the point when your dog may notice the sound and react. If this happens it is important to go back several steps and start with the noise at a much lower volume.

Keep repeating the process, increasing the volume only slightly each time.

What should I expect?

It is important not to expect too much, too soon. As a general rule you should not try to do more than three or four sessions in a block.

How long will this training program take?

You have to accept from the outset that the program will take days if not weeks or even months but eventually your dog should remain relaxed at full intensity noises. Once you have reached this point it is important to reinforce the good response on an occasional basis.

How often do I have to do this revision program?

Initially it has to be quite frequently but with time this can be less often. Reinforcements should be done shortly before the festive season. Do not expect your dog to remember everything until the next big party!

What should I do if I don't appear to be making any progress?

If you seem to be having any problems, consult your veterinarian for further advice or help. Sometimes sound sensitivity may be associated with both medical and more general psychological problems.

What happens if I haven't managed to get my dog trained in time?

This is not an uncommon problem (see the following fact sheet for just such a situation). Drugs may be an option to help the dog improve more quickly or to help the dog better handle fireworks and thunderstorm events that arise before the program has been successfully completed.

FIREWORK & THUNDERSTORM PHOBIAS – TREATMENT
HOW TO DEAL WITH THE PROBLEM IN AN EMERGENCY

Drugs

These may be useful in some cases but should only be given under veterinary supervision. Remember they should be given so they take effect BEFORE any noise starts or panic sets in. This is usually at least an hour prior to the event. Sedatives may help the pet sleep through the event or be less aware of the stimuli but do not reduce anxiety. Anti-anxiety drugs may reduce anxiety and panic but may not calm the dog sufficiently. There are also drugs that can be used on an ongoing basis to try and prevent or reduce the effect of the stimulus should it arise. Short term drugs on the day of the fireworks (or storm) may be added to some of these drugs if needed.

Please contact your veterinarian for further advice if necessary.

Punishment

Don't punish your dog when he is scared, it only confirms to him that there is something to be afraid of and will make him worse. In addition, if you are upset or anxious about your pet's behavior, this will also make your dog more anxious.

Reassurance

Don't fuss, pet or try to reassure your dog when he is scared since he may regard this as a reward for the behavior. Although it may be difficult, try to ignore any fearful behavior that occurs.

Training devices and commands

Practice training your dog to settle and focus on commands for favored treats and play toys. Try and associate this training with a favored location in the house (one where the noise of the fireworks and storm might be less obvious), and use some training cues (e.g. a favored CD, a favored blanket) each time you do the training (so that the command, location and cues help to immediately calm the dog). A head halter can also be used to help control, distract and calm the dog during training. Then at the time of the storm, use your commands, location, cues and head halter to try and calm the dog, while avoiding punishment or reassurance of the fearful response .

Feeding

Feed your dog a good meal, rich in carbohydrate with added vitamin B6 a few hours prior to the expected fireworks (or storm). If necessary don't feed him at any other time during the day to ensure a good appetite.

However, if your dog is prone to diarrhea when scared or at other times, please consult your veterinarian for advice regarding this strategy.

Environment

Make sure that the environment is safe and secure at all times. Even the most placid dog can behave unpredictably when frightened by noise and should he bolt and escape he could end up in a much worse state.

Can I do anything to reduce the impact of the noise and flashes from the fireworks or storms?

When the season begins, try to ensure that your dog can reside in a well-curtained or blacked out room when it starts to go dark. Blacking out the room removes the potentially additional problems of flashing lights, flares etc.

Provide plenty of familiar toys and games that might help to distract the pet.

Try to arrange company for your dog so that he is not abandoned in the room.

Make sure that all the windows and doors are shut so the sound is deadened as much as possible. Try taking your pet to a room or area of the house where the stimuli will be at their mildest and the dog can be most easily distracted.

Try to provide background sounds from the radio or television. Rap or similar music with a lot of constant drum beats does help. It does not necessarily have to be loud as long as there is a constant distracting beat to the music that will prevent him from concentrating on the noises outside.

Ignore these noises yourself and try to involve your pet in some form of active game.

My friend down the street has a dog that is not scared of loud noises and gets along well with mine. She has offered to lend me her dog for support. Should I accept?

This may be an excellent strategy. Keeping the two together during the evenings may help. Playing with the non-fearful dog when your own becomes scared may help to encourage him to join in and reduce his fear.

Is there anything else that I can do that is worthwhile?
Don't just ignore the problem because it only happens intermittently or for a few days each year. Instigate a desensitization program once the season is over so that you ensure your dog loses fear of the situation.

HOUSE-SAFETY & CRATE TRAINING

Why do dogs need to be confined?
Dogs are highly social animals that make wonderful pets. They can be effective as watchdogs, are excellent companions for play and exercise, and are sources of affection and comfort. However, with the lifestyle and schedule of the majority of families, dogs must learn to spend a portion of the day at home, while their human family is away at school, work, shopping or recreational activities. During those times when you are away and unavailable to supervise, the pet may still feel the need to chew, play, explore, eat, or eliminate.

How can this misbehavior be prevented?
Preventing such inappropriate behaviors when you are absent involves both scheduling and prevention. Scheduling means insuring that the pet has had the opportunity to play, eat, and eliminate before you leave it in its confinement area or crate. Prevention involves keeping the pet in a confined area where it is secure, safe, and can do no damage to itself or your possessions.

What are my options for confinement?
Depending on the structure of your home, it may be possible to dog-proof the house by closing a few doors, or putting up some child gates or barricades. The dog can then be allowed access to the remaining areas of the house. Another option is to use avoidance devices that keep the pet away from selected areas using motion detectors, citronella spray collars or other forms of "booby-traps" (see our handout on 'Behavior management products'). If this dog-proofing is not possible when you have to leave, confine the dog to a single room, pen, or crate. This smaller confinement area not only provides safety for the dog and protection of the home from damage, but also provides a means of teaching the dog what it is supposed to chew, and where it is supposed to eliminate.

Isn't crate training cruel?

Crate training is neither cruel nor unfair. On the contrary, leaving the dog unsupervised to wander, investigate, destroy, and perhaps injure itself is far more inhumane than confinement. Ensure that the crate is large enough so the dog gets sufficient food, play, exercise and attention before it is confined, and you return before the dog needs to urinate or defecate.

What are the benefits of crate training?

The two most important benefits are the safety it affords the pet, and the damage that is prevented. The cage also provides a place of security; a comfortable retreat where the dog can relax, sleep, or chew on a favorite toy. Behavior problems can be immediately prevented by confining the pet to a crate or room, when the owner is not available to supervise. When you are at home, supervision and rewards can be used to prevent undesirable behavior, and to teach the dog where to eliminate, what to chew, and what rooms and areas are "out of bounds."

Will cage confinement help with house-training?

Yes. Crate training is one of the quickest and most effective ways to house-train a dog. Since most dogs instinctively avoid eliminating in their sleeping and eating areas, dogs that use their crate as a bed or "den" will seldom eliminate inside unless they have been left in the crate for too long. Crate training can also help teach the dog to develop control over its elimination (see 'puppy – getting started and house training guide').

As soon as your dog is released from its crate, take it to the designated area and reward elimination at acceptable locations. Since the crate prevents chewing, digging, and elimination on the owner's home and property, owners of crate trained puppies have fewer behavior concerns, the puppy receives far less discipline and punishment, and the overall relationship between pet and owner can be dramatically improved.

Will the crate provoke barking?

No. The crate can also be a useful way to reduce or eliminate distress barking. Rather than locking the puppy up and away from the owners at night time or during mealtime, the puppy can be housed in its crate in the bedroom or kitchen. In this way the puppy cannot get into mischief, and is less likely to cry out or vocalize, if the owners are in the room. If the puppy is locked away in a laundry room or basement with no access to the owners, distress vocalization is far more likely. If the owner then goes to the puppy to quiet it down or check it out, the crying behavior is rewarded.

What about caging and travel?

Of course, throughout its life, whether travelling or boarding, the dog may require crate confinement. Those dogs that are familiar and comfortable with caging are more likely to feel secure, and far less stressed, should caging be required.

PUPPY CRATE TRAINING

What type of crate or confinement area works best?

A metal, collapsible crate with a tray floor works well, as long as the crate is large enough for the dog to stand, turn, and stretch out. Some dogs feel more secure if a blanket is draped over the crate. A plastic travelling crate or a homemade crate can also be used. Playpens or barricades may also be successful as long as they are indestructible and escape proof.

Where should the cage be located?

Because dogs are social animals, an ideal location for the crate is a room where the family spends time such as a kitchen, den, or bedroom rather than an isolated laundry or furnace room.

How can crating or confinement become a positive experience?

Most dogs quickly choose a small area, such as a corner of a room, in a dog bed, or on or under a couch, where they go to relax. The key to making the crate the dog's favorite retreat and sleeping area, is to associate the crate with as many positive and relaxing experiences and stimuli as possible (food, treats, chew toys, bedding) and to place the dog in its cage only at scheduled rest and sleep periods. You must therefore be aware of the dog's schedule, including its needs for exploration, play, food, and elimination, so that the dog is only placed in its cage, when each of these needs is fulfilled. You must then return to the dog to release it from its cage before the next exercise, feeding or elimination period is due.

A radio or television playing in the background may help to calm the dog when it is alone in its cage, especially during the daytime. These may also help to mask environmental noises that can stimulate the dog to vocalize.

The crate should never be used as punishment.

How do I crate-train my new puppy?

1) Introduce the puppy to the crate as soon as it is brought home and as early in the day as possible. Place a variety of treats in the cage throughout the day so that the puppy is encouraged to enter voluntarily. Food, water, toys and bedding could also be offered to the puppy in the open cage.

2) Choose a location outdoors for the puppy to eliminate. Take the puppy to the location, wait until the puppy eliminates, and reward the puppy lavishly with praise or food. After some additional play and exercise, place the puppy in its crate with water, a toy and a treat and close the door.

3) If the puppy is tired and calm, it may take a "nap" shortly after being placed in its crate.

4) Leave the room but remain close enough to hear the puppy. Escape behavior and vocalization are to be expected when a dog is first placed into

its crate. If the "complaints" are short or mild, ignore your puppy until the crying stops. Never release the puppy unless it is quiet. This teaches that quiet behavior, and not crying will be rewarded. Release the puppy after a few minutes of quiet or a short nap.

5) Punishment may be useful to deter crying if it does not subside on its own. A shaker can (a sealed can filled with coins or marbles) can be tossed at the crate when the pup barks. Other methods include water sprayers or alarms (audible or ultrasonic). The owner should remain out of sight. By plugging in an alarm, tape recorder, water pik, or hair dryer beside the crate and turning it on with a remote control switch each time the dog barks, the dog can be taught that barking leads to punishment whether the owner is present or not. When the barking ceases, the punishment is stopped. Bark collars and alarms or water sprayers that are activated by the barking are also available for persistent problems. Punishment must always be used with caution, since it can exacerbate the vocalization problem of a very anxious pet.

6) Repeat the cage and release procedure a few more times during the day before bedtime. Place the puppy in its crate a few times before the end of the day. Each time, increase the time that the dog must stay in the crate before letting it out. Always give the puppy exercise and a chance to eliminate before locking it in the crate.

7) At bedtime, the dog should be exercised, locked in its crate, and left for the night. Do not go to the dog if it cries. Remote punishment can be used to deter crying. Alternately, the crate can be kept in the bedroom.

8) If the pup sleeps in one end of its crate and eliminates in the other, a divider can be installed to keep the puppy in a smaller area.

9) Never leave the puppy in its crate for longer than it can control itself or it may be forced to eliminate in the crate.

10) If the pup must be left for long periods during which it might eliminate, it should be confined to a larger area such as a dog-proof room or pen, with paper left down for elimination. As the puppy gets older, its control increases and it can be left longer in its crate.

11) Although there is a great deal of individual variability, many puppies can control themselves through the night by 3 months of age. During the daytime, once the puppy has relieved itself, a 2-month old puppy may have up to 3 hours control, a 3-month puppy up to 4 hours, and a 4 month old puppy up to 5 hours.

12) A crate is not an excuse to ignore the dog!

CRATE TRAINING ADULT DOGS

What is the best technique for crate training older pets and adult dogs?
1) For adult dogs or older puppies that have not been crate trained previously, set up the crate in the dog's feeding area with the door open for a few days. Place food, treats, and water in the crate so that the dog enters the crate on its own. Another alternative is to place the crate in the dog's sleeping area with its bedding. Once the dog is entering the crate freely, it is time to close the door.

2) Using the same training techniques as for 'sit' and 'stay' training, have the dog enter its crate for short periods of time to obtain food, treats, or chew toys. Once the pet expects treats each time it enters the crate, train the dog to enter the crate on command (e.g. kennel!), and have the dog remain in the kennel for progressively longer periods of time, before the dog is allowed to exit. Give small rewards each time the dog enters the cage at first, and give the dog a favored chew toy or some food to help make the stay more enjoyable. At first, the door can remain open during these training sessions.

3) When the dog is capable of staying comfortably and quietly in the crate begin to lock the dog in the crate at nighttime. Once the dog sleeps in the crate through the night, try leaving the pet in the crate during the daytime. Try short departures first, and gradually make them longer.

Is crate training practical for all dogs?
An occasional dog may not tolerate crate training, and may continue to show anxiety, or even eliminate when confined. These dogs may adapt better to other types of confinement such as a pen, dog run, small room, or barricaded area. Of course, if the dog is being left alone for longer than it can control (hold in) its elimination, it will be necessary to provide an area much larger than a cage, so that the pet has a location on which to eliminate, away from its food and bedding.

Continued anxiety, destruction or vocalization when placed in the crate may indicate separation anxiety. The intervention of a behaviorist may be needed.

Why is my dog soiling the house?

There are numerous reasons that a dog might soil the house with urine and/or stools. Determining the specific reason is essential for developing a treatment program. Dogs that soil the home continuously or intermittently from the time they were first obtained may not have been properly house-trained. Follow the steps in 'puppy – getting started and house training guide' for success.

Dogs that have been previously house-trained, may begin to soil the home for medical reasons or behavioral reasons. Assuming medical causes can be ruled out, some of the behavioral causes can be a change in owner schedule, a change in housing or any change in the pet's home that might lead to anxiety. For example, if you leave the dog alone for longer than the dog is accustomed, or significantly change the daily schedule or routine, your dog may begin to house-soil. Dogs that are exhibiting an increase in anxiety may begin to eliminate in the home, due primarily to a loss of control when anxious and not due to spite. Dogs that exhibit separation anxiety (see 'separation anxiety') may soil the home, and require an intensive retraining program.

Why am I finding urination on upright objects?

Marking is urination on upright objects. It is most likely to occur on or near the odors, especially the urine, left by other dogs. The volume of urine is usually small. The problem is much more common in intact males, but some neutered males and spayed females will mark. Dogs may mark territory for a number of reasons including male hormonal influences, other dogs entering the property, moving to a new household or getting new furniture, or as a response to increased stress or anxiety.

Why does my dog urinate when he meets new people or I come home?

Two specific types of house-soiling, submissive and excitement urination, differ from most other forms of house-soiling in that the dog has little control over its elimination. Submissive urination occurs when a person approaches, reaches out, stands over or attempts to physically punish it. The dog not only urinates but may show other signs of submission such as ears back, retraction of lips, avoidance of eye contact, and cowering. Although this problem can be seen in dogs of any age, submissive urination is most commonly seen in puppies and young female dogs. Owner intervention in the form of verbal reprimands or punishment, only serve to aggravate the problem by making the dog act more submissive which leads to further urination. Excitement urination is similar to submissive urination except the stimuli that lead to elimination are those that lead to excitement, particularly greeting and giving affection to the dog. These dogs may also be overly submissive, but not necessarily.

What medical problems could cause my dog to house-soil?

There are numerous medical problems that could cause or contribute to house-soiling, and these become increasingly more common as the dog ages. Medical problems that cause an increased frequency of urination such as bladder infections, bladder stones or crystals, or bladder tumors, those that cause a decrease in control or mobility such as neurological deterioration or arthritis, and those that cause an increase in urine volume (amount) such as kidney disease, liver disease, diabetes, or Cushing's disease could all contribute to indoor elimination. Certain drugs such as steroids may also cause a dog to drink more and therefore urinate more. For dogs that defecate in the house, any condition that leads to more frequent defecation such as colitis, those that cause an increased volume of stool such as problems with absorption or lack of digestive enzymes, and those that affect the dog's mobility or control such as arthritis or neurological deterioration must be ruled out. As dogs age, cognitive brain function declines, contributing to indoor elimination (see 'behavior problems of older pets').

How can the cause of house-soiling be determined?

For dogs that are house-soiling, a physical examination and medical history are essential. For most cases a urinalysis and general blood profile will also be needed, and additional tests such as radiographs and contrast studies, may be indicated based on the results. If there is any abnormality in elimination frequency or amount, stool color or consistency or urine odor, more comprehensive laboratory tests may be necessary. Once medical problems have been ruled out, it will then be necessary to determine if your dog was ever completely house-trained, whether there were changes in the pet's household or schedule at the time the problem started, whether the dog is marking or eliminating on horizontal surfaces, whether or not the pet is exhibiting anxiety when the owners leave or when it is locked in its confinement area, and whether there is any evidence of submissive or excitement urination.

How can house-soiling be treated?

Training techniques for house-soiling dogs are virtually identical to those needed to house-train a new puppy. However, even if house-soiling dogs are retrained to eliminate outdoors, indoor sites may continue to be used, since the odor, substrate, and learned habit may continue to attract the dog back to the location. In addition, dogs that eliminate indoors are in essence, performing a self rewarding behavior since they relieve themselves and do not perceive that the area they have used is inappropriate.

The key to effective house-training is constant supervision. Prevent access to indoor elimination sites. Mildly correct the pet if it is caught eliminating in an inappropriate location. Redirect the dog to appropriate areas at times when elimination is necessary. Reinforce the acceptable behavior with lavish praise or food rewards when the dog eliminates in the designated area. If a word cue is used prior to each elimination-reward sequence, the dog may soon learn to eliminate on command. If you have trouble keeping the dog in sight leave a remote indoor leash attached to the dog. This leash can also be used to deter any elimination or pre-elimination behaviors (such as sniffing, circling or squatting) in the act and to direct the dog to the appropriate area without delay. Whenever you are not available to supervise, the dog should be housed in either a confinement area where it does not eliminate (such as a bedroom, crate, or pen), or in an area where elimination is allowed (such as a dog run, papered pen or room, or outdoors).

Your dog must never be allowed access to indoor sites where it has previously eliminated unless you are there to supervise. Access to these areas can be denied by closing doors, putting up barricades or booby-trapping the areas. Odors that might attract the pet back to the area can be reduced or removed with commercial odor counteractants. Be certain to use a sufficient amount of the odor eliminator to reach all areas where the urine has had time to soak in. The appeal of the substrate can be reduced by changing the surface covering (a plastic runner with nubs up, taking up the carpet, or electronic mats).

Feeding schedules can be regulated to improve owner control over the elimination of stool. After a dog eats, it will usually need to eliminate in 15-30 minutes. Dogs that eat free-choice often need to relieve themselves at a variety of times throughout the day. Dogs that eat one or two scheduled meals each day often void in a more predictable manner. Feeding a low-residue diet may also be of benefit because the dog often has less urgency to defecate and produces less stool.

The dog that eliminates in its crate poses special problems. In these cases, crates and cages may not be the ideal training aid. Since the purpose of the crate is to provide a safe, comfortable area for the dog to "curl up and relax", it is not appropriate for dogs that are anxious about entering or staying in their cage. While this can be overcome with training techniques, it may be better to confine these dogs to a small room such as a laundry room or kitchen where the dog is fed, or a bedroom where the dog sleeps.

If the dog has reduced control due to its physical health, scheduling changes may need to be made. Some owners may be able to arrange their schedules so that more frequent trips to the elimination area can be provided. Alternatively, a dog walker or doggy day care, may need to be considered. If the owner cannot accommodate the dog's decreased control, installing a doggy door, or providing a papered area may be necessary.

When age related cognitive decline is suspected, a drug trial with selegiline or feeding a diet enriched with antioxidants and designed to help with cognitive impairment may be useful in conjunction with retraining techniques.

How can separation anxiety be treated?

To try and differentiate house-soiling from separation anxiety, it may be necessary for the owner to keep records of when the elimination occurs. If the elimination takes place when the owner is gone, or the dog is prevented from being near the owner, separation anxiety should be considered. If the house-soiling dog exhibits separation anxiety, treatment should be directed not only at re-establishing proper elimination habits, but also at the underlying separation anxiety (see 'separation anxiety'). Drug therapy may be useful in those cases where anxiety is a contributing factor. It should be noted that punishment at homecoming is not only useless for correcting a problem that has occurred during the owner's absence, but also serves to add to the pet's anxiety during future departures and homecomings.

How can submissive and excitement urination be treated?

For submissive urination, it is important that the owner and all visitors interact with the pet in a less dominant or threatening manner. The pet should be allowed to approach the owner. Kneeling down and speaking softly, rather than standing over the dog and petting the chest instead of the head, may help reduce submissive responses. Physical punishment and even the mildest verbal reprimands must be avoided. In fact, owners who attempt to punish the pet for urinating submissively will make things worse, since this intensifies fearful and submissive behavior. When greeting a very submissive dog, the owner may initially need to completely ignore it at greeting, even to the extent of avoiding eye contact. Counter-conditioning can be very helpful in controlling submissive urination. The dog is taught to perform a behavior that is not compatible with urinating, such as sitting for food or retrieving a toy when it greets someone. If the dog anticipates food or ball playing at each greeting, it is less likely to eliminate.

For excitement urination, those stimuli that initiate the behavior should be avoided. During greetings, owners and guests should refrain from eye contact, and verbal or physical contact until the pet calms down. Greetings should be very low key and words spoken in a low, calm tone. Counter-conditioning, distraction techniques and drug therapy might be useful. Caution must be taken to only reward appropriate competing behaviors (e.g. sit up and beg, go lie on your mat, retrieving a ball). Inappropriate use or timing of rewards might further excite the dog and serve as a reward for the excitement urination.

For refractory cases, the use of drugs to increase bladder sphincter tone might also be considered as an adjunct to behavior therapy. Another important aspect of treating over-excitement to visitors, is repeated presentations of the stimulus so that the dog learns the correct response. If visitors come only infrequently, the dog does not have the opportunity to learn a new behavior. By scheduling visitors to come, visit briefly, then leave by another door and re-enter, the dog may learn to be less excited and/or submissive with each entrance. Each time the person returns they are more familiar and less likely to stimulate the urination behavior. This allows the dog to "practice" the good behavior and reinforce the appropriate response.

How can marking be treated?

Neutering will reduce male marking behavior in over 80% of dogs but only eliminate it in about 40% of dogs. It is also recommended for female dogs that mark during estrus. Confining the pet so that it is unable to watch other dogs through windows in the home may be helpful. Urine residue must be removed from around doors, windows or other areas where stray dogs have been marking. The owner should give rewards to reinforce marking at outdoor sites where marking is permitted and marking should not be permitted anywhere else. New upright objects that are brought into the home should not be placed on the floor until the pet is familiar with them. During retraining, the owner must closely supervise the pet and when it cannot be supervised it should be confined to its crate or bedroom area, away from areas that have been previously marked. It might also be possible to booby-trap those areas that the pet might mark. If anxiety is an underlying factor in the marking behavior, then treatment of the anxiety with desensitization and counter-conditioning may also be helpful.

Why should I muzzle my dog?

If you know your dog has aggressive tendencies, then it is irresponsible to risk the health of others by not taking suitable precautions. Muzzles can also be used to test the dog's response to potentially problematic situations, to help introduce dogs that might be aggressive to people or other animals, and to temporarily prevent damage to the household in dogs that ingest or destroy objects in the environment.

Aren't muzzles cruel?

Muzzles themselves are not cruel, but they may cause welfare problems if they are not used appropriately. If the guidelines below are followed, your pet will actually enjoy being muzzled. The most common errors are to only use a muzzle when something nasty is going to happen to your pet, e.g. when he is about to be injected; to expect your dog to instantly accept the muzzle; or to leave the muzzle on excessively.

What types of muzzle are there?

There are two common types of muzzle. The basket muzzle and the nylon muzzle. Both have their uses. The basket muzzle allows your dog more freedom to pant and drink if properly fitted. The nylon muzzle prevents the dog from opening its mouth, but may lead to overheating if left attached too long since it restricts panting and drinking. Some nylon muzzles have a mesh over the end to provide for a looser fit and more opportunity to pant, while others have a medium size opening at the end for the nose and mouth where small tidbits can also be given. However, the dog may still provide a small nip with this latter type of muzzle.

How do I train my dog to enjoy being muzzled?

1) It is important to find an effective and comfortable muzzle for your dog. This may take a bit of time but it is worth shopping around. Some muzzles can be slipped off by pawing so that a proper fitting muzzle should be difficult if not impossible for your dog to remove. Some muzzles come with (or can be affixed with) a strap that attaches from the muzzle over the top of the dog's head (passing between the eyes) to the dog's collar so that it cannot be pulled off by the dog.

2) Your dog should not be muzzled initially in a conflict or fearful situation. Show your dog the muzzle, let him sniff to investigate it and give him a treat before putting the muzzle away. Repeat this procedure several times. This starts to build a positive association with the muzzle.

3) Next turn the muzzle to face your dog and place some treats inside and encourage him to take them out. Gradually place the treats further inside so that he sticks his head all the way into the muzzle.

4) Next slip the muzzle on without fastening it for a few seconds and reward your dog when you take it off. Slowly increase the time you leave it on from a few seconds to a minute or more and no longer reward your pet every time unless he remains calm. Be sure to set things up so your dog succeeds, by only placing the muzzle on for short periods of time. We want the muzzle to be removed when the dog is calm and quiet, not fussing or pawing.

5) Now that your dog accepts the muzzle, you can try fastening it. Again the length of time that it is left on needs to be increased gradually. While the muzzle is on the dog your dog can be rewarded with affection or play if it can be sufficiently distracted so that it does not show any fear. If your dog enjoys walks or games of chase, this might be a sufficient enough diversion to help him or her adapt to the muzzle more quickly. The longer the time that the muzzle is left on the greater the reward should be when it comes off, particularly if your dog has made no effort to remove it. You should aim to work towards keeping your dog muzzled for about thirty minutes. The goal is to only remove the muzzle when the dog is calm and quiet, not struggling. If you remove the muzzle immediately after the dog struggles or paws at it, the dog may learn that these actions get the muzzle removed.

6) Start muzzling your dog before you go for walks, but continue to avoid situations that might lead to fear, anxiety or conflict for your dog. If you feel you must take the muzzle off for some of the time, do it when you start to head home and get your dog to keep to a close heel on the lead as long as the muzzle is removed. Always give him lots of praise when you take the muzzle off.

Once this routine has been established, your dog should be muzzled before you encounter known conflict or problem situations. Your pet should still be muzzled at other times for play and walks so that it does not start to resent or predict these few necessary occasions.

You should never remove the muzzle when your pet is trying to remove it. He can be encouraged to leave it alone by a slight tug on a lead. When he relaxes, the muzzle can be removed and take note that you may have been expecting too much too soon. The important rule is to work at a rate that your pet can accept and cope with. This may mean that the whole program may take a few weeks rather than a few days.

Most male animals (stallions, bulls, boars, rams, and tomcats) that are kept for companionship, work, or food production are neutered (castrated) unless they are intended to be used as breeding stock. This is a common practice to prevent unacceptable sexual behavior, reduce aggressiveness, and prevent accidental or indiscriminate breeding. However, many dog owners choose not to neuter their male dogs, despite the benefits.

How does neutering affect behavior?

The only behaviors that will be affected by castration are those that are under the influence of male hormones. A dog's temperament, training, personality and ability to do "work" are a result of genetics and upbringing, not its male hormones. Castration does not "calm" an excitable dog, and unless a castrated male dog is overfed or under-exercised, there is no reason for it to become fat and lazy.

What is castration?

Castration or neutering of male dogs is surgical removal of the testicles (orchidectomy). The procedure involves general anesthesia. An incision is

made just in front of the scrotal sac and both testicles, leaving the sac intact. Vasectomies are not performed since it is both sterilization and removal of the male hormones that provide the behavioral and medical benefits.

Which of my dogs' behavior problems can be expected to improve following castration?

As mentioned, only those behaviors that are "driven" by male hormones, can be reduced or eliminated by castration. Although the hormones are gone from the system almost immediately following castration, male behaviors may diminish quickly over a few days or gradually over a few months.

Undesirable sexual behavior: Attraction to female dogs, roaming, mounting, and masturbation can be reduced or eliminated by castration.

a) Case studies show that for roaming there was moderate improvement in 70% of dogs with marked improvement in 40%. For mounting there was moderate improvement in 70% of dogs with marked improvement in 25%.

b) In one study, castration led to reduced aggression toward other dogs in the house in 1/3 of cases, towards people in the family in 30% of cases, towards unfamiliar dogs in 20% of cases and towards unfamiliar people in 10% of cases.

Urine Marking: Most adult male dogs lift their legs while urinating. Instead of emptying their bladders completely, most male dogs retain some urine to deposit on other vertical objects that they pass. Some males have such a strong desire to mark that they also mark indoors. Castration reduces marking in 80% of dogs with a marked improvement in 40%.

Aggression: Every aggressive dog should be castrated. At the very least this will prevent reproduction and passing on of any genetic traits for aggression. Castration may also reduce or eliminate some forms of aggression (i.e. those that are influenced by male hormones).

Are there any additional benefits to castration?

Medical benefits: Castration eliminates the possibility of testicular cancer and greatly reduces the chance of prostate disease, two extremely common and serious problems of older male dogs. Most older dogs will develop prostate disease or testicular tumors if they survive to an old enough age. Castration can also reduce the risk of perianal tumors and perineal hernias.

Population control: Perhaps the most important issue is that millions of dogs are destroyed annually at animal shelters across the United States and Canada. Neutering males is as important as spaying females when it comes to population control.

Are there any risks?

Nowadays, with the broad selection of anesthetic agents and state of the art monitoring, it is extremely rare for there to be anesthetic or surgical complications during a canine castration.

Most young and healthy animals recover without incident. Often, the biggest concern is not the surgery and anesthesia, but the recovery, since we need to ensure that the dog does not lick excessively at its incision line until it is fully healed. Constant monitoring, bitter tasting creams, or a protective collar, known as an Elizabethan collar, will be required if excessive licking is observed following castration.

When castration is being considered for an older dog, the benefits must be weighed against any risks associated with anesthetic and surgery. Since castration surgery is seldom associated with any complications, it is the anesthetic that is the primary concern. If castration is being considered as a separate procedure for a medical reason (prostatic enlargement, testicular tumors, perianal tumors), then there is a significant benefit to the dog's health, comfort and perhaps longevity, in having the castration performed. If the dog is exhibiting any undesirable behaviors that might be improved by castration (roaming, masturbation, mounting, interdog aggression, excessive sexual interest or marking), there may also be a significant benefit to be gained from castration. Although not infallible, a physical examination, a series of blood and urine tests and any additional screening that your veterinarian may feel is warranted for your dog (e.g. EKG, chest radiographs), can help to determine if your pet has any significant anesthetic risks. These tests can also help the veterinarian determine which anesthetic protocol would be safest for your pet. Since many older pets require anesthesia for other procedures (e.g. growth removal, preventive dentistry), the benefits can often be further increased, and the number of anesthetic procedures reduced by performing the castration along with the other procedure.

What age is best for preventive castration?

A number of studies have shown that castration is just as effective at reducing male associated behavior problems as it is at preventing them. This means that whether the pet is castrated post-pubertally (e.g. 1 year or older) or pre-pubertally (e.g. 2 months of age) the behavioral effects are likely to be the same. There is, however, anecdotal evidence that dogs that are sexually experienced are more likely to retain their sexual habits after castration, compared to those dogs that have had little or no sexual experience prior to castration. It has been advocated recently that castration be performed at as young an age as is practical, to ensure that it is done before the pet has a chance to breed. This is most important in animal shelters since it allows them to ensure that every dog adopted has already been castrated. To date, studies have shown that castration is safe, and has no long-term effects on health or behavior, regardless of the age that it is performed. Many shelters and some veterinary clinics begin neutering as young as two months of age. They report that the surgery is often shorter and that recovery is quicker and with less post-operative discomfort for these younger animals. Once dogs are adopted into their new homes, most veterinarians recommend waiting until all vaccinations are complete before admitting the pet into the hospital for surgery. However, if general anesthesia were needed prior to the vaccinations being completed for any other reason (e.g. suturing a cut, removing quills) this would be an excellent time to consider castration. In summary, there seems to be no behavioral or medical benefit to waiting until a dog is "mature" to perform a castration.

My dog has retained testicles – what does this mean?

During fetal development or shortly after birth, the testicles will descend into the scrotal sac. In some dogs, likely due to a genetic predisposition, the testicles may not descend into the scrotal sac. These dogs are known as either unilateral (one testicle) or bilateral (both testicles) cryptorchids. The testicle may be retained in the abdomen or anywhere between the abdominal cavity and the external sac. Retained testicles do not usually produce sperm, but they will produce hormones, which can lead to any of the behavioral changes or medical problems previously discussed. In fact, some studies have shown that retained testicles may be more prone to developing cancer. At the very least, it would be extremely difficult to determine if a testicle, which is located in the abdomen, begins to develop cancer, since it cannot be palpated. All dogs with retained testicles should be neutered (and both testicles removed) for medical and behavioral reasons, and to ensure that this genetic abnormality is not perpetuated.

PLAY & EXERCISE

Why are play and exercise important?

Play with owners and with other dogs, not only provides the dog with some of its exercise requirements, but also helps to meet social needs. Insufficient exercise can contribute to problem behaviors including destructiveness (chewing and digging), investigative behavior (garbage raiding), hyperactivity, unruliness, excitability, attention-getting behaviors, and even some forms of barking. It is especially important to ensure that a dog's need for exercise has been met prior to leaving the dog alone at home and prior to lengthy crating or confinement sessions.

What are good ways to play with and exercise my puppy?

Taking your dog for a walk is a good way to accomplish exercise and can be enjoyable and healthy for you as well. From an early age you should acclimate your puppy to a collar and leash. A flat nylon or leather collar is fine. Keep your puppy away from stray dogs and neighborhood parks until all vaccinations are finished. Practice your walking skills in your own yard first. Put your puppy on a leash and with your voice and a small tug, or perhaps a food or toy reward as a prompt, encourage it to follow you. Reward the good behavior with praise. Keep initial walks short to encourage compliance.

Playing with your pet is an enjoyable activity for both of you. Not only does the puppy get exercise, but positive interactions take place. Training sessions are also an excellent way to gain owner leadership and control, while providing interaction between you and your pet.

How much exercise and play is appropriate?

Selecting an appropriate amount and type of play and exercise will depend on the type of dog. Puppies and even adult dogs from breeds that have been bred for their stamina or to do "work" often have higher exercise requirements. For purebred dogs, consider their traditional work when deciding the type and amount of play to provide. For example, the retrieving breeds do best with lengthy games of fetch or "Frisbee", while the sledding breeds might prefer pulling carts, or running or jogging with an active owner.

The length and type of play and exercise for your dog will depend on its behavioral requirements and health limitations. While some dogs may still be ready for more after a five mile jog and a game of fetch, others may be tired and satisfied after a short walk around the block.

How can I keep my dog occupied when I am away?

When you are out, or you are busy at home with other activities and responsibilities, it would be ideal for your dog to be relaxed and sleeping, but this will not always be the case. Exploring the environment, stealing food items, raiding garbage cans, chewing or digging, are just a few of the ways that dogs will find to keep themselves occupied. When you are confident that you have provided your dog with sufficient play and interactive exercise, and you must leave your dog alone, provide sufficient toys and distractions to keep your dog occupied and confine your pet to a safe, dog-proofed area. Some dogs do best when housed with another dog for play and companionship. Others prefer objects to chew (see 'destructiveness – chewing'), areas to dig (see 'destructiveness – digging'), self feeding toys, or even a video to keep themselves occupied and "busy" while you are unavailable.

What type of play should be avoided?

Try to avoid games that pit your strength against your puppies. Tug-of-war games seem to be an enjoyable diversion for many puppies and they do help to direct chewing and biting toward an acceptable play object, rather than an owner's hands or clothing. On the other hand, some puppies get very excited, overly stimulated and become far too aggressive during tug-of-war games. A general rule of thumb for tug-of-war (or any other game for that matter) is to avoid it, unless you are the one to initiate the game, and can stop it as soon as the need arises. Teaching the dog to "drop" on command can help to ensure that you remain in control of object play sessions such as fetch and tug -of -war (see 'controlling stealing and teaching give'). A variety of types of interactive toys are also available for throwing, retrieving, playing kickball etc.

Although games like chase are good exercise, they can often result in wild exuberant play that gets out of control. Again, a good rule of thumb is to only play these games, if you are the one to initiate the game, and are capable of stopping the game immediately should it get out of control. Many dogs can be taught to play "hide and seek" without becoming too excited. Other dogs like to "search" for their toys and bring them to you.

How can I teach my puppy to play fetch?

Most young puppies, even those that do not have an inherent instinct to retrieve, can be taught how to play fetch from an early age. You will need to train your puppy to do three things; go get the toy, bring it back, and relinquish it to you so that you can throw it again. First, make the toy enticing. Try a squeaky toy or a ball. Toss the toy a short distance, 1-2 feet, and encourage your puppy to go to it. When it gets there give it praise. If your puppy picks up the toy in its' mouth, say 'good dog'. Then, move backwards a short way, clap your hands and entice your puppy to come towards you. All the while you should be encouraging verbally with a happy tone of voice and lots of praise. When your puppy returns to you, say 'give it' or 'release' and show another toy or even a small food treat. Most puppies will gladly give the toy to get the new toy or treat and at the same time will quickly learn the 'give' or 'release' command. Then, by repeating the entire sequence of events again, the game of fetch itself, should soon be enough of a reward that food and toys will no longer be necessary to entice the puppy to give the toy. At the end of each fetch play session, have the puppy return the toy and give a toy or chew treat for the puppy to play with as a final reward for releasing the toy.

Punishment is the application of a stimulus that decreases the chances that a behavior will be repeated. It must be timed to coincide with the undesirable behavior, and must be unpleasant enough to deter the dog from repeating the behavior. Keep in mind that you are punishing the behavior not the dog. Therefore punishment to dissuade an undesirable behavior might be acceptable, especially if the dog immediately and consistently stops when punished. However punishment as a form of training is inappropriate and can lead to fear and avoidance. Punishment should never be considered unless the pet has the means to satisfy its nature and its needs. For example, the chewing dog should be provided with appropriate exercise and appealing toys to chew on, before any attempts to punish undesirable chewing are initiated. If however, we can train our pets to do what they are supposed to do and provide outlets for their needs, then it will seldom be necessary to punish inappropriate behavior.

How can punishment be used to correct behavior problems?

The key to successful punishment is to associate an unpleasant consequence with the undesirable behavior. Remember that punishment must take place while the behavior is occurring, not after. Physical or direct interactive punishment is likely to lead to fear of the owner and fear of the hand. Therefore the use of punishment products may be more appropriate and more effective, since they are less likely to be associated with the owner, and are more specific and immediate than an owner's voice or physical handling. Most of these devices actually serve to interrupt or disrupt the inappropriate behavior, so that the dog can be directed to perform an appropriate behavior, and as such may not be a true form of punishment. For example, the dog that is barking could be interrupted with an air horn or shaker can and immediately taught to approach the owners to play with a favored toy. On the other hand, if the pet is frightened of repeating a behavior because the environment is set up (booby-trapped) to deter the pet, then the owner does not even need to be present to stop the behavior.

Punishment should never be used to train a pet. The pet should be taught what we want using lure reward methods, rewards and shaping or prompting and rewards. It is illogical to wait until the pet misbehaves and then administer something unpleasant. Punishing the pet can lead to fear of the owner, fear of handling or fear of particular stimuli (approach, reaching out, pulling leash). If punishment is effective it can at best stop the behavior from recurring in that location but will not stop the behavior (e.g. chewing, elimination) from being repeated at other times or locations. With owner initiated punishment the pet may soon learn to inhibit the behavior in the owner's presence (and continue the behavior in the owner's absence). On the other hand, where punishment is not sufficiently unpleasant it may serve as a reward (attention). Therefore, if the pet continues the behavior after one or two applications of the punishment then it is ineffective and should be discontinued.

Punishing the dog while the owner remains out of sight is a better way of teaching the pet to avoid the behavior altogether, whether the owner is present or not. This is known as 'remote punishment' (punishment administered by the owner while remaining out of sight) and takes a great deal of preparation, time and forethought. Perhaps the only practical application of punishment is to booby-trap the area (sometimes known as 'environmental punishment'), so that the dog is punished even in the owner's absence.

What is 'direct interactive punishment' and how does it work?

If you catch your puppy engaging in an incorrect behavior, try a loud noise such as clapping your hands or a loud "uh-uh". Remember, reprimands need to occur while the behavior is happening, preferably just as it begins, and never after. Often puppies will be startled when they hear these noises and temporarily stop the behavior. At that time you need to quickly redirect the puppy to a more appropriate task.

Another way to interrupt your puppy is with various types of noise devices. One such device is a "shaker can". This is an empty soda can that has a few pennies inside and then is taped shut. When given a vigorous shake it makes a loud noise that will often interrupt the puppy's behavior. Other devices that make a loud noise are ultrasonic trainers, battery operated alarms, and air horns (see 'behavior management products').

How does remote punishment work?

For remote techniques to be successful there are two key elements. The owner must be able to monitor the dog to determine when the undesirable behavior begins and must be able to administer the "punishment" while remaining out of sight. A long range water rifle, a remote citronella collar or a long leash left attached to the dog's head halter often work best. To know when the problem begins you will need to watch your dog closely while remaining out of sight (from around a corner, or perhaps through a window if the dog is outdoors). A one way mirror, intercom, or motion detector might also be practical methods of remotely monitoring behavior. Then as soon as the dog enters the area or begins to perform the undesirable behavior, the remote punishment device can be activated. If your dog finds the noise or spray unpleasant and cannot determine where it is coming from it should quickly learn to stay away from the area whether the owner is present or not.

How can I booby-trap the environment to punish the pet?

Punishing the behavior remotely, with the owner out of sight, is impractical if the owner is away from home or unavailable to supervise. Booby-traps are a way of teaching the pet to avoid the area, or the behavior itself. Some innovative ways to discourage a dog from entering an area where an undesirable behavior is likely to be performed (garbage raiding, chewing, entering rooms) would be to make the area less appealing by placing balloons set to pop, a pyramid of empty cans set to topple, or a bucket of water set to dump as the pet enters the area. Mousetrap trainers, motion detectors, alarm mats, shock mats, and indoor electronic "fencing", are also effective at keeping dogs away from problem areas (see 'behavior management products').

Taste deterrents might also be helpful for destructive chewing, provided they are unpleasant enough to deter the behavior. Products such as bitter apple, bitter lime or Tabasco sauce are often recommended, but many dogs do not mind, or learn to enjoy the taste. A little water mixed with cayenne pepper, oil of eucalyptus, any non-toxic mentholated product, or one of the commercial anti-chew sprays often work best. To be effective, the first exposure to a product must be as repulsive as is humanely possible, so that the dog is immediately repelled whenever it smells or tastes that product again. Never leave any objects or areas untreated until the dog learns to leave the object or area alone.

What is negative punishment and how does it work?

All of the punishment techniques discussed above are forms of positive punishment, in which the application of an unpleasant stimulus decreases the chance that the pet will repeat the behavior. Another form of punishment occurs when a reward is removed as a consequence for a behavior. In other words, the removal of something pleasant is punishing the pet because it is learning that good things are taken away if the behavior is repeated. For example, if the puppy is playing and this escalates to play biting and you stop the game and walk away this is known as negative punishment.

What should I do if I find the problem after it has already occurred?

If you find something that your puppy has done (destruction, elimination), but you did not catch him in the act, just clean it up and vow to supervise your puppy better in the future. Do not get your puppy and bring him over to the mess and yell and physically discipline him. Remember that you need to punish the behavior you wish to change. If you did not see your puppy chew up the object, all you are doing is disciplining your puppy for being present at a mess on the floor. Since that makes no sense to your puppy, your reprimands could create fear and

anxiety, which could lead to aggression and owner avoidance.

If I must not punish my dog after the problem has occurred, what can be done?

Other than designing appropriate environmental booby-traps, the only thing that you can do to avoid undesirable behavior is to supervise your puppy when you are around, and to prevent access to potential problems when you are not available to supervise. Keeping a leash attached to a head halter will allow you to maintain good supervision and interrupt problems immediately when you are around and supervising. Remember that problems such as chewing and other forms of destructiveness are part of the puppies' normal curiosity and desire to chew. Always provide suitable play objects designed to entertain your puppy so that he will not want to destroy your possessions (see 'destructiveness – chewing').

PUPPY – GETTING STARTED & HOUSE TRAINING GUIDE

When you bring a new puppy into your home there will be a period of adjustment. Your goals are to help your puppy to quickly bond to its new family, and to minimize the stress associated with leaving its mother, littermates, and former home. If there are already dogs in the new home the transition may be a little easier as the puppy is able to identify with its own kind. Obtaining two puppies would be another option. However, most puppies, especially those obtained before 12 weeks of age, will form attachments almost immediately to the people and any other pets in the new home, provided that there are no unpleasant consequences associated with each new person and experience.

How do I prevent my puppy from doing damage or getting into mischief?

The rule of thumb for dog training is "set the dog up for success". Supervise the puppy at all times until it has learned what it is allowed to chew, and where it is supposed to eliminate. Keeping the puppy on a 10 foot remote leash is an excellent way to keep it in sight, and to train it not to wander off. This is particularly helpful with a highly investigative puppy or for a very busy household.

At any time that the puppy cannot be supervised, such as throughout the night or when you need to go out, house it in a secure area. An escape-proof crate, a dog run, or collapsible pen are simple, highly effective, and most important, safe. The puppy could also be confined to a room that has been carefully dog-proofed. When selecting your dog's confinement area it is useful to consider a number of factors. The dog will adapt fastest to the new area if it is associated with rewards. Have the puppy enter the area for all its treats, toys, and perhaps food and water. The area should have some warm, dry, comfortable bedding, and should never be used for punishment (although it can, and should, be used to prevent problems). Housing the puppy in isolated areas where there is minimal human contact, such as in a laundry room or basement, should be avoided. In fact, often the best area is a kitchen (so that this can also be the dog's feeding area) or a bedroom (so that it becomes the dog's sleeping area). Each time the puppy needs to be confined, it should first be well exercised and given an opportunity to eliminate. Another consideration in selecting the type of confinement area is how long you may need to leave the dog alone. You must provide an area for elimination anytime the puppy will be left alone for longer than it can control its elimination. A room or collapsible pen with a paper-covered area would be needed. A cage or crate could be used for owners that do not have to leave their puppies confined for longer than 2 or 3 hours.

What is the best way to punish my puppy for misbehavior?

Every effort should be made to avoid punishment for new puppies as it is generally unnecessary and can lead to avoidance of family members, at a time when bonding and attachment is critical. By preventing problems through confinement or supervision, providing for all of the puppy's needs, and setting up the environment for success, little or no punishment should ever be required. If a reprimand is needed, a verbal "no" or a loud noise is usually sufficient to distract a puppy so that you can then redirect the puppy to the correct behavior. Puppies that are supervised with a remote leash can be immediately interrupted with a pull on the leash (see 'punishment' for further details).

How can I prevent problems?

Supervise the puppy at all times that it is not confined to ensure that the puppy does not get itself into mischief, or cause damage to itself or the home. Leaving a remote leash attached is all that is usually needed to prevent or interrupt inappropriate behavior such as garbage raiding, chewing on household items, house-soiling, or wandering off into rooms or areas that are out of bounds. If the leash is attached to a head halter you can quickly correct other problems that might arise, such as nipping, play biting, and jumping up. When the puppy cannot be supervised, confinement (discussed above) will be necessary.

What must I do to provide for my puppy's needs?

Chewing, play, exercise, exploration, feeding, social contact and elimination are basic requirements of all puppies. By providing appropriate outlets for each of these needs, few problems are likely to emerge. Puppies should be given chew toys that interest them and occupy their time. When supervised, the owner can allow the puppy to investigate and explore its new environment and can direct the puppy to the appropriate chew toys (and away from inappropriate areas). Play, exercise, affection, training, and handling must all be part of the daily routine. New tasks, new routines, new people and new forms of handling can be associated with rewards to ensure success. And, of course, the puppy will need to be provided with an acceptable area for elimination, and will need guidance until it learns to use this area.

How do I house-train my puppy?

All it requires are a few basic rules to house-train puppies within a few days. This does not mean that the puppy will be able to be trusted to wander throughout the home without eliminating. What the puppy should quickly learn is where it should eliminate, and the consequences of eliminating indoors when the owner is supervising.

A. Puppies have a strong urge to eliminate after sleeping, playing, feeding and drinking. Prepare to take your puppy to its selected elimination area within 30 minutes of each of these activities. In addition, although some puppies can control themselves through the entire night, most puppies need to eliminate every 3 to 4 hours during the daytime. With each passing month, you can expect your puppy to control itself a little longer between elimination times. The puppy should be taken to its elimination area, given a word or two of verbal encouragement (e.g. 'Hurry up') and as soon as elimination is completed, lavishly praised and patted. A few tasty food treats can also be given the first few times the puppy eliminates in the right spot, and then intermittently thereafter. This teaches the puppy the proper place to eliminate, and that elimination in that location is associated with rewards. Some puppies may learn to eliminate when they hear the cue words ('Hurry up'). Always go outdoors with your puppy to ensure that it has eliminated and so that rewards can be given immediately upon completion, and not when the dog comes back indoors (too late!).

B. When indoors the puppy must be supervised so that you can see when it needs to eliminate and immediately take it outdoors to its elimination area. Should pre-elimination signs (circling, squatting, sneaking-off, heading to the door) occur, immediately take the dog to its elimination site, give the cue words, and reward the puppy for elimination. If the puppy begins to eliminate indoors, use a verbal reprimand or shake can, and immediately take the puppy outdoors to its proper site, so that it can complete the act. Rather than using punishment, it is best to always supervise your puppy. One of the best techniques is to leave a remote lead attached.

C. When you are not available to supervise, the puppy should be confined to its confinement area (see 'house-safety and crate training'). Be certain that your puppy has had a chance to eliminate, and has had sufficient play and exercise before any lengthy confinement. If the area is small enough, such as a pen or crate, many puppies will have sufficient control to keep this area clean. This means that when you come to release the puppy from confinement, it must be taken directly to its elimination area. If the area is too large for the puppy to keep clean, or the puppy is left alone too long for it to control itself, the entire area, except for the puppies bed and feeding spot, should be covered with paper for elimination. Once the puppy starts to limit its elimination to some selected areas, unused areas of the paper can be taken up. For owners that intend to continue to use paper for training, even when home, the puppy should be supervised when released from confinement, and then returned to this area when pre-elimination signs are seen.

Why does my puppy refuse to eliminate in my presence, even when outdoors?

Puppies that are not supervised and rewarded for outdoor elimination, but are constantly being disciplined and punished for indoor elimination, may soon begin to fear to eliminate in all locations in your presence. These puppies do not associate the punishment with indoor elimination; they associate the punishment with the presence of the owners.

What do I do if I find some stool or urine in an inappropriate spot?

There is no point in punishing or even pointing out the problem to the puppy. Only if the puppy is in the act of elimination will it understand the consequences (rewards or punishment). In fact, it is not the puppy that has erred, it is the owner who has erred by not properly supervising.

How can I teach my puppy to signal that it needs to go out to eliminate?

By regularly taking the dog outdoors, through the same door, to the same site, and providing rewards for proper elimination, the puppy should soon learn to head for the door each time it has to eliminate. If you recognize the signs of impending elimination and praise the puppy whenever it heads for the doorway, the behavior can be further encouraged. Puppies that have been interrupted or reprimanded on one or more occasions as they begin to eliminate indoors, may begin to try to sneak away, whine or show some form of anxiety, when they feel the urge to eliminate, but cannot escape from the owner's sight. If you can pick up on these cues, and take the puppy directly to the outdoors for elimination and reward, the puppy may consistently begin to show these signals when he or she needs to eliminate, and may even begin to take you to the exit door.

When will I be able to trust my puppy to wander loose throughout the home?

Generally you will want your dog to have been error free around the house for about a month before you can begin to decrease your confinement and supervision. The first time you leave the puppy unsupervised should be just after taking the dog outdoors for elimination. Gradually increase the length of time that your dog is allowed to roam through the home without supervision. If the dog has been able to go unsupervised for a couple of hours without an "accident", it might then be possible to begin going out for short periods of time. Of course, if the dog still investigates and chews, then confinement and supervision may still be necessary.

PUPPY – TRAINING BASICS

At what age can I start training my new puppy?

You will be training your puppy from the moment you bring it home and start to house train. Puppies start learning from birth. Good breeders encourage handling and socialization from birth. Some training can begin as soon as the puppy can open its eyes and walk. Young puppies have short attention spans but expect them to begin to learn simple obedience commands such as 'sit', 'down' and 'stay', from as young as 7 to 8 weeks of age (see 'rewards – learning and reinforcement', 'puppy training – sit, down, stand, and stay'; and 'puppy training – come, wait and follow' for training on the specific tasks).

Formal dog training has traditionally been delayed until 6 months of age. Actually this juvenile stage is a very poor time to start. The dog is beginning to solidify adult behavioral patterns, dominance behavior is beginning to emerge, and behaviors learned in puppyhood may need to be changed. In addition anything that has already been learned or trained incorrectly will need to be undone and retaught.

When training is started at 7 to 8 weeks of age, use methods that rely on positive reinforcement and gentle teaching. Puppies have short attention spans, so training sessions should be brief, but daily. Puppies can be taught to 'sit', 'down', and 'stand' using a method called food-lure training. We use food treats to entice the dog to follow its nose into the proper positions for 'sit', 'down', 'stand', and 'stay'.

How do I get started using food lure training?

Small pieces of food or a favored toy can be used to motivate your puppy to perform most tasks. Provided the reward is sufficiently appealing, the puppy can be prompted to get the desired response by showing the puppy the reward, giving a command, and moving it to get the desired response. For example, food held up over the puppy's nose and moved slowly backwards should get a 'sit' response; food drawn down to the floor should get a 'down' response; food brought back up should get a 'stand' response; food held out at a distance should get a 'come' response; and food held at your thigh as you walk should get the puppy to 'heel or 'follow'. By pairing a command phrase or word with each action, and giving the reward for each appropriate response, the puppy should soon learn the meaning of each command (see 'rewards – learning and reinforcement for dogs and cats'; 'controlling stealing and teaching the "give" command'; 'teaching – sit, down, stand and stay'; and 'training puppies – come, wait and follow').

How often should I give the command?

Ideally you should give the command phrase once and then use your food to move the puppy into positions. Once the puppy has performed the task, add in verbal praise and an affectionate pat, which are known as secondary reinforcers. Some trainers also use clickers as secondary reinforcers. If the puppy does not immediately obey on the first command, then you are likely proceeding a little too quickly. If you keep repeating the command, the puppy will learn that several repetitions are acceptable before it needs to obey. Keeping a leash attached can help to gain an immediate response if the puppy does not obey.

Remember that early in training your puppy does not know the meaning of the word. Therefore you could just as easily teach your puppy to sit with the word bananas, (or sit in any other language) as you could with the word sit. The key is to associate the word, in this case "sit", with the action of placing the hind end on the floor.

How should I phase out the lure and food rewards?

At first you are going to let the puppy see the food in your hand so that you will have her attention and can use it to guide her into position. As your puppy begins to comply more readily, you can start to hide the food in your hand, but give the command and repeat the motion or signal that she has learned to follow. Soon the puppy will come to expect the treat each time she performs the task. Then, signal and give the command, but when she performs the task, reward only with praise and give the puppy an affectionate pat. Next, you can begin to vary the frequency, giving praise with; 'good dog' and perhaps patting each time, but giving the food randomly, perhaps every 3 or 4 times. In time, the puppy should respond to either the hand signal or the command

Over time, the words "good dog" or the affectionate pat become secondary reinforcers. Because they have been paired with food in the past, they take on more meaning and become a reinforcement in themselves. It is important to use secondary reinforcement because you will not always have food with you when you need your pet to obey. In addition, if you rely on food to always get your puppy to comply, you will have a puppy that will only do the task when you have a treat.

At first training may begin in designated sessions throughout the day, with a variety of family members. All rewards should be saved for these training sessions. Over time however, you should begin to ask your puppy to perform the tasks at other times.

How much time should I spend training my puppy every day?

You do not necessarily need to train in a set session daily. Rather, integrate these tasks throughout the day. A goal to strive for is at least 15 minutes of training every day. These can be short 5 minute sessions spread throughout the day. Try to have all family members ask your puppy to do these tasks. Remember to try and train in every room of your house. You want your puppy to 'sit', 'lie down' and 'stay' everywhere, not just in the training location.

Use these training tasks as you integrate the puppy into your life. For example, ask your puppy to 'sit' prior to receiving her food, 'sit' before you let her in or out the door, and 'sit' before you pet her. These are times when your puppy wants something and is more likely to comply. In this way you are training your dog all the time, throughout the day and also establishing yourself as the leader, the one who controls the resources. Training your puppy prior to getting each reward also helps to prevent problems. Having your puppy sit before getting a food or treat prevents begging, while teaching your dog to sit before opening the door can prevent jumping up or running out the door. Be creative. The time you spend training your puppy now will pay off when you have an adult dog. To have a well-trained dog, you need to be committed to reinforcing the training tasks on nearly a daily basis for the first year of your puppy's life. The more you teach and supervise your puppy, the less opportunity it will have to engage in improper behaviors. Dogs do not train themselves, when left to choose their behavior they will act like dogs.

What can be done if my puppy is too distracted or excitable to control?

Training should begin in a quiet environment with few distractions. The reward chosen should be highly motivating so that the puppy is focused entirely on the trainer and the reward. Although a small food treat generally works best, a favorite toy or a special dog treat might be more appealing. It might also be helpful to train the puppy just before a scheduled mealtime when it is at its hungriest. For difficult puppies or headstrong puppies the best way to ensure that the puppy will perform the desired behavior and respond appropriately to the command is to leave a leash attached and to use a head collar for additional control. In this way, the puppy can be prompted into the correct response if it does not immediately obey and pressure released as soon as the desired response is achieved (see 'management devices in dog training'). Clicker training is also an excellent way to immediately and strongly reinforce the desired response (see 'rewards – learning and reinforcement').

Should I also consider training classes?

Pet owners who are novices at training can begin a training program with these few simple steps. It takes repetition, time and perseverance for the puppy to be able to predictably and reliably respond to commands in a variety of situations. The training class serves many functions. Of course trainers can demonstrate techniques and help guide you through the steps in training. They can help advise you on puppy training problems, and can help you advance your training to more difficult exercises. The puppy will be learning in a group situation, with some real life distractions. And, considering human nature, the pet owner who takes his or her dog to a puppy class, will be forced to practice (do their homework) throughout the week, if they do not want to fall behind by the next class. A training class is a good place to meet and talk to other new puppy owners and see how all puppies behave.

Training classes for young puppies are also an excellent way to socialize your new puppy to a variety of people, other dogs, and stimuli, in a controlled environment. In addition, you will learn how to prevent problems before they can begin, or deal with them as they emerge, rather than having to find a way to correct problems that have already developed. Your puppy might also make some new friends of the same age. You could then visit these friends (or vice versa) with your puppy for social play and exercise sessions. Since the primary socialization period for dogs ends by 3 months of age, puppy socialization classes are most valuable for puppies 8 weeks of age and older. If all puppies in the class have had initial vaccinations, are healthy and parasite free, the health risks are low and the potential benefits are enormous. Discuss when to start and the location of classes in your area with your veterinarian.

PUPPY TRAINING – TAKING CHARGE

Dogs are a highly social "grouping-living" species that in the wild is often referred to as a pack. Packs have a leader that the other members follow and look to for "direction." In fact, each individual in the pack generally develops a relationship with each other pack member so that they are either dominant or subordinate to that individual. When puppies enter our homes the family becomes the new social group. Allowing behaviors that are pushy, disobedient or inappropriate may lead to problems that become increasingly difficult to correct. Therefore it is essential that all owners take control over the puppy and gain a position of leadership in the family pack. This control must be achieved by the proper use and timing of rewards and by directing the puppy to display appropriate responses rather than through physical techniques that can lead to fear and anxiety.

When is the best time to begin training my puppy?
Formal dog training has traditionally been delayed until 6 months of age. Actually, this juvenile stage is a poor time to begin training. The dog is beginning to solidify adult behavioral patterns, dominance behavior is emerging, and behaviors that they have learned in puppyhood may need to

be changed. Therefore, it is best to begin teaching puppies from the time they are obtained. One important task to begin early is to establish yourself as the leader. This can be done by rewarding desirable responses, training the dog to obey commands, avoiding the reinforcement of behaviors that are initiated by your dog and training the dog to accept some simple body handling techniques.

Are physical exercises necessary for gaining control?

Although there are many physical techniques that have been advocated for gaining control, it is the owners' attitudes, actions, and responses to the new puppy (along with the puppy's genetics) that are most important in the puppy becoming either well-mannered and responsive, or stubborn, disobedient and "domineering".

Dog training literature has often discussed using scruff shakes and rollover techniques to discipline puppies. However, these physical techniques do not necessarily mimic how dogs would communicate with each other and such handling by a human could lead to fear, anxiety and even retaliation. Training is intended to train the dog what you want, rather than discipline what you don't want. This makes a positive, learning environment for the puppy to grow up in. There may be a number of advantages to teaching your puppy to assume subordinate postures (on their side, on their back, hands on neck, hand stroking the top of the head, hand grasping muzzle) but this does not mean that they teach your dog to be subordinate in its relationship to you. Having an obedient, well-behaved dog that enjoys handling and accepts restraint is best accomplished through reward based obedience training, avoiding punishment and confrontational based training techniques.

How can I gain control without physical exercises?

The best way for each family member to take control is to teach your puppy that each reward must be earned. This is also the best way to insure that undesirable puppy behaviors are not inadvertently reinforced. The puppy should learn to display subordinate postures through reward training, rather than through any type of force. Begin with some basic obedience training, teaching the puppy to 'sit', 'stay' and 'lie down' for rewards. Practice short sessions, multiple times each day. Whenever the puppy is to receive anything of value (affection, attention, food, play and walks) the puppy should first be taught to earn its reward by performing a simple obedience task such as 'sit' or 'stay'. Teach the puppy that rewards of any sort will never be given on demand. Also known as 'nothing in life is free', a term coined by veterinary behaviorist, Victoria Voith, or "learn to earn" as described by William Campbell, the puppy must be taught that vocalization, nipping, mouthing, overly rambunctious, or demanding behaviors of any sort will never earn rewards. In fact, these behaviors should be met by inattention, by confining the puppy for a few minutes until it settles down, or with training devices and commands that get the puppy to exhibit the desired response. Another option is to immediately control and calm the puppy with a head collar (see 'biting – play biting and mouthing in puppies' for details). Rewards should be given as soon as the puppy is performing an appropriate response.

You should also handle your puppy so that it will learn to accept all forms of physical contact and restraint. Do this when the puppy is calm, such as after a nap. Avoid any exercise that leads to fear and struggling. Be gentle, progress slowly and only make the puppy be still for a few seconds in the beginning. Gradually you can increase the time you make your puppy comply.

Set limits on the puppy so that it does not learn that it can control you. Having the puppy sleep in its own bed or own cage rather than on your bed or couch, helps to prevent the dog from gaining control or becoming possessive of your resources. When the puppy is taken for walks it should be taught to follow. This should begin at the front door where the puppy should be taught to sit, wait, and follow, and never allowed to lead or pull you through the doorway.

What should I do if my puppy misbehaves?
Undesirable misbehavior must be prevented, or corrected in the act. Allowing the puppy, even once to perform an undesirable behavior such as entering a restricted room, jumping up, mounting or jumping onto the couch will serve to reward and encourage the repetition of the behavior.

There will be times when your new puppy misbehaves. How you respond to the puppy will often influence later interactions. Young puppies are very impressionable. Harsh physical reprimands are contraindicated. They only serve to frighten the puppy and perhaps make them hand shy. Unfortunately, animals can learn in one trial if something is aversive enough. We want young puppies to look toward a human hand as something pleasant that brings comfort, food and affection. Most puppies can be easily interrupted with vocal intonation and loud noises. What is equally important is to redirect the puppy to the correct behavior after you interrupt what you do not like. Remember that punishment must take place while the behavior is occurring, not after.

If you catch your puppy misbehaving, try a loud noise such as clapping your hands or a loud "uh-uh". Remember, reprimands need to occur while the behavior is happening, preferably just as it begins, and never after. Often puppies will be startled when they hear these noises and temporarily stop the behavior. At that time you should redirect the puppy to a more appropriate task and reinforce with an immediate and positive 'good dog'.

Another way to interrupt your puppy is with various types of noise devices. One such device is a "shake can". This is an empty soda can that has a few pennies inside and then is taped shut. When given a vigorous shake it makes a loud noise, which will interrupt the puppy's behavior. Another device that makes a loud noise is the so-called "rape alarm". When activated they make a shrill, loud, piercing noise, which will startle the puppy. Ultrasonic and sonic dog training devices are also available (see 'behavior management products').

The most important thing that you can do to avoid undesirable behavior is to supervise your puppy. Unsupervised puppies will chew and destroy objects as part of their natural curiosity and play. Rather than finding yourself with the need to reprimand your puppy, keep your puppy on a leash to avoid bad behaviors. Always provide suitable play objects designed to entertain your puppy so that it will not want to destroy your possessions (see 'destructiveness – chewing' for ideas).

Most importantly, if you find something that your puppy has destroyed but you did not catch him in the act, just clean it up and vow to supervise your puppy better in the future. Do not go get your puppy and bring him over to the mess and yell and physically discipline him. Remember that you need to punish the behavior you wish to change at the time it occurs. If you did not see your puppy chew up the object, all you are doing is disciplining your puppy for being present at a mess on the floor. Since that makes no sense to your puppy, your reprimands could create fear and anxiety, which could lead to aggression and owner avoidance.

What can be done for the particularly stubborn, disobedient, or headstrong puppy?

Puppies that are particularly headstrong and stubborn might need some fairly stringent rules. Tug-of-war games should only be allowed if the owner initiates the game, and can successfully call an end to the game, with an 'out', or 'give' command when it is time to call it quits (see 'controlling stealing and teaching give'). Rough play must not escalate to uncontrollable play biting that cannot be controlled by the owner.

One of the best management tools for gaining safe and effective control at all times is a head collar. The puppy can be supervised and controlled from a distance by leaving a long line or leash attached to the head halter. The principle of halter training is to gain control over the dog with as much natural communication as possible and without the use of punishment. Positive reinforcement is used to encourage proper behavior. A pull on the leash is used to disrupt misbehavior. Since the halter is attached to the dog's muzzle, common behavior problems (nipping, barking, jumping up, pulling, stealing food, etc.) can immediately be interrupted without fear or pain by pulling on the leash. The halter places pressure around the muzzle and behind the neck. This simulates the muzzle and neck restraint that a leader or mother dog might apply to a subordinate, and therefore is a highly effective and natural form of control (see 'management devices in dog training').

What types of handling should I begin with when I start to train my puppy?

A. Body Handling

You will do yourself and your new pet a favor by teaching your new puppy to allow you to handle his body. Throughout the life of your dog there will be times that you need to restrain your dog, lift your dog or handle various parts of the dog's body. This may become necessary when its time to brush your dog's teeth, trim its nails, give medication, or clean its ears. Yet if you have never handled an adult dog these simple tasks could become impossible. Handling also serves to simulate the physical communication that is exhibited by a bitch controlling her puppies or a leader dog over a subordinate group member. The young puppy must be taught to feel comfortable with this type of handling.

Gently handle your puppy daily. Pick a time when your puppy is calm, like just after a nap. Do not try to start a body handling exercise when your puppy is excited, rambunctious or in the mood for play. Place the puppy in your lap and touch the feet, open the mouth, look in the ears and under the tail. All the while, praise your puppy for being good, even offer a few tasty food treats. Be sure to keep initial sessions very short, since you want your puppy to succeed and not struggle. If the session is too long you run the risk of the puppy struggling and getting free. This could send a message to your puppy that it can "win". Always set up the puppy to succeed, but on your terms. Gradually increase the amount of time you control your puppy so that no struggle ensues. Soon the puppy will allow and perhaps anticipate these handling sessions. All family members should participate in this exercise. An adult should supervise young children. If you see any hesitance or reluctance on the part of the puppy, you will want to repeat the exercise, until you can accomplish the handling without resistance. Do the same exercise a little more gently or in a slightly different location, and give some tasty treats for compliance, and progress gradually to more difficult situations. Never force the puppy to the point that it exhibits fear or attempts escape. On the other hand if you do not gradually overcome the resistance the puppy may never allow the handling as an adult. Over time your puppy should allow you to place pressure on the back of its neck while it is in a down position, to roll it onto its side, to grasp its muzzle and to be lifted (if it is small enough). These forms of handling should not be used for punishment.

B. Food guarding, toy guarding

Another exercise that is so important is to acclimate your puppy to having his food and possessions touched by humans. Dogs in the wild will guard their food to prevent its loss but that is not necessary in the home. We are not going to take away our pet's food and not give it back. Handle the food bowl while your puppy eats, pet the puppy and perhaps lift the bowl, place in a special treat, and return it. When walking past the puppy while it is eating you can place a treat in its food bowl, or reach down, pat the puppy and give a treat. This way the puppy learns to tolerate intrusions and disturbance while it eats and will not be startled and react aggressively should something unexpected happen when eating. If the treat you add is tasty enough, the puppy may even look forward to your approaches during feeding. If any growling should emerge you should seek professional guidance immediately.

You should also practice gently taking toys from the puppy. Quietly and calmly place your hand on the toy and tell your puppy "give" as you remove it from its mouth. Then say 'thank-you' and return the object as you tell your puppy to 'take it'. Repeat this training task multiple times daily in multiple locations. At times take the object and offer a treat instead. This will let your puppy know that sometimes something better comes from relinquishing the object. You should be able to handle any toy that your puppy has. This sends the message to the puppy that it is okay for you to handle its possessions, and that you will give them back. The puppy will trust you and then when you need to remove something from the mouth, your dog should accept your interference.

How can I get my puppy to 'come' when called?

Teaching a puppy to 'come' on command is a very difficult but important task. Start early because a puppy that will come when called is safer! In addition, most young puppies do not like to stray too far from their owners. So all it takes is a kneeling owner and a happy 'come' command and your puppy may willingly approach (without the need for any food or toy prompt). Similarly most young puppies will automatically come and follow as you walk away. However, by 3 to 4 months of age, as puppies become a little more independent and exploratory, more appealing rewards may be needed. The two most important rules about teaching your puppy to come to you are to set up the puppy for success (so that you never fail) and that each training session is simple, fun and pleasurable. NEVER CALL YOUR PUPPY TO YOU FOR DISCIPLINE!

Start by backing away from your puppy 1-3 feet and wiggle a food treat or a favored toy (prompt) in front of its nose. At the same time say the puppy's name and 'come'. Use a happy inviting tone of voice. When your puppy comes to you, praise it lavishly and give the treat. Then repeat. Start by only moving short distances, and then gradually have the puppy come further to reach you. Reinforce this task by calling your puppy over multiple times daily, giving a pat or a food treat and sending it on its way. Try to avoid only calling the puppy to you to bring it inside, to put it in its crate or otherwise end something fun. Be sure to spend time calling the puppy over and then releasing it, this will help the puppy learn that by coming to you, good things happen. Remember it is critical to succeed with every training session. Stay close, make certain that there are no distractions and proceed slowly.

Over time, the puppy should be very slowly taught to come from progressively farther distances and in environments with a greater number of distractions. If there is any chance that the puppy might escape or disobey, have the puppy wear a long remote leash (which can be left dangling as the puppy wanders and investigates). Then if the puppy does not immediately obey the 'come' command, a gentle tug of the leash can be used to get the puppy's attention, and a repeated command in an upbeat, happy voice (along with a food or toy prompt) should be able to ensure that the 'come' command is successful and rewarding.

How can I teach my new puppy to 'wait' or 'follow'?

Teaching a puppy to 'wait' or 'follow' are extensions of the other tasks you should have already taught. To teach your puppy to follow at your side (heel), use a food treat, place it by your thigh and entice the puppy both vocally and with the food to 'heel'. As the puppy follows its nose to stay near the treat, it will also be learning to heel.

For dogs that constantly walk ahead or pull, teaching your dog to follow should begin where there are few distractions, such as in your backyard. To ensure success you should keep a leash or leash and head collar on your dog. Begin with a 'sit-stay' command and give a reward. Start to walk forward and encourage your dog to follow or heel as above, using a food reward held by your thigh. Be certain to allow only a few inches of slack on the leash so that if your dog tries to run past you, you can pull up and forward on the leash so that the puppy returns to your side. Once back in the proper position (by your side for 'heel' or behind you for 'follow'), provide a little slack in the leash and begin to walk forward again. Continue walking with verbal reinforcement and occasional food rewards given as the dog follows. Each time the dog begins to pass you or pull ahead, pull up and forward on the leash, and release as the dog backs up. Although the dog could be made to sit each time it pulls forward, the goal is to have the dog return to your side. If the dog "puts on the brakes" and will not follow, all you need to do is release the tension and verbally encourage the dog to follow. Once you have the dog successfully heeling in the yard with no distractions, you can proceed to the front yard and the street, at first with no distractions, until good control is achieved.

How can I teach my dog to 'wait'?

Although much the same as 'stay', this command is important for the dog that might otherwise bound out the front door, lunge forward to greet people and other dogs, or run across a busy street. Begin with 'sit-stay' training, until the dog responds well in situations where there are few distractions such as indoors or in your backyard. Next, find a situation where the dog might try to pull ahead, such as at the front door, so that you can begin to teach the 'wait' command. Training sessions should begin when there are no external stimuli outdoors (other dogs, people) that might increase your dog's motivation to run out the door. Use a leash or leash and head collar to ensure control. Begin with a 'sit-stay' by the front door. While standing between your dog and the door, and with only a few inches of slack on the leash, give the wait command and open the door. If the dog remains in place for a few seconds, begin to walk out the door and allow your dog to follow. Then repeat, with longer waits at each training session. If however, when you open the door or begin to walk out, your dog runs ahead of you, you should pull up on the leash, have your dog sit, release, give the 'wait' command and repeat until successful. Once your dog will successfully wait for a few seconds and follow you out the door, gradually increase the waiting time, and then try with distractions (dogs or people on the front walk). This training should also be tried as you walk across the street, or before your dog is allowed to greet new people or dogs it meets.

PUPPY TRAINING – SIT, DOWN, STAND & STAY

How do I teach my puppy to 'sit' on command?

Using a food treat, hold the food over the dog's nose and slowly move it up and back over the dog's head. As the puppy follows the food with its head it will sit down. Now couple the word 'sit' with the action. The upward motion of the hand as you hold the food treat also serves as a visual command for the puppy. If the pup lifts its front legs you are holding the food treat too high. As soon as the puppy sits say 'good sit' and give the treat. Many repetitions will be necessary for the pup to learn the association. Gradually, as the puppy understands what you want it to do, only give the treats intermittently. You should practice sit in many places throughout your home. It is especially important to teach your puppy to sit by the front door. A dog that readily sits by the front door will do better when greeting guests.

How do I teach my puppy to lie down on command?

Start with your puppy in a sit position. To get the puppy to lie down, take a treat and lower it between the puppy's front paws and say 'down'. Usually the puppy will follow the treat and go down. If the puppy does not lie all the way down, slowly push the treat between the paws and if the puppy lies down give it the treat and of course add 'good dog'. If the puppy stands up, start over.

For some puppies, teaching the 'down' command can be very difficult. An alternative method is instead of pushing the food treat backwards, slowly pull the treat forward. If that does not work, sit on the floor with your legs straight out in front of you and slightly bent at the knees. Take a hand with a treat in it and push it out under your knee from between your legs. As the puppy tries to get the food treat, slowly bring it back under your knee. As the puppy tries to follow, it will usually lie down.

Once the puppy understands the 'down' command, make sure that you vary the starting position. You should try to get your puppy to 'down' from both a stand and a sit.

How can I teach my puppy to 'stay' on command?

Puppies can be taught to stay for short periods of time at a young age. Once they sit on command each and every time they are asked, without the need for food inducements, training can proceed to more difficult concepts such as "stay".

First the pup is taught to stay without moving as you stand in front for 1-2 seconds. Initially give the puppy the 'sit' command, say 'stay' (using a hand as a stop sign can be a good visual cue), take one step away, and then return to the puppy and reward it for not moving. Be very careful that the puppy does not stand up or move as you present the reward because then you will have rewarded 'getting up'. Gradually increase the distance by a step at a time and the length of the stay by a few seconds at a time, until the puppy can stay for a minute or more with you standing at least 10 feet away. It is important to set up the puppy to succeed. Proceeding very slowly, and keeping a long lead attached to the puppy so that it can not run away can help ensure success. Be patient. It can take a week or more of daily training to get a puppy to 'sit' and 'stay' for 1-2 minutes. Over a few months it should be possible to increase the 'stay' to 15 minutes or more, and to be able to leave the room and return without the puppy rising from its 'stay'. For these longer stays it may be better to use a 'down-stay' (lying down and staying in place) combination, and to train the dog in a favored resting or sleeping area.

Once extended 'sit-stays' are accomplished, the command can be used to prevent many potential behavior problems. For example, if you practice 'sit and stay' by the front door, this command can then be used to prevent running out the door and jumping on company. Have your puppy sit and stay while you place the food on the floor and then give him an OK or release command. This will help establish your leadership and control.

How can I teach my dog to stand on command?

Place your puppy in a 'sit' position. Take the food treat palm facing up and move it forward and away from the pup as you say 'stand'. Your puppy should again follow his nose and stand up. Don't pull your hand so far away that the puppy follows you, but just until it stands up.

What else can I teach my dog?

Using the concepts discussed above a dog can be trained to perform anything that it is physically capable of. A 'down' or 'sit' can be extended from several seconds to many minutes as long as we progress gradually or "shape" the dog's behavior. In shaping, we determine our ultimate goal, such as a 20 minute stay, and reward successive increments of the behavior until we reach that goal. For example, once the dog will sit for 3 seconds before the reward is given, we can repeat the command and when the puppy sits we wait for 4 seconds before the reward is given. Proceed very slowly, ensuring that the puppy is performing the behavior properly a few times in a row before proceeding to the next step.

What is socialization?

Socialization is the process during which the puppy develops relationships with other living beings in its environment. Two other important terms in a pup's development are "habituation" and "localization".

What is habituation?

As all animals develop there are numerous stimuli (sounds, smells, sights and events) that when unfamiliar can lead to fear and anxiety. Habituation is the process whereby dogs get used to repeated stimuli, and stop reacting to them provided that there are no untoward consequences.

What is localization?

Localization is the process by which the puppy develops attachment to particular places.

Why are these terms important?

To reduce the possibility of fearful responses as a puppy grows and matures, it is essential to expose young puppies to many stimuli (people, places and things) when they can most effectively socialize, localize, and habituate to these stimuli. Early handling and events that occur during the first 2 to 4 months of life, are critical factors in the social development of the dog. Dogs that receive insufficient exposure to people, other animals and new environments during this time may develop irreversible fears, leading to timidity and/or aggression.

What can I do to improve my chances of having a social, non-fearful dog?

PEDIGREE

The genetics of the breed and of the parents in particular play an important role in how sociable, playful, fearful, excitable, or domineering a puppy becomes. Choose a breed and parents (both male and female) that have the type of behavior that you would like the puppy to have. Of course, there is a great deal of variability between individuals, so that breed and parental behavior will not always be indicative of what the puppy will be like.

PUPPY ASSESSMENT

Even the most social and playful of puppies may become fearful and aggressive as they develop out of puppyhood. Avoid selecting puppies that are shy, withdrawn or fearful. But selecting a friendly and non-fearful puppy does not ensure that this behavior will persist into adulthood. In fact, little or no predictive value has been found in assessing puppies under 3 months of age, since these puppies are still developing their social skills and many problem behaviors do not begin to emerge until sexual or social maturity. However, as puppies age these criteria do begin to become more reliable. Assessing the behavior of the parents, and understanding the behavior of a breed are far more critical than assessing an individual puppy.

EARLY HANDLING

Puppies that are stimulated and handled from birth to five weeks of age are more confident, social, exploratory, faster maturing and better able to handle stress as they develop. Puppies obtained from a breeder or home where they have had frequent contact and interaction with people are likely to be more social and less fearful as they develop.

PRIMARY SOCIALIZATION

There is a sensitive period in the development of most species when they develop social attachments with their own and other species, independent of punishment and rewards. In fact, both positive and negative events seem to accelerate socialization. The events that occur during this socialization period determines the puppy's future social partners, as well as to what species it feels it belongs. By recognizing the critical time frame in which canine socialization develops, you can help to ensure a healthy social attachment to people and other animals, including other dogs.

The primary socialization period for dogs begins at 3 weeks of age and is diminishing by 12 weeks. Peak sensitivity is at 6 – 8 weeks. Beyond 12 weeks there is a tendency to act fearfully towards new people, animals and situations. Many young dogs will regress or become fearful again if they do not receive continued social interaction as they grow and develop. The 6-8 month period is another important time for socialization.

To help a healthy social relationship with other dogs throughout life, dogs should maintain their social contacts with their mother and littermates until 6 – 8 weeks of age. They should continue to have regular social interaction and play sessions with other dogs after it is taken into a new home. The puppy would likely do best if there was another dog in the new home, or if it had playmates in the neighborhood that it could interact with on a daily basis.

What is the best age to obtain my new puppy?

Since it is so important for the puppy to develop and maintain social attachments to their own kind, puppies ideally will remain with their mother and littermates until about 7 weeks of age. Then when placed in the new home they can expand their social contacts to new people and species while still in their primary socialization period. Also by this time puppies will begin to develop preferences for elimination sites, so that this timing can be helpful for house-training.

What can I do to assist my puppy in its social development?

There should be little problem with a puppy that is less than 12 weeks of age developing healthy and lasting attachments to the people, sights and sounds in its new home. Your puppy is most likely to become fearful of stimuli that are not found in its day-to-day routine. Make a conscious effort to identify those people and situations that the puppy is not regularly exposed to. For example, if there are no children in the home, you might arrange regular play sessions with children. If you live in the country, make a few trips into the city, so that the puppy can be taken for walks on city streets, or through neighborhood plazas. Conversely, a puppy that grows up in the city might become fearful or aggressive toward farm animals that it was not exposed to during its early development.

Introduce your puppy to as many new people and situations as possible, beginning in its first three months of development. People in uniforms, babies, toddlers, the elderly, and the physically challenged are just a few examples that might lead to fear and anxiety, unless there is sufficient early exposure. Similarly, car rides, elevators, stairs, or the noises of cars, trains, airplanes, or hot air balloons are some examples of events and experiences to which the puppy might be usefully exposed.

One way to facilitate the introduction of the puppy to new situations and people is to provide a reward such as a favorite toy or biscuit each time it is exposed to a new stimulus. Having a stranger offer a biscuit to the puppy will teach it to look forward to meeting people and discourage hand-shyness since the puppy will learn to associate new friends and an outstretched hand with something positive. Once the puppy has learned to 'sit' on command, have each new friend ask it to 'sit' before giving the biscuit. This teaches a proper greeting and will make the puppy less likely to jump up on people.

Be certain that the puppy has the opportunity to meet and receive treats from a wide variety of people of all ages, races, appearance and both sexes during the formative months. There will of course, be times when your puppy is in a new situation and you do not have treats. Be sure then to use a happy tone of voice and encourage your puppy.

If your puppy seems to panic, back off a little and try again later, rather than aggravating the fear. Never reassure the fearful dog as this might serve to reward the fearful behavior.

Is it healthy to take my puppy out in public at such a young age?

There is always a concern about the risks of taking the puppy out of its home before it is fully vaccinated because it may be exposed to infection before the vaccines have had time to become protective. However benefits gained from these new and early public appearances can be enormous and without them the risk of the puppy developing permanent fears or anxiety is a serious concern.

One solution is to have people and healthy vaccinated animals visit the puppy in its own home, until it is sufficiently vaccinated to be taken out. A compromise is to take the puppy out to meet people and other pets in low risk environments. As long as vaccines are up-to-date, taking the puppy for walks along the sidewalk and avoiding neighborhood parks where stools and urine might accumulate is generally safe.

Another valuable aid is to enroll the puppy in puppy socialization classes. If these classes are held indoors in a room that can be cleaned and disinfected, and all puppies are screened for vaccination and health prior to each class, then these classes provide good exposure to people and other dogs, in a low risk environment. Not only do these classes offer an opportunity for play and socialization with a variety of people and dogs, they also help guide the owners into proper training techniques from the outset.

SEPARATION ANXIETY

How do I know if my pet's problem is due to separation anxiety?
Separation anxiety describes dogs that usually are overly attached or dependent on family members. They become extremely anxious and show distress behaviors of vocalization, destruction, house-soiling or inactivity when separated from the owners. Most dogs with separation anxiety try to remain close to their owners and become increasingly anxious the greater the separation. They may follow the owners from room to room and begin to display signs of anxiety as soon as the owners prepare to leave. Some of these dogs crave a great deal of physical contact and attention from their owners and can be demanding. During departures or separations they may begin to salivate or pant profusely, vocalize, eliminate, refuse to eat, become destructive or become quiet and withdrawn. Most often these behaviors occur within about 20 minutes of the owner's departure. While typically the behavior occurs each and every time the owner leaves, it can only happen on selected departures, such as work-day departures, or when the owner leaves again after coming home from work.

Are there other reasons that my dog may engage in these behaviors?
Many dogs, especially puppies enjoy chewing and engage in the behavior when they have nothing better to keep them occupied. House-soiling may be due to medical problems, leaving the dog alone for longer than it can control its bladder, or inadequate house-training. Vocalization may be due to territorial intrusion by strangers or other animals, and can be a rewarded behavior if the dog receives any form of attention when it vocalizes or

rewarded by the stimulus leaving. Some dogs will attempt to escape or become extremely anxious when confined, so that destructiveness or house-soiling when a dog is locked up in a crate, basement, or laundry room, may be due to confinement or barrier anxiety and associated attempts at escape. In addition, noise phobias such as a thunderstorm that passes through during the owner's absence, may lead to marked destructiveness, house-soiling, salivation and vocalization. Old dogs with medical problems such as loss of hearing or sight, painful conditions and cognitive dysfunction may become more anxious in general, and seek out the owner's attention for security and relief. While giving attention to help calm your dog may seem to be the best alternative, this may greatly increase your dogs need to be with you and around you at all times.

What can I do immediately to prevent damage?

This is an extremely difficult question. The goal of treatment is to reduce your pet's level of anxiety by training it to feel comfortable in your absence. This can be a long intensive process. Yet, most owners will need to deal with the damage or vocalization immediately. During initial retraining its usually best to hire a dog sitter, take the dog to work, find a friend to care for the dog for the day, board the dog for the day, or arrange to take some time off from work to retrain the dog. Crate training or dog proofing techniques may work especially well for those dogs that already have an area where they are used to being confined. Crates should be used with caution however, with dogs that have separation anxiety and/or also have barrier frustrations because they can severely injure themselves attempting to get out of a crate. It is important to choose a room or area that does not further increase the dog's anxiety. The dog's bedroom or feeding area may therefore be most practical. Booby-traps might also be used to keep the dog away from potential problem areas (see 'behavior management products' and 'canine punishment').

For vocalization, anti-bark devices may be useful (see 'barking'), but the dog will continue to remain anxious, and the motivation to vocalize may be too strong for the products to be effective. Tranquilizers and anti-anxiety drugs may also be useful for short-term use, until the owner has effectively corrected the problem.

Lastly, punishment for destruction or house-soiling when you return is contra-indicated (see 'canine punishment'). The destruction or house-soiling is a result of the pet's anxiety, not "spite" or being "mad" that you left. Punishment will only serve to make the pet more anxious at your return.

How can the dog be retrained so that it is less anxious during departures?

Since the underlying problem is anxiety, try to reduce all forms of anxiety, prior to departure, at the time of departure, and at the time of homecoming. In addition, the pet must learn to accept progressively longer periods of inattention and separation while the owners are at home.

What should be done prior to departures?

Before any lengthy departure, provide a vigorous session of play and exercise. This not only helps to reduce some of the dog's energy and tire it out, but also provides a period of attention. A brief training session can also be a productive way to further interact and "work" with your dog. For the final 15-30 minutes prior to departure, the dog should be ignored. It would be best if your dog was trained to go to its rest and relaxation area with a radio, TV, or video playing, as the owner could then prepare for departure while the pet is out of sight and earshot of the owner. The key is to avoid as many of the departure signals as possible, so that the dog's anxiety doesn't heighten, even before the owner leaves. Brushing teeth, changing into work clothes, or collecting keys, purse, briefcase or schoolbooks, are all routines that might be able to be performed out of sight of the dog. Owners might also consider changing clothes at work, preparing and packing a lunch the night before, or might even consider leaving their car at a neighbor's so the dog wouldn't hear the car pulling out of the driveway. The other alternative is to expose your puppy to as many of these cues as possible while you remain at home so that they no longer are predictive of departure. A few minutes prior to departure the dog should be given some fresh toys and objects to keep it occupied so that the owner can leave while the dog is distracted. Saying goodbye will only serve to bring attention to the departure.

What can be done to reduce anxiety at the time of departure?

As you depart, the dog should be kept busy and occupied, and preferably out of sight, so that there is little or no anxiety. Giving special food treats that have been saved for departure (and training) times can help keep the dog distracted and perhaps "enjoying itself" while you leave. Dogs that are highly aroused and stimulated by food may become so intensively occupied in a peanut butter coated dog toy, a fresh piece of rawhide, a dog toy stuffed with liver and dog food, or some frozen dog treats, that they may not even notice you leave. Be certain that the distraction devices last as long as possible so that the dog continues to occupy its time until you are "long gone". Frozen treats placed in the dog's food bowl, toys that are tightly stuffed with goodies, toys that are designed to require manipulation and work to obtain the food reward, toys that can maintain lengthy chewing, and timed feeders that open throughout the day are a few suggestions. Determine what best motivates your dog. For example, if a particular toy is highly successful provide two or three of the same type rather than toys that do not maintain your dog's interest. It may also be helpful to provide some or all of the dog's food during departures with a few special surprises in the bottom of the bowl. On rare occasions a second pet can help to keep the dog occupied and distracted during departures. Food will not be of interest to dogs that are too anxious.

What should I do when I come home?

At homecomings, ignore your dog until it calms and settles down (this may take 10-15 minutes). Your dog should soon learn that the faster it settles the sooner it will get your attention. Exuberant greetings or any type of punishment for misbehavior will only serve to heighten the dog's anxiety surrounding homecomings.

My dog starts to get anxious even before I leave. What can I do?

There are a number of activities that we do consistently prior to each departure. The dog soon learns to identify these cues or signals with imminent departure. On the other hand, some dogs learn that certain other signals mean that the owners are staying home or nearby and therefore the dog stays relaxed. If we can prevent the dog from observing any of these pre-departure cues, or if we train the dog that these cues are no longer predictive of departure, then the anxiety is greatly reduced. Even with the best of efforts some dogs will still pick up on "cues" that the owner is about to depart. Train your pet to associate these cues with enjoyable, relaxing situations (rather than the anxiety of impending departure). By exposing the dog to these cues while you remain at home and when the dog is relaxed or otherwise occupied, they are no longer predictive of departure. This entails some retraining while you are home. You get the items (keys, shoes, briefcase, jacket etc.) that normally signal your departure, and walk to the door. However, you do not leave, just put everything away. The dog will be watching and possibly get up, but once you put every thing away, the dog should lie down. Then, once the dog is calm, this is repeated. However, only 3-4 repetitions should be done in a single training session. Eventually, the dog will not attend to these cues (habituate) because they are no longer predictive of you leaving and will not react, get up or look anxious as you go about your pre-departure tasks. Then, the dog will be less anxious when you do leave. This often allows the next step in re-training, planned departures.

What can be done to retrain the dog to reduce the dependence and following?

The most important aspect of retraining is to teach the dog to be independent and relaxed in your presence. Only when you have taught the dog to stay in place in its bed or relaxation area, rather than constantly following you around, will it be possible to train the dog to begin to accept actual (or mock) departures.

First and foremost the dog must learn that attention-getting behaviors do not pay off. Any attempts at attention must be ignored. On the other hand, lying quietly away from you should be rewarded. Teach your dog that it is the quiet behavior that will receive attention, and not following you around, or demanding attention. Your dog should get use to this routine when you depart. Teach your dog to relax in its quiet area and to accept lengthy periods of inattention when you are home. You may have to begin with very short periods of inattention and gradually shape this to 30 minute periods or longer. For some dogs this may mean a formal program of 'down'–'stays'. Be sure to schedule attention, interaction and play that you initiate.

How can I teach my dog to accept my departures?

Formal retraining should be directed at teaching your dog to remain on its mat, in its bed, or in its crate or den area, for progressively longer periods of time (30 minutes or more). Start by using a favored treat as a prompt. Hold it in front of your dog, give the 'sit' or 'lie down' commands and then give the treat, praise and petting. At the next few commands, hold your hand out, but hide the food so that the dog is not certain whether it is there or not. Progress from a 1 second sit, to 2 seconds then 3 seconds, etc., until the dog will sit for at least 60 seconds.

Next practice the 'stay' command, holding up the hand prompt saying 'sit', then 'stay' and walk 2 or 3 steps away. Have the dog stay for 60 seconds and then walk back and give the reward with the dog staying in position. Once your dog will stay in place for 1 minute while you go across the room, sit and return, switch to intermittent rewards. Patting and praise is given every time, but food is only given every 2nd, 3rd or 4th time. However for each new step in training, use the food reward the first time or two. If you have trouble proceeding to this step, change to a leash and head halter to ensure success. Increase gradually to 30 minutes or more. The goal is to teach the dog to stay in its bed or confinement area for progressively longer periods of time before you return and give the reward and never to give attention or rewards unless the dog is leaving you alone or lying in its resting area. Next, you begin to leave the room. Hold up your hand as prompt, give the 'down-stay' command, walk across the room, and go out of sight for a short time before returning to give the reward. Gradually make departures longer until the dog will tolerate leaving for up to 30 minutes. From this point on, your dog should be encouraged to stay in its bed or crate for extended periods of time rather than sitting at your feet or on your lap. If your dog can also be taught to sleep in this relaxation area at night rather than on your bed or in your bedroom, this may help to break the over-attachment and dependence more quickly.

During these training exercises use as many cues as possible to help relax the dog. Mimic the secure environment that the dog feels when the owner is at home. Leave the TV on. Play a favorite video or CD. Leave a favorite blanket or chew toy in the area. These all help to calm the dog.

How do I progress to leaving the house?

Finally, practice short "mock" departures. During "mock" or graduated departure training, the dog should be exercised, given a short formal training session, and taken to its bed or mat to relax. Give the 'down-stay' command, a few toys and treats and leave. The first few "mock" departures should be identical to the training exercises above, but instead of leaving the room for a few minutes while the dog is calm and distracted, you will begin to leave the home. The first few departures should be just long enough to leave and return without any signs of anxiety or destructiveness. This might last from a few seconds to a couple of minutes. Gradually but randomly increase the time (e.g. 30 seconds, 1 minute, 2 minutes, 1, 2, 3, 2, 5, 7, 4, 7, 10, etc.). As the time of departure approaches 10 or 15 minutes, begin to include other activities associated with departure such as opening and closing the car door and returning, turning on and off the car engine and returning or pulling the car out of the driveway and returning.

How come my dog gets so anxious when I leave home, but is just fine when I leave the car?

Many dogs that destroy the home when left alone will stay in a car or van without becoming anxious or destructive. This is because the dog has learned to relax and enjoy the car rides, without the need for constant physical attention and contact. And, when the owner does leave this relaxed dog in the car, the departures are generally quite short. The owner may occasionally leave the dog in the car during longer absences. The owner has trained the dog using inattention, relaxation and a graduated departure technique. The dog has learned that when he is in the car, the owner returns quickly and he can be good and not be anxious. What is very important is to progress slowly through the series of departures. If when you return, the dog is anxious or extremely excited, then the departure was too long and the next one should be shorter. This is an effective technique, but very slow in the beginning. The goal is to teach the dog "my owner is only going to be gone for a short time; they are coming right back; I can be good."

Is drug therapy useful?

Drug therapy can be useful especially during initial departure training. Tranquilizers alone do not reduce the pet's anxiety and may only be helpful to sedate your dog so that it is less likely to investigate and destroy. Often the most suitable drugs for long term use are anti-depressants, anti-anxiety drugs or a combination. Drugs alone will do little or nothing to improve separation anxiety. It is the retraining program that is needed to help your dog gain some independence and accept some time away from you.

THE USE OF MANAGEMENT DEVICES IN DOG TRAINING – TO CHOKE OR NOT TO CHOKE

What is a good way to train my dog?

The goal of training is to teach the pet to respond to a variety of commands. To be successful, the owner must first be able to get the pet to exhibit the desired response when the command is given. To achieve this, the owner can use a lure such as a food or toy (lure-reward training) or a closed hand target (target training) to encourage or lead the dog to the correct response. Alternately, training devices such as a head halter and leash can be used to prompt the dog into the response. The dog should then be rewarded. Although primary reinforcers such as food or a favored toy are generally used first, over time secondary reinforcers (e.g. clicker, praise) should intermittently replace these. Clicker training pairs a clicker with food so that the clicker soon becomes a consistent predictor of food. It can then be used to immediately mark and reward desired responses. Over time the training can then progress to gradually more complex or more accurate responses (shaping). If you are interested in clicker training see an obedience instructor or check www.clickertraining.com on the web.

What about punishing the incorrect behavior so the dog learns to do the right thing?

Unfortunately, many trainers still advocate punishment, which is intended to discourage or "reduce" undesirable behavior rather than train and encourage desirable behavior. This is not really training because punishment does not teach the dog what it is "supposed" to do. Punishment can also cause fear, anxiety, increased aggression and discomfort or harm to the pet. Some dogs may even retaliate or defend themselves by attacking the person who is administering the punishment. Therefore, it is not a logical, scientifically sound, or acceptable method of training and may in fact be counterproductive.

What is perhaps confusing is that many dogs have been successfully trained with punishment. In fact, many of these dogs are actually trained with negative reinforcement where the pain or discomfort is released as soon as the desired behavior is exhibited. This is a difficult concept to teach and requires "impeccable" timing. In addition, dogs that have been trained with punishment may be fearful of misbehaving in the trainer's presence. Some of these dogs are then labeled as "one-man-dogs" because the dog is only responsive to a trainer who can successfully administer the punishment. On the other hand, dogs trained with rewards and shaping should respond to the commands of any family member as long as the commands are consistent and positive.

What types of training devices are available to me?

There are a wide variety of leash, halter, and harness systems that can be used for walking and training. In fact, a control device attached to either the head, neck or body is essential when leash control is mandatory, as well as for those dogs that do not heel or come consistently on verbal command.

Choke, pinch and prong collars have been designed to control and train in a manner that makes it increasingly uncomfortable if the dog does not obey. The more forceful the owner's pull, the more discomfort for the pet. Choke collar training may be useful as a means of applying negative reinforcement. This can be accomplished by issuing a command, pulling on the choke collar to get the desired response and then immediately releasing as soon as the dog complies (obeys). In other words release from discomfort indicates to the dog that the desired response is now being exhibited. Unfortunately, since many owners are unskilled, untrained or unsuccessful in the use of negative reinforcement, the choke, pinch, and prong collars are primarily used to correct or punish undesirable behavior. In the short run, these corrections may cause sufficient discomfort for the behavior to cease. However, with repeated exposure and training, the dog's fear and anxiety may actually increase each time it is exposed to the stimulus (because previous exposures have been uncomfortable or aversive). Conversely, some dogs may become so accustomed (desensitized) to the effects of the choke or pinch device that it becomes ineffective. Although many trainers still train with devices that are intended to pull, jerk, choke, punish or "correct", the most effective and humane means of training is through motivation, positive reinforcement and shaping.

Body harnesses or head halter restraint are two alternatives to neck collars. Some body harnesses merely serve as restraint devices while others such as the K9 Pull Control™, Lupi™ and No Pull Halter™ have been specially designed to stop pulling since they pull the forelegs back when the dog attempts to lunge forward. However these devices do little to aid in training or control. There are also a number of devices that utilize head control.

Since the Gentle Leader™ (also known as the Promise System™) has both a neck and nose strap adjustment, it can be used either to control the dog when the owner is holding the leash, or with a leash or "drag" line left attached and dangling, for immediate "remote" control. Therefore it might also be referred to as a head collar. The Halti™ is a head halter, which is an effective leash control device but cannot be fitted to leave attached to the dog. The Snoot Loop™ is a head halter with side adjustments to allow for a snugger muzzle fit, thereby reducing the chances that the pet can remove it. Other products such as the NewTrix™ head halter are designed to stop pulling but do not aid in training or control.

How might I use a headcollar/head halter for control?

One of the most effective means of gaining control, and ensuring that the pet responds quickly to each command is to use a leash and head halter such as the Gentle Leader™ for training. With the Gentle Leader™, the owner gains control naturally through pressure exerted behind the neck and around the muzzle. The head halter acts as a tool to help achieve the desired response without punishment and to communicate the owner's intentions. The proponents of head halters point to the fact that horses can be successfully and humanely controlled with head devices since "where the nose goes the body follows". Yet dog owners continue to try and control dogs with neck restraint (often with limited success). With a head halter the owner can gain eye contact and reorient the dog to perform the desirable response (sort of a power steering option for dogs). With the head halter properly fitted and the leash slack, the dog is not restricted from panting, eating, drinking, chewing, barking, jumping up, biting, lunging forward, or stealing from the table or the garbage. On the other hand, since the halter encircles the head and muzzle, a pull on the leash can immediately curtail pulling, barking, chewing, stealing, stool eating and even some forms of aggression. The head halter and remote leash can also be used to prompt the dog to respond to a command (e.g. "Quiet" for barking or "Off" for puppy nipping). A release indicates to the dog that it is performing the desired behavior. With a 10-foot leash attached the head halter also provides the owner with a mechanism for interrupting and deterring undesirable behavior immediately (e.g. garbage raiding, jumping up, house-soiling). A longer rope can be used for outdoor training.

How exactly does the head halter work?

Pets tend to oppose or pull against pressure. Dogs that walk or lunge ahead of their owners are therefore more likely to pull even harder if the owner pulls back on the leash. There are three basic ways of pulling on the head halter to achieve most goals. If the dog is walking at the owners side or slightly behind the owner with a minimum of slack on the leash, all the owner has to do is pull forward to get the dog to back up (heel, follow). A pull upward will close the mouth (barking, nipping) while continuing to pull up and forward will back the dog into a sit. Of course, with the leash attached to the head halter, the owner can immediately turn the head to achieve eye contact. A continuous pull rather than a tug or jerk should be used until the desired behavior is achieved. The second hand can also be used to gently guide the head into position. Immediately releasing tension then indicates to the dog that it is now responding acceptably.

Training should begin in calm environments with minimal distractions. The dog is given the command and if it responds appropriately, a favored treat can be given as a reward. A lure reward or closed hand target can be used to help guide the pet into the correct response. After a few successful responses the treat can be phased out and given intermittently but the praise and stroking should continue. Clicker training (as discussed) would be another option. If the command is given and the desired response cannot be achieved, an immediate pull on the head halter can be used to ensure success. The tension is then released and the dog rewarded.

What are the most important elements to be successful with a headcollar?

THERE ARE FIVE KEY ELEMENTS TO SUCCESSFUL HEAD HALTER TRAINING

1. Fit: The neck strap should be high and snug, and the nose strap adjusted so it can't be pulled over the end of the nose. Use rewards and distractions to help the dog to adapt quickly. The dog can then be taken for a walk or played with to keep it distracted while getting used to the head device.

2. Be prepared: Keep a short amount of slack on the leash (less than 3 cm/1 inch) and be prepared to immediately pull the dog into position if it does not respond to a command. A gentle pull (not jerk) up and forward can get eye contact (for target training, control and calming), close the mouth, and get the dog to back up into a heel or sit. Using the second hand to guide or support the head can help the dog to respond faster and calm quicker.

3. Motivate: Remember the goal is to encourage the dog to respond to the command. An appealing tone of voice, positive eye contact, target training, primary reinforcers such as special treats and toys, and secondary reinforcers such as praise, clickers and stroking can be used to improve success. The rewards (stroking, clicker, food, toy) should not be given until the dog responds appropriately.

4. Release: Release immediately as soon as the desired response is exhibited

5. Reward or repeat: As soon as you begin to release the tension (a very small amount of slack), be prepared to reward or repeat. If the dog remains in a position with some slack in the line, give rewards. If the dog does not maintain an acceptable position on the slackened leash, take up the slack by pulling once again to obtain the desired response. Release and either reward the desirable response or repeat the pull and release until the acceptable response is achieved.

Once these steps are accomplished, the owner can proceed to more complex tasks or more difficult environments. For example, the dog can be taught to 'sit' and 'stay' for gradually longer periods of time before the reward is given. The owner can gradually move farther from the dog [still maintaining only a few centimeters (1 inch) of slack] to train the dog to stay and not to follow or lunge forward. And, once the dog will walk by the owner's side, the 'heel' or 'follow' can be practiced at times when the dog might lunge forward on a walk or jump up at visitors at the door or bark.

Feline Behavior

Aggression is a serious and dangerous behavior problem for cat owners. There are many different types of aggression. Making a diagnosis, determining the prognosis (the chances of safe and effective correction) and developing an appropriate treatment plan are usually best handled by a veterinary behaviorist. In some cases medical conditions can contribute to aggression. Before a behavior consultation your cat must have a thorough physical examination and blood tests to rule out organ dysfunction. To treat aggression, it is necessary to determine which type of aggression your cat displays; fear, territorial, parental, play, redirected, predatory, petting-induced, pain-induced, social status, medical or learned. Also determine in what circumstances the pet is aggressive and whether the aggression is toward family members, strangers, other pets in the household, or strange pets. Keeping a diary can be particularly useful. More than one form of aggression may be exhibited. Behavior modification techniques and/or changes to the pet's environment will be necessary to correct most aggressive problems. Drug therapy can be a useful part of treatment for some forms of aggression.

Fear aggression: what is it and how is it diagnosed?

Fear aggression arises when a cat is exposed to people, other animals, places or stimuli (e.g. noises) that the cat is unfamiliar with, or to situations previously associated with an unpleasant experience. Although many cats may retreat when fearful, those that are on their own territory or are prevented from retreating because they are cornered are more likely to fight. If the stimulus (person or animal) retreats or the pet is harmed or further frightened in any way (e.g. a fight, punishment), the fear is likely to be further aggravated and the fearful behavior is reinforced. In addition people or animals that do not approach in a calm, confident or friendly manner are more likely to be met with a fearful response. Fear aggression toward family members might arise out of punishment or other unpleasant experiences associated with them. Many cases of fear aggression are seen as combinations or complicating factors of other forms of aggression (territorial, maternal, redirected, etc.). Fearful body postures in conjunction with aggression are diagnostic of fear aggression. Behavior therapy perhaps in combination with drug therapy can be used to treat most cases of fear aggression (see 'fear in cats').

Play aggression: what is it and how is it diagnosed?

Play aggression is commonly shown by young cats toward people or other pets in the family. Overly rambunctious play along with grabbing, stalking, pouncing, nipping or biting of people or their clothing are common signs of play aggression. Although it is a normal behavior it can lead to injuries. If handled incorrectly it could lead to more serious forms of aggression as your cat matures.

Territorial aggression: what is it and how can it be treated?

Territorial aggression can be exhibited toward people or other animals (usually other cats) that approach or reside on the pet's property. Territorial aggression can occur towards cats outside of the home, but also towards cats that live in the household. This may be with the addition of another cat,

or when resident cats reach social maturity at 1-2 years of age. Since the person or other animal entering the property may also be causing fear or anxiety, territorial aggression often occurs in conjunction with fear aggression.

Predatory behavior: what is it and how can it be treated?

Predation is the instinctive desire to chase and hunt prey. Predatory behaviors include stalking, chasing, attacking, and ingestion of prey animals, but may occasionally be directed at people or other pets. Although the desire to chase can be reduced by using desensitization and counter-conditioning in the presence of the stimuli (see 'behavior modification desensitization, counter-conditioning and flooding'), this can be dangerous behavior, which is best prevented. If the behavior is directed toward small pets in the home, confining those pets to a room where the cat does not have access is best. If the behavior is directed to animals outside, then keeping the cat indoors is a solution. Predatory behavior toward family members may be a form of play aggression for some cats.

Pain-induced and irritable aggression: what is it and how can it be treated?

Pain-induced aggression is usually elicited by handling or contact that elicits pain or discomfort. However, even if your cat is not exhibiting pain, certain medical conditions (endocrine imbalances, organ disease, etc.) may make the pet more irritable and prone to aggression. Fear and anxiety further compound many of these cases. Once your cat learns that aggression is successful at removing the stimulus, aggression may recur when similar situations arise in the future, whether or not the pain is still present. Treatment requires first that the medical or painful condition be resolved.

Next, identify the types of handling and situations that have led to aggression in the past. With desensitization and counter-conditioning (see 'behavior modification desensitization, counter-conditioning and flooding'), your cat can slowly and gradually be accustomed to accept and enjoy these situations. Once the cat learns that there is no further discomfort associated with the handling, and that there may be rewards, the problem should resolve.

Maternal aggression: what is it and how can it be treated?

Maternal aggression is directed toward people or other animals that approach the queen with her kittens. With desensitization, counter-conditioning, good control and highly motivating rewards, it may be possible to train your cat to accept handling of the kittens. Once the kittens are weaned, spaying should be considered to prevent recurrence.

Redirected aggression: what is it and how can it be treated?

Aggression that is directed toward a person or pet that did not initially evoke the aggression is classified as redirected. This is likely to occur when the cat is aroused and a person or other pet intervenes or approaches. Cats that are highly aroused must be avoided. Since redirected aggression arises out of other forms of aggression, it is important to identify and treat the initial cause of aggression (e.g. fear, territorial, other animals outside), or to prevent the problem by avoiding exposure (see 'redirected aggression').

Petting induced aggression: what is it and how can it be treated?

Some cats bite while being petted. Some cats are intolerant of all handling, but most cats with petting aggression accept a certain amount of petting but then become highly agitated and attack when they have had enough. This can be difficult to understand since many of these cats seek attention and at the outset seem to enjoy physical contact from the owner. It seems that these cats have a certain threshold for the amount of physical interaction that they can tolerate. Although the aggression may be a specific form that arises from arousal related to petting, fear and social status may also play a role. First, identify and avoid responses that might increase your cat's fear or anxiety (e.g. punishment, uninvited approaches and handling) and make all handling experiences positive. When handling, physical restraint must be avoided as cats that are placed in a position where they feel constrained or unable to escape might become aggressive. The cat that assumes a leadership role in relationship to a family member may bite or attack that person, while avoiding aggression to a person who is more "dominant" in the relationship.

In order to resolve petting induced aggression, make sure that the initiation and termination of petting is under your control. In addition, your cat needs to learn that petting is not associated with excessive restraint or anything unpleasant but rather with rewards. Do not approach, confront, or lift your cat, unless it approaches for affection. At this point call the cat onto your lap (perhaps with a command, or bell), and begin light stroking without any physical restraint. After a brief session put the cat on the floor and give a reward such as food, play, or a catnip toy. At each subsequent session, when the cat is ready for affection, call the cat onto your lap, and pat or stroke a little longer before putting the cat down and providing the reward. Be aware that as you approach the limit of your cat's tolerance of petting, anxiety and aggression will recur. This limit can often be evidenced by a change in the cat's demeanor. Usually the cat will begin to rapidly move the tail back and forth, the pupils may dilate and the ears go back, or the cat may begin to lick or act agitated. Try and stay below this threshold and cease petting before the cat becomes anxious. Although shaping may greatly increase the number and length of petting sessions your cat will accept and enjoy, you will need to learn and accept your cat's limitations.

Social status aggression: what is it and how is it treated?

Information on the social structure and relationship between cats is continually being updated with new research. Cats do maintain social relationships when living in groups leading to the speculation that some form of social structure also exists. Social structures in groups are often maintained with aggressive displays and actions. Some cats may display aggression toward their owners or other cats when displaying assertiveness. This type of aggression is infrequently described in the veterinary literature but is a consideration in those cats that bite or attack their owners or other cats in order to control a situation. Since cats are now known to be a social species, it is not surprising that some cats will assert themselves when challenged by a subordinate cat or family member in the home. Social status aggression in most cases is a complicating factor of other forms of aggression. Assertive displays, soliciting attention through attacks or biting, aggression during petting, attempts to control the environment by blocking access to doorways or refusing to be moved from sleeping areas, stalking family members, and threats or aggression to owners when walking or passing by the cat, may be displays of social status. A diagnosis of social status aggression is also a strong consideration when the cat attacks family members that have not assumed a position of control and leadership but does not threaten those that have good control.

Attaining leadership over assertive cats must be accomplished without physical force and confrontation, as this would lead to fear and retaliation. Take control of all rewards, and teach the cat that obedient and compliant behavior is the only way to earn them. A few basic training commands using food reward training techniques can go a long way in gaining control over some cats. By teaching a cat that each play session, treat, or piece of food must be earned from its "owners", the cat will learn that the owner is in control of all resources and all that is positive. Conversely, the cat must learn that its demands or attempts to control resources (attention-getting behavior, play or food soliciting behavior) must never be rewarded. An observant owner should be able to determine when a cat is ready and desiring food, treats, affection or play. This is usually a cat that looks relaxed, tail up and pupils normal size. Using a command or audible signal such as a bell, the cat can be trained to come to the owner and receive these rewards. Once the cat learns to come or approach on command or signal, the desired behavior (e.g. petting) can then be shaped by gradually making the task more difficult at each training session. Demanding, assertive, or any other forms of undesirable behavior should never be physically punished. Inattention or walking out of the room often works best, but if this is not possible an immediate disruption with a can of compressed air, water

pistol, or air horn, should quickly deter the behavior without causing fear of the owner. Another way to ensure immediate control without the need for direct contact is to fit your cat with a harness, and attach a long leash when you are at home and supervising.

Learned aggression: what is it and how can it be treated?

Learning is an important component of most types of aggression. Whenever a cat learns that aggression is successful at removing the stimulus, the behavior is further reinforced. Some forms of aggression are inadvertently rewarded by owners who, in an attempt to calm the pet and reduce aggression, actually encourage the behavior with patting or verbal reassurances. Pets that are threatened or punished for aggressive displays may become even more aggressive each time the situation recurs especially if that stops the threatening behavior.

Treatment with flooding is intended to teach the pet that the stimulus is not associated with any harm and that aggression will not successfully remove the stimulus. With desensitization and counter-conditioning, the cat is not only taught that the stimulus is safe, but that it is associated with a reward (see 'behavior modification desensitization, counter-conditioning and flooding').

What are some of the other causes of aggression?

Aggression associated with medical disorders may arise at any age, may have a relatively sudden onset and may not fit any feline species typical behavior. Some medical conditions can, on their own, cause aggression, but in many cases a combination of behavioral factors and medical problems cause the pet to pass a certain threshold at which aggression is displayed. Infectious agents such as rabies, hormonal imbalances such as hyperthyroidism, psychomotor epilepsy, neoplasia, and a variety of genetic and metabolic disorders can cause or predispose a cat to aggression. Painful conditions such as dental disease, or arthritis, and medical conditions causing fever, fatigue or sensory loss might increase the pet's irritability.

In rare circumstances, aggression has no identifiable etiology (idiopathic) and no particular stimuli that initiate the aggressive displays. There may be a genetic propensity to aggression.

AGGRESSION – PLAY

My cat's play is starting to lead to injuries. What can be done?

Understimulation, an excess of unused energy, and lack of appropriate opportunities for play can lead to play aggression. This may be exhibited as overly rambunctious or aggressive play, which inadvertently leads to injuries to people. In some cases, the play can include a number of components of the cat's predatory nature including the stalk, pounce, and bite, which can be extremely intense. Although play is usually more common in kittens, it may persist through adulthood especially in cats under two years of age that are only cats.

As mentioned, cat play is best stimulated by moving objects that can be stalked, chased, swatted, or pounced upon (see 'feline play and investigative behaviors'). Providing ample opportunities for self-play aids in reducing inappropriate play with owners. In addition, before you consider using one of the interruptions (water sprayer, alarm, and compressed air), the cat should first receive a sufficient number of play alternatives. Anticipate your cats need to play and initiate interactive play sessions. Play directed toward the owners, which is initiated by the cat, should not be tolerated. Owners that allow the cat to initiate affection and attention-getting behaviors run the risk of these behaviors escalating into more aggressive sessions, should the owner refuse the cat's demands. Successful interactive toys include wiggling ropes, wands, dangling toys, and those that are thrown or rolled for the cat to chase. Exercise care and choose toys that cannot be ingested or swallowed.

For self-play the cat can be provided with toys that roll such as ping pong balls or walnuts, toys that dangle, battery-operated and spring-mounted toys, scratching posts, and toys within containers that deliver food when scratched or manipulated. For cats that enjoy exploration, climbing and perching give opportunity for these. Hiding treats in various locations stimulates searching behavior that cats enjoy. Bird feeders outside of windows occupy some cats, while others might be interested in videos for cats. Catnip toys and toys with food or treats that can be obtained by scratching or manipulation, help to stimulate play and exploration. Cats with a strong desire for social play benefit from the addition of a second kitten to act as a playmate, provided both cats have been adequately socialized to cats.

How can I tell if play is about to become aggressive?

Often it is possible to see a change in your kitten's behavior that will signal to you that the play session is getting out of control. The first sign may be intense movement of the tail from side to side. The ears may go back and the pupils, the dark part of the eye, may become larger. At this point it is best to end the play session before the kitten becomes too agitated.

What should I do if the cat begins to exhibit play aggression?

Wherever possible ignoring the cat, or perhaps even walking out of the room, will teach the cat that there will be no interaction or reward when he or she initiates play. Play with you should be initiated by you, and not by the cat.

Physical punishment must be avoided! First, pain can cause aggression so if you hit your cat, you may increase the aggressive behavior. Second, painful punishment may cause fear and owner avoidance. Third, owners that attempt to correct the playful aggression with physical contact may actually serve to reward the behavior.

For a deterrent to be effective it must occur while the behavior is taking place and be timed correctly. Punishment also should be species appropriate. Noise deterrents are often effective in cats. For very young kittens, a "hissing" noise may deter excessive play behavior. The noise can be made by you, but if not immediately successful a can of compressed air used for cleaning camera lenses may be more effective and is less likely to cause fear or retaliation.

Some cats need an even more intense deterrent. Spray cans with citronella spray, water sprayers and commercially available "rape" alarms or air horns should be sufficiently startling to most cats to interrupt the behavior. What is most important in using these techniques is the timing. You must have the noise-maker with you so that you can immediately administer the correction (see 'controlling undesirable behavior in cats'). However without providing ample appropriate play opportunities punishment and distraction techniques will not be successful on their own.

What should I do about my cat that hides, stalks or jumps out at family members and me?

Another component of aggressive play behavior is hiding and dashing out and attacking people as they walk by. Often the kitten or cat waits around corners or under furniture until someone approaches. This can be a difficult problem.

First, keep a journal of occurrences, time of day and location. This can help identify a pattern that can be avoided. Second, you need to be able to know where your cat is. An approved cat collar (one that has a quick release catch or is elastic) with a large bell on it is helpful. If the cat always attacks from the same location, you can be ready, anticipate the attack and become pre-emptive. As you prepare to walk by the area, toss a small toy to divert the cat to an appropriate play object. Another tactic is to use your noise deterrent to get the cat out of the area or block access to the location such as under the bed so that the cat is unable to hide there and pounce out at your feet. Again, these techniques are most successful when combined with plenty of opportunities for appropriate play.

Is there a way to prevent this behavior?

Treatment for this problem is much the same as for other forms of play aggression. You must provide ample outlets and opportunities for play on your terms. Perhaps schedule play sessions. These should be aerobic play sessions so that the cat gets plenty of exercise.

If your cat does not seem to be interested in these play sessions, try other toys. Some cats prefer small, light toys that are easy to manipulate. Others prefer balls or small stuffed toys. Make sure the toys are safe and not small enough to be swallowed. Provide play sessions when the cat seems interested and avoid sessions at all other times. For example, if the cat seems to be interested in nighttime play, try and circumvent problems by offering play at approximately the same time that the cat would begin. Should the cat begin to initiate the play "session" before you are ready, remember that you must ignore the cat (or use one of the interruption devices) and restart the session after the cat has calmed down. Next evening begin a little earlier so you can "beat the cat to the punch". It can also be helpful to try and keep up your cat's interest in the toys. This can be accomplished by a daily rotation of toys so that the cat is presented with a few new items daily. Pick up all the toys and place them in a box or basket out of the cat's reach. Every day take out a few toys, or a bag or box and set then out for the cat to play with. Set aside some time for interactive play with you as well.

Cats can also be trained to do a number of tricks. This is an excellent way to stimulate your cat, to interact with your cat in a positive way and to gain some verbal control over your cat. Using a few choice food tidbits as rewards, most cats can be taught to sit, come, fetch, or "give 5".

AGGRESSION – REDIRECTED

What is it?

Redirected or misdirected aggression happens when the cat is in an arousing situation, but is unable to direct aggression toward the stimulus. For example, your cat is sitting on a windowsill and sees another cat out on the property. Your cat becomes very agitated, begins to focus on the other cat and shows aggressive body postures, hisses, or growls. If a person or animal in the home were to walk into the room, they may be the recipients of an aggressive attack. When this happens between resident cats, sometimes they will no longer tolerate being together and fight whenever they see each other. The initial stimulus that arouses the cat is most frequently another cat, but it could be any sight, sound, or a source of discomfort that leads to a heightened level of anxiety.

What should I do if that happens?

First, avoid the cat until it calms down. If the aggression is being redirected toward a second cat in the household, the two cats may have to be separated. In some cats this separation may only need a few minutes, but it is not unusual for it to take hours. In rare cases it may take several days or the cat may remain aggressive. This is most likely if the redirected aggression was met with retaliation, punishment or other form of fearful event (perhaps in an effort to separate the cat from the victim). In addition if the attack leads to a change in relationship between the cat and the victim (fear, defensiveness) then the aggression may persist. The best way to calm an agitated cat is to put the cat in a darkened room and leave it there. If locking up the aggressor is dangerous, it may be necessary to use a large blanket, a thick pair of gloves, and a large piece of cardboard to safely maneuver the cat into the room. If the problem is recurrent, leaving a body harness with a long leash attached to the cat can be a safe way to control the cat from a distance without the need for direct contact. Some cats may need to be kept in the room anywhere from several minutes to several days. The owner can go in, turn on the light, offer food to the cat, and if the cat remains fearful or does not accept the food, the owner should turn out the lights and leave. If the aggression has been directed toward a second cat in the home it is very important to wait until the cats are calm before re-introducing them. The biggest mistake that owners make in trying to resolve this problem is to try and bring the cats together too soon.

How should I get my cats back together again?

Re-introductions are best done slowly. Food rewards should be used to facilitate calm, non-anxious behavior. The cats need to be far enough apart (10 to 20 feet) so that they are relaxed and will take food or a treat while in the presence of the other cat. For safety and control it is often advisable that the cats have harnesses and leashes on them. If the cats will not eat then they are too anxious and probably too close together. Try moving the dishes further apart. If the cats still will not eat, separate them until the next feeding. If the cats eat at that time, allow them to remain together while they eat and then separate them. Repeat the same distance the next feeding. If things go well the next time the dishes can be moved slightly closer together. If the cats are comfortable, you can leave them together to let them groom and then separate them.

This is a slow process; you cannot rush things. Allowing the cats to interact in an aggressive manner sets the program back. The cats are separated except when they are distracted, occupied, and engaged in an enjoyable act (feeding or playing). The goal is to make sure that good things are associated with the presence of the other cat. It also may be helpful to switch litter pans between the cats. Another technique is to rub the cats with towels and switch from one to the other, mixing their scents.

If the aggression has not been severe it may be possible to get the cats reacclimated to one another through play. The best toy is a rod-type handle with a catnip mouse or feathers on the end for chasing and pouncing. With each cat on either side of a slightly open door introduce the toy and see if they will play with each other.

Another possible way to re-introduce cats is with the use of a crate. Place one cat in the crate while the other cat is loose in the room. This might best be done at feeding or play times. Allow the cats to become comfortable with the presence of one another. Then the next time switch occupants of the crate. An alternate method is to use a screen door on a room to separate the cats but allow them to visualize each other and get used to the sight of one another. Feeding the cats on either side of the door can also be used to facilitate the process.

If the problem is severe, one or both of the cats may need to be medicated. This is a step that needs to be discussed with your veterinarian and all the risks and benefits explored.

Can redirected aggression be directed towards people?
Yes. When redirected aggression is directed toward people the problem has often arisen because the people interacted with the cat when it was very agitated. Avoidance of the aggression-producing situation is necessary. Situations include the sight or sound of intruder cats on the property, especially in the spring and fall, new people or pets in the household, loud or unusual noises and a variety of other new or novel stimuli that are sometimes difficult to identify. If the situation cannot be entirely avoided then the owner must learn to avoid the cat, or find a safe way to maneuver the cat into a quiet room until it calms down, as previously discussed.

How can redirected aggression toward people be treated?
Resolving the aggression requires that the source of the agitation be identified and avoided. Since redirected aggression arises out of some other form of aggressive arousal that is then directed toward people, identifying and treating the primary source of aggression (e.g. territorial, fear) is required (see 'aggression – diagnosing and treating'). Avoiding exposure can be achieved by confining your cat away from the doors and windows, where the stimulus might be seen, heard, or smelled. Keep it out of the room (this may only be necessary at times when the stimuli, such as other cats, are likely to be around) or use booby-traps such as motion detectors to keep your cat away from the doors and windows. Installing vertical blinds or shutters, or placing sticky tape or upside down carpet runners along the windowsills or in front of the doorway may be sufficient. Alternately remove the stimulus or keep an intruder off the property by using repellents or outdoor booby-traps such as ultrasonic devices or motion detector alarms or sprinklers. Keeping garbage locked up and removing bird feeders can reduce the chances that animals will enter your property and disturb your

cat. If it is not practical to prevent exposing your cat to the stimulus, it might be possible to reduce the anxiety and arousal with drug therapy along with a desensitization and counter-conditioning program. Discuss this with your veterinarian.

AGGRESSION – TERRITORIAL

What is territorial aggression?

Territorial aggression may be exhibited toward people or other animals (usually cats) that approach or reside on the pet's property. Aggression can occur towards outside cats and also to cats that live in the household, especially new cats coming into the territory. This can occur with the addition of another cat, or when resident cats reach social maturity at 1-2 years of age. Another situation is when one cat is removed from the household (perhaps for routine surgery or boarding), and aggression is exhibited when the cat is brought back into the home. This may be either one or both of territorial and fear aggression (perhaps the returning cat smells, looks or acts unfamiliar in some way).

Territorial aggression can manifest as stalking, chasing and aggressive encounters, which may lead to injury. At times the aggressor will prevent the victim from having access to certain areas of the home resulting in a cat that lives on top of furniture or bookshelves or under beds. This may in part be related to the social relationship (status) of each cat (see 'aggression – introduction to aggressive behavior').

How can territorial aggression be prevented?

Territorial aggression can be prevented or minimized with early socialization, patient and slow introductions of new cats and adequate space, litter boxes and food bowls for cats. However, when a new cat is introduced (or reintroduced) into a household with existing cats, problems can best be prevented by slowly introducing the new cat to the environment, by keeping the new cat in a separate room with water and kitty litter, and supervising all interactions. If both cats have had adequate socialization with other cats, and are not too timid or fearful, it is usually only a matter of time before the cats work things out on their own, and are able to share the territory with little or no aggressive displays. However, in some homes, the aggression between cats persists and a more formal desensitization and counter-conditioning program may be required.

What is the best way to safely introduce (or reintroduce) a cat into the

household?

In order to ensure that there are no injuries and that all introductions are positive a desensitization and counter-conditioning program is the best way to ease a new cat into a household. Begin by confining the new cat to a room or portion of the home with its own litter box, food and water. Allow the existing cat to continue to have access to the rest of the home. This arrangement provides a separate territory within the home for each cat, and allows both cats an opportunity to adapt to the smell and sounds of each other, without the possibility of direct contact or physical confrontation. If the new cat is housed in a screened-in porch or a room with a glass door, it may also be possible to allow the cats to see each other through a safe partition. When the cats show no fear, anxiety, or threat toward each other, then progress to controlled exposure exercises.

Training should occur when the cats can be occupied in a highly "rewarding" activity such as feeding, play, or treats. Provided both cats are far enough apart to minimize the possibility of aggression, and the reward is sufficiently appealing, the cats will focus on the rewards rather than each other.

In addition, if the rewards are saved exclusively for these introduction times, the cats will quickly learn to expect "good things to happen" in the presence of each other. In addition to ensuring that the cats are at a safe enough distance to minimize fear, both cats (or at least the one that is likely to be the aggressor) can be confined to an open wire mesh cage or a body harness and leash. This will ensure that the cats can neither escape nor injure each other. It is safest to begin the first few introductions, not only at sufficient distance to reduce fear, but also with one or both cats in cages or on body harness and leash, so that they can neither retreat, or injure the other cat (see 'behavior modification – reducing fear and anxiety – desensitization, counter-conditioning and flooding'). If the cats have been in cages during the first training session, they can be placed in each other's cages at the next session (so that the cats are exposed to the other cat's odor). The cages can be moved progressively closer, provided the cats show no fear or anxiety and remain interested in the food. Once the cats will eat and accept exposure in either cage when close together, keep one cat in the cage and the other out during feeding. The situation is then reversed at the next session. As a final step the distance between cats can be increased again, with both cats out of their cages. A body harness and leash can be used to ensure additional safety. Over time the cats are fed closer together until a point where the cats can eat, or take treats, in each other's presence.

Another way to integrate cats is with play therapy. Some cats are more interested in play, toys or catnip than they are in food. One of the best toys is a wand type or fishing rod type handle with a stimulating play toy such as a catnip mouse or feathers on the end for chasing and pouncing. Begin by having both cats play at a distance from each other. Over time, introduce the toys between the cats and let them play with the toys together.

What if the aggression between the cats persists?

Introductions must be done slowly. The cats need to be far enough apart that they are relaxed and will take food or a treat while in the presence of the other cat. If the cats will not eat then they are too anxious and probably too close together. Try moving the dishes further apart. If the cats still will

not eat, be certain that they remain apart and do not give any food until the next feeding session. If the cats eat at that time repeat the same distance at the next feeding. If things go well, the next time the dishes can be moved closer together, but only by a small amount.

This is a slow process; you cannot rush things. Allowing either cat to interact in an aggressive manner sets the program back. The cats must remain separated except for times such as feeding when the cats are distracted, occupied, and engaged in an enjoyable act. In other words, good things are associated with the presence of the other cat. Another technique, which may help, is to rub the cats with towels and switch from one cat to the other to mix their scents.

Despite slow and careful progression, some cats may continue to display aggression, and it may be necessary to accept that they may never be compatible housemates. The only way to avoid territorial competition in these cats may be to find a new home for one of the cats, or to provide separate living quarters for each cat within the home. If the cats get along at certain times of the day, they can then be allowed limited exposure and interaction at these times. A leash and harness, or perhaps an air horn or water rifle, could be used to safely separate the cats should any aggressive displays emerge. If the problem is too severe, it may be helpful to medicate one or both cats. The option of drug therapy should be discussed with your veterinarian.

CONTROLLING UNDESIRABLE BEHAVIOR

Punishment is the application of a stimulus that decreases the chance that a behavior will be repeated. It must coincide with the undesirable behavior, and must be unpleasant enough to deter the cat from repeating that behavior. Keep in mind that you are punishing the behavior not the cat. Punishment should never be considered unless the pet has the means to satisfy its nature and its needs. For example, the scratching cat should be provided with an appropriate scratching post, before any attempts to punish undesirable scratching is initiated.

What is the best way to physically discipline my cat?

One of the most frequently utilized and least successful forms of punishment is where the owner uses a direct swat or hit. Hitting a cat can lead to hand-shyness, fear of the owner, and potential injury for both the owner and the cat. The cat will continue to perform the undesirable behavior in your absence since it learns that it can perform the behavior without punishment when you are out of sight. Physical punishment is therefore ineffective, potentially dangerous, and totally unnecessary.

How can I punish my cat for rough play?

Perhaps the only place where interactive punishment might be successful is for the cat that swats or scratches the owners in play. Even here, species appropriate punishment such as "hissing" or the use of a punishment device is better than using any physical techniques. Before punishment is considered however, the cat must be given ample opportunity to play. Toys that can be chased, swatted, and batted should be provided. Realize that if you give any form of attention (including physical punishment) to a cat that is swatting, or attacking in play, the behavior may actually be rewarded and further encouraged.

Whenever the cat begins to swat or play attack, immediately stop the play by walking away or by using some non physical form of punishment such as a water sprayer, can of compressed air, cap gun, hand held alarm or perhaps a loud hiss. Under no circumstances should a cat ever be punished unless it is caught in the act of performing the behavior. Remember, physical punishment should never be used as it is generally ineffective, and could cause harm to your relationship with your cat, or to the cat itself.

How can I punish my cat for other behaviors?

The key to successful punishment is to associate an unpleasant consequence with the undesirable behavior. However, unless the owner remains out of sight while administering punishment the cat may learn to cease the behavior only when you are present. Punishing the cat remotely, while you remain out of sight, is an effective means of deterring undesirable behavior. It takes a great deal of preparation, time and forethought. Another effective means of punishment is to booby-trap an area, so that the cat learns to "stay away".

How does remote punishment work?

For remote techniques to be successful there are two key elements. First, you must monitor the cat while out of sight so that you know when the problem begins. The second element is that the punishment must be delivered while the inappropriate behavior is occurring (while you remain out of sight).

1) Keep a close watch on the problem area while hidden around a corner, in a nearby closet, or behind a piece of furniture. Or, monitor your cat using an intercom, a motion detector or even just a set of bells that might "jingle" when disturbed.

2) As soon as the cat enters the area or begins to perform the undesirable behavior (climb, scratch), use a long range water pistol, noise device or remote control device to chase the cat away.

3) If the cat cannot determine where the noise or water is coming from, it should quickly learn to stay away from

the area whether the owner is present or not.

A commercial remote device is the citronella spray collar. It can be attached to a harness on the cat or just placed in the area and activated remotely as the cat enters the area. Another option is to set up a remote control switch near the problem area and have a device such as a water pik, alarm, or hair dryer plugged in.

When the owner is not around to supervise and monitor, booby-trap devices can be utilized or the cat should be confined to an area of the home that has been cat-proofed and supplied with a litter box, bedding area, toys for play and areas for scratching or climbing.

How can I booby-trap the environment to punish the pet?

Punishing the behavior remotely, with you out of sight, is impractical if the cat cannot be prevented from performing the undesirable behavior, when you are not there to supervise and monitor. Booby-traps are a way of teaching the pet to avoid the area or the behavior itself. One of the simplest ways to discourage a cat from entering an area where an undesirable behavior is likely to be performed (scratching, eliminating), is to make the area less appealing (or downright unpleasant) for scratching or eliminating. If the cat is scratching furniture, a large piece of material draped over the furniture may do the trick, since the cat won't be able to get its claws into the loose fabric. A small pyramid of empty tin cans or plastic containers could also be balanced on the arm of a chair so that it topples onto the cat when scratching begins. A piece of plastic carpet runner with the "nubs" facing up can be placed over a scratched piece of furniture to reduce its appeal, or a few strips of double-sided sticky tape would send most cats looking for another place to scratch (hopefully the scratching post). Mousetrap trainers, shock mats, or motion detectors are also very effective at keeping cats away from problem areas. A motion-detecting sprinkler is also available to keep other cats or animals off of the property (see 'behavior management products' for more details).

Most of these same booby-traps would also be effective for destructive behaviors such as chewing and sucking. Taste deterrents might also be helpful, provided they are unpleasant enough to deter the behavior. Products such as bitter apple, bitter lime or Tabasco sauce are often recommended, but many cats quickly learn to accept the taste. A little water mixed with cayenne pepper, oil of eucalyptus, any non-toxic mentholated product, or one of the commercial anti-chew sprays often work. To be effective, the first exposure to a product must be as repulsive as is humanely possible, so that the cat is immediately repelled whenever it smells or tastes that product again. Never leave any objects or areas untreated until the cat learns to leave the object or area alone.

Perhaps most important, punishment whether interactive or remote should never be a substitute for good supervision and the opportunity to engage in the proper behavior. This is very important with kittens that are learning what is acceptable in a new home.

For very active animals, a room that has been "cat-proofed" and supplied with toys, and objects to scratch and climb, is a good solution when owners are unable to supervise.

DESTRUCTIVE CHEWING & SUCKING

What can I do to stop my cat from chewing?

During exploration and play, kittens (and some adult cats) will chew on a variety of objects. Not only can this lead to damage or destruction of the owner's possessions, but some chewing can be dangerous to the cat. The first step is to ensure that the cat has appropriate opportunities and outlets for play, scratching, climbing, chewing and exploration (see 'feline play and investigative behaviors'). Next, potential targets of the cat's chewing should be kept out of reach. When this is not possible the cat may need to be confined to a cat proof room, or the problem areas may have to be booby-trapped (see 'behavior management products'). String and thread, electric cords, plastic bags, twist ties, and pins and needles are just a few of the objects that cats may chew or swallow resulting in intestinal foreign bodies and possibly the need for surgery.

Another common target of feline chewing is houseplants. The best solution is to keep the cat away from household plants whenever the cat cannot be supervised. booby-traps may also be effective. Placing rocks or gravel in the soil, mothballs, or a maze of wooden skewers can help to keep the cat from climbing on, digging in, or eliminating in the soil. Some cats may be interested in chewing on dog toys or biscuits, and feeding a dry cat food may help satisfy some cats need to chew. In some cats the desire for chewing plant material can best be satisfied by providing some greens (e.g. lettuce, parsley) in the food, or by planting a small kitty herb garden for chewing.

What can I do for my cat that sucks on wool and fabrics?

Sucking on wool or other fabrics may be seen occasionally in any cat, but is most commonly a problem of Burmese and Siamese cats, or Oriental mix breeds. Although some cats do grow out of the problem within a few years, the problem may remain for life. The first step in correction is to provide alternative objects for chewing and sucking. Some cats may be interested in one of the many chew toys or chew treats designed primarily for dogs. A well-cooked bone with some gristle and meat could be considered, provided the cat is well supervised and sucks and gnaws on the bone without causing it to splinter. Feeding dry and high fiber foods or dental foods and dental treats may also be helpful. Making food more difficult to obtain by placing large rocks in the food dish encourages the cat to "forage". Second, be certain that the cat has plenty of play periods with the owners, or even a playmate to keep it exercised and occupied. This may require the owner to not only schedule play time, but to control the cat toys and every 1 – 3 days provide a rotating inventory of toys to stimulate usage. Other cats will respond well to training interactions with their owner, and cats can be taught tricks. Finally, cat proofing techniques or booby-traps will likely be required whenever the owner cannot supervise.

Some cats are so persistent in their desire to suck wool that more drastic measures may be required. Covering chew toys with a small amount of a product containing lanolin (such as hand cream) for licking is occasionally helpful. For some cats, it may be necessary to leave the cat with one or two woolen objects to suck on, provided no significant amounts are swallowed. It has even been suggested that a raw chicken wing a day might be tried as a last resort. However, given the prevalence of Salmonella in uncooked chicken, microwaving would seem prudent. If these techniques do not help, then it may be necessary to use a cat cage with perches when the cat is unsupervised to avoid continued ingestion of material.

Some cats have such a strong and seemingly uncontrollable desire to suck that the condition has been compared to compulsive disorders in people. The same drugs used for human compulsive disorders may be useful for some of these cases. If your cat shows persistent efforts to suck, chew or ingest material, a consultation with a veterinary behaviorist, or applied animal behaviorist may be necessary to control the behavior.

EXCESSIVE NOCTURNAL ACTIVITY

Why does my cat seem to be most active at nights?

Some cats are active at night or awake and "raring to go" very early in the morning. Since many owners are out at work or school during the day the cat may spend the daytime hours in rest and relaxation, especially if it is the only pet in the household. The cat's day then begins when the owner arrives home to provide the cat with feeding, play and social interaction. This is also the most natural time for cats to be active since they normally are most active in hunting and exploration at dusk and dawn (this is known as crepuscular). Typical complaints are cats that nibble or even attack the owner's ears or toes in bed, walking across the sleeping owners, nighttime vocalization, or explosive, uncontrollable play sessions across the furniture and/or owners, during the night or early morning. Some owners inadvertently reward the behavior by giving the cat a little food, affection, or attention to try and calm the cat.

How can I stop my cat from keeping me up at night?

You must learn to schedule and encourage play and feeding during the daytime and evening hours, so that the cat's schedule more closely matches that of yourself. Adjusting the timing of feeding or the type of food may help to alter the cat's sleep schedule. For example, eating a few hours earlier or later, or increasing the evening meal to one that is higher in carbohydrates may help to alter the cat's schedule just enough that it sleeps through the night.

Some cats can be retrained by keeping the cat awake and active by playing, feeding and interacting with the cat throughout the afternoon and evening. Catnaps in the evening should be discouraged.

If the cat continues to disturb you during the night, confining your cat out of the bedroom, and providing it with a comfortable sleeping area and litter may do the trick. Do not provide food through the night as this encourages the cat to stay awake. On the other hand, if the cat remains awake, providing the cat with ample opportunity for scratching, climbing and play in a confined area may occupy the cat until it becomes tired.

Cats that are vocal when locked out of the bedroom must be ignored. Going to the cat or giving attention in any way will only serve to reward the demanding behavior. Cats that scratch or bat at the bedroom door can be kept away by the use of an upside down carpet runner, electronic pet mat or perhaps a motion detector (although it might disturb the owner). Citronella spray avoidance units are also available (see 'behavior management products'). If the cat is overly vocal, lock it away in as sound proof an area as possible such as a washroom, or a cat carrier in a distant bedroom. Nested corrugated cardboard boxes around the cage help to further reduce the noise.

What if it is necessary to have the cat sleep in the bedroom?

If you decide that your cat would do best if allowed to stay in the bedroom, you must remember that any attention whatsoever will further reinforce the behavior. React to the demanding cat with inattention. However if the cat persists or the behavior escalates to a point where it cannot be ignored, punishment may be effective.

It should first be noted that punishment is generally contraindicated in cats because punishment that is too mild is likely to be ineffective and may actually serve to provide enough play or attention to reward the behavior. Punishment that is too harsh on the other hand could lead to an increase in anxiety, fear of the owner and even aggression. If punishment is to be used, devices that quickly deter the cat without the need for owner contact, such as a water sprayer, air horn, ultrasonic device or compressed air or a spray of citronella are usually the safest and most effective.

Is there medication that might help?

If all else fails and the cat does not sleep through the night with behavioral techniques alone, your veterinarian may be able to provide some medication to help your cat fall asleep for the first few nights.

My cat seems to be afraid of people and or other animals – why might that be?

There are many reasons that cats can develop such fears. Your cat may have had limited exposure to people and other animals when it was young. Socialization is an important aspect of raising a kitten. Without adequate, continuous and positive interactions with people and other animals, cats may develop fears. Because the socialization period in cats begins and ends earlier (generally between 3-9 weeks) than it does in dogs, the early environment of the kitten is most important. Because of this, cats adopted as strays or from shelters may not have had adequate early exposure to many new and novel things. Cats can also learn through the effect of even just one unpleasant experience ("one trial learning") that was intense or traumatic. This learning may then generalize to similar situations. For example, a bad experience with a small child could result in a cat that is fearful of all small children. Sometimes a number of unpleasant events "paired" or associated with a person or animal can lead to increasing fear. For example, if a pet is punished or some disturbing event occurs in the presence of a particular person or other animal, it may begin to pair the stimulus (the person or other animal) with the unpleasant consequence (punishment). Genetics and the early environment are other important contributing factors to the development of fear. Cats that are handled frequently and regularly during the first few weeks of life are generally more exploratory and more social. There are some cats that are inherently timid and fearful. These may never become outgoing and highly sociable. Still other cats experienced poor nutrition during development or while kittens and this affected their emotional development.

Can I prevent fears from developing?

Early, frequent and pleasant encounters with people of all ages and types can help prevent later fears. Genetics plays a role in the development of fears, therefore select kittens that are non-fearful and sociable. Since some evidence has indicated the father's role in personality, assessing and observing the kitten's parents will give some insight into the personality that a kitten may develop when it grows up.

What are the signs of fear?

When frightened a cat may hide, try to appear smaller, place its ears back and be immobile. On the other hand, a cat may show signs of agitation or aggression such as dilated pupils, arched back, pilo-erection (hair standing on end) and hissing (see 'fears, phobias and anxieties' for a detailed description).

What information do I need to identify and treat my fearful pet?

A behavioral consultation is needed for cats that are showing extreme fears and/or aggression. If the fears are mild, then owner intervention may help to prevent them from progressing. First identify the fearful stimulus. This is not always easy and needs to be very exact. Which person(s) or animal(s) is the cat afraid of and where does the fearful behavior occur? Often there are certain situations, people and places that provoke the behavior more than others.

For treatment to be most successful, it is important to be able to place the fearful stimuli along a gradient from low to high. Identify those situations, people, places and animals that are least likely, as well as most likely, to cause the fear.

Next, examine what factors may be reinforcing the behavior. Some owners reward the fearful behavior by reassuring their pets with vocal intonations or body contact. Aggressive displays are a successful way of getting the fearful stimulus to leave and thus also reinforce the behavior. Any ongoing interactions that provoke fear need to be identified and removed. This could be teasing behavior, painful interactions, and punishment or overwhelming stimuli.

After I have identified the stimuli, what next?

Before a behavior modification program can begin you must be able to control your cat. This can be accomplished with a figure eight harness and leash, or if needed a crate. Next, teach your cat to pair a non-fearful situation with food rewards. The goal of this training is to allow the cat to assume a relaxed and happy body posture and facial expression in the presence of the stimulus.

For mild fears, cats may settle down with constant (flooding) exposure to the fearful situation, provided there are no consequences that aggravate the fear. For example, cats kept in a cage for a few days in a boarding facility will often get used to the situation and settle down, provided there are no events that add to the fear.

For most cats a program of counter-conditioning and desensitization will be the most successful way to acclimatize the cat to the stimuli that cause the fearful response. Do this slowly. Start by exposing the cat to very low levels of the stimulus that do not evoke fear. Reward the cat for sitting quietly and calmly. Save all favored rewards for these retraining sessions so that the cat is highly motivated to get the reward. The cat soon learns to expect rewards when placed in the cage and exposed to the stimulus. Gradually the stimulus intensity is increased (see 'behavior modification, desensitization, counter-conditioning, differential reinforcement and flooding'). If the cat acts afraid during training it should be stopped. Set up the cat to succeed. Over time, the stimulus can be presented at closer distance, or in a louder or more animated manner. The situation may then need to be changed to advance the training. For example, if your cat is fearful of a particular person, once

the person can sit beside the cage while your cat eats, the person could then attempt to feed the cat favored treats through the bars of the cage. Next, the cat might eat and take rewards while out of the cage wearing a leash and harness if necessary, but go back to an increased distance to ensure success and safety. Over time the person can move closer at feeding times until he or she can give the cat its food. Cats that are fearful of other cats might be fed in two different cages in the same room. Once the cats will eat with the cages next to each other during feeding times, you could begin to keep one cat in the cage during feeding with one out, and alternate at future feedings. Next, both cats could be fed while out of the cages at a distance with one or both on halters and then progress to having the cats side-by-side at feedings (see 'aggression – territorial'). This can then advance to play sessions, catnip and treat times, and other times when the cats could "enjoy" themselves in each other's company.

My cat still encounters the fearful stimulus when we are not in a training exercise. What should I do then?

Each time the cat experiences the fearful stimulus and reacts with fear, the behavior is reinforced. Try and avoid the fear-producing stimulus, if possible. This may mean confining the cat when children visit, or the house is full of strangers. Drug therapy can also be useful to reduce fears and anxieties during times when the stimulus cannot be avoided. Drug therapy can be discussed with your veterinarian.

Do I need to train my new kitten to use a litter box?

Most cats by nature use a soil type surface for elimination. By providing a litter box with an appropriate and appealing substrate (material), most cats do not need to be trained to use it. At about 30-36 days of age kittens leave the nest to search out a loose substrate for elimination. The kitten learns specific areas and substrates to use by observation of the queen (mother). Although some cats, especially those on their own property will dig and bury their wastes, many cats only partly cover their feces especially if they are off of their home territory. Some cats do not bury urine or stools at all, even on their own property and, for obvious reasons these cats may prove harder to litter train.

Is there anything that I need to do to aid this process?

Initially it is best that the kitten be confined to a small area with an appropriate sized litter box. This allows you to take advantage of a cat's tendency to eliminate in a loose material. As long as the kitty litter is easily accessible and is the only loose substrate available, very little effort should be required to litter box train the kitten. About the only other indoor area that might be equally or more appealing to some cats is the soil around houseplants. Ensuring that the cat is prevented from getting into houseplants, except when you are around to supervise deals with this problem. Kittens, like dogs, will need to eliminate after they eat, after they wake up and after play. At those times place the kitten in its litterbox and praise her for elimination. A kitten does not need to be confined continuously, but should be supervised to prevent accidents and frequently brought back to the appropriate elimination location. A little of the urine or stool odor from previous elimination should help to attract the cat back to the box. In fact, if the kitten soils in a location other than its box on the first attempt, clean up the area thoroughly using a product that is designed to neutralize cat urine odor, and perhaps even move a small amount of the stool or a few drops of the urine to the box to attract the cat to that area.

What type of litter material should I use?

There are many types of litter materials available today. These include plain clay litters, fine "clumping" litters, plastic pears, recycled newspapers, wood shavings and many others. Some have materials added to control odor although scented litters may be aversive to some cats. The type you choose is up to you. Since the kitten will first start eliminating by following the cues of the queen, continuing with the same litter as used in the first home is helpful.

What size and type of litter box should I buy?

Initially, the size of the litter box should be determined by the size of the kitten or cat. A very small kitten may need a box with shorter (lower) sides or a ramp for easier access. As the kitten grows, a larger box is generally more appropriate. Some owners prefer litter boxes with covers on them. This is acceptable if it is acceptable to the cat. You need to be sure that the cat can negotiate the opening by stepping into it and that the cat is not too large to fit into the opening.

Where should I put the litter box?

The litter box should be placed in a location that is easily accessed by the cat, yet out of the way. Try to avoid congested household areas. The cat should have some privacy and quiet to eliminate. Laundry and furnace rooms are often used, but be sure that noise from household equipment is not disruptive and aversive to your cat. Make sure that the cat does not get locked out of the room at a time when it may have to eliminate. Try to put the litter box in an area that is convenient for you to check on and keep clean. Do not put food and water bowls right next to the litter box. If there are dogs in the home, then the litter box should be located where the cat can eliminate without being bothered by them.

How often should I clean the litter box?

One of the most important factors in continued litter box usage by house cats is cleanliness. Cats are very fastidious animals, and spend time each day making sure their coat, feet and face are clean. One can assume that they would like a clean place to eliminate. The number of cats in the home and litter usage determines the time between litter cleaning. Fecal material should be removed on a daily basis, whether the litter material type is clumping or plain. Litter boxes should ideally be cleaned each day, and except for the clumping types the litter should be changed and the box should be cleaned out once per week. Remember that each cat is an individual. Your cat may like more frequent cleaning of the litter box to maintain good usage patterns. Some cats dislike the odor of the cleansers used to clean litter boxes, so rinse the box thoroughly after each cleaning. A number of products are self-cleaning and this can be particularly appealing to some cats. However some cats might be frightened of the motors and cleaning mechanisms.

How many litter boxes do I need in my home?

The number of litter boxes needed depends on the number of cats, the size of the home, the temperament of the cat, and other pets in the home. When there are multiple cats, multiple pans should be available in different locations, not all side-by-side in one place. Because there can be varied interactions between individuals, multiple boxes in multiple locations allow housemates to avoid one another if they so choose. Even for only one cat, two boxes may be appropriate depending on the layout of the home and the individual preferences of the cat. Some cats prefer one box for urine and one for stool. Some physical limitation may prevent a cat from climbing stairs and so a box in the location the cat frequents is needed. In general, there should be at least one litter box per cat, and some behaviorists advise one more box than the number of cats in the house.

What if the kitten does not use its litter box?

Should the kitten begin to eliminate in locations other than its litter box, first review the steps above. Is the litter in an area that is appealing and easily accessed by the cat? Is the litter box being cleaned often enough? Are there enough litter boxes for the number of cats? Try and determine what there is about the area that your cat is soiling that is so appealing to your cat. And perhaps most important is there anything about the area, box or litter that might be preventing its use (or scaring your cat)? To determine the most appealing litter for your cat, offer two or more different litters in the same type of box, side-by-side and see which one, if any, the cat uses most frequently. Next, determine the type of litter box the cat prefers by offering two or more litter box types side-by-side (each with the preferred type of litter). You can determine the cat's preferred location by offering the preferred litter box with the preferred litter in two or more locations and determining which one, if any, the cat uses more frequently. If litter box problems then persist, additional guidance and perhaps a behavior consultation might be required (see 'house-soiling in cats').

HOUSE-SOILING

House-soiling in cats, also often called feline inappropriate elimination, is the most common behavioral complaint of cat owners. Problem behaviors can be urine and/or stool deposited outside of the litter box, or marking behaviors such as spraying or horizontal urination in small amounts. Spraying and marking behaviors are covered separately in 'marking behaviors in cats'.

Could there be a medical reason that my cat is house-soiling?

Medical diseases of the urinary tract can cause inappropriate elimination. There are many such conditions, including stones and crystal formation in the bladder, bacterial infections, and a group of inflammatory diseases of the bladder and urinary tract of unknown origin that cause pain and an increased urgency to urinate. Diseases of the kidneys and liver can cause the cat to drink more and urinate more frequently. In addition, age related cognitive (brain function) decline and endocrine disorders such as hyperthyroidism and diabetes, may lead to changes in elimination habits including house-soiling. Medical problems that lead to a difficulty or discomfort in passing stools, poor control or an increased frequency of defecation could all contribute to house-soiling with stools. Colitis, constipation, and anal sac diseases, are just a few of the medical problems that need to be ruled out when diagnosing the cause of inappropriate defecation. Another consideration is the pet's mobility and sensory function. Medical conditions affecting the nerves, muscles, or joints, could lead to enough discomfort, stiffness or weakness that the cat may not be able to get to the litterbox, climb into the litterbox, or get into a comfortable position for elimination.

In summary, if elimination is associated with pain or discomfort, or if access to the litterbox is difficult or uncomfortable the cat may begin to eliminate outside of the box. In addition, those cats with increased frequency of elimination (especially if the litter box is not cleaned more frequently) and those with decreased control may begin to soil the house. A complete physical examination, urinalysis and in some cases additional diagnostic tests such as blood tests, radiographs or a urine culture, will be needed to rule out medical problems that could be causing or contributing to the cat's elimination problem. Some problems may be transient or recurrent so that repeated tests may be needed to diagnose the problem. Once a cat has persistently eliminated outside of the litter box for medical reasons, the cat may learn to eliminate in the wrong location.

What could the problem be if it is not medical?

Diagnostic possibilities for elimination problems in cats include litter, litter box, and location aversions, and substrate and location preferences. Frustration or stress can also influence feline elimination behavior. Keep in mind that the initiating cause of non litter box use may have been medical or a change in the environment. However, the problem could now be maintained by the cat having learned to eliminate somewhere other than the litter box. When frustration, stress, anxiety, or marking are suspected to be the cause, drug therapy and behavior modification techniques may be effective (see 'marking behaviors in cats' for treatment).

How do we determine the behavioral cause?

When all medical problems have been treated or ruled out and the house-soiling persists, a complete and comprehensive behavioral history will be necessary in order to establish a diagnosis and treatment plan. This includes information about the home environment, litter box type and litter used, litter box maintenance and placement, and the onset, frequency, duration and progression of problem elimination behaviors. Other factors to note include new pets in the household, any household changes that might have occurred around the time the problem began, and any patterns to the elimination such as the time of day, particular days of the week, or seasonal variations. Relationships between the soiling cat and other animals and people in the home need to be examined. The number and placement of litter boxes is extremely important in multi-cat households and if inappropriate or undesirable for one or more of the cats, may contribute to the house-soiling.

Other information required is whether the cat is using the litter box at all, and the location of inappropriate elimination including types of surface, whether on horizontal or vertical surfaces, and whether it is urine, stools or both.

How do I determine which cat is eliminating when there is more than one cat?

When there are multiple cats in the home, it may be difficult to determine who is actually soiling. Confinement of one or more cats may be necessary to discover who is not using the litter box. However, if social conflicts between cats contribute to the problem, separating cats may make the problem diminish or stop. A fluorescent dye can be administered to one cat, and the soiled areas can then be evaluated with a "black" light to determine if that is the cat that is house-soiling.

What factors should I look at to correct this problem?

Two areas that need to be addressed are litter box maintenance and litter box location. Litter box maintenance refers to how the box is cleaned. For some cats, it is necessary to keep the litter box scrupulously clean. This may mean changing the box daily, or at least removing fecal matter every day. All litter boxes should periodically be totally emptied and cleaned. If clumping litter is used, daily scooping is needed and at least semi weekly emptying and cleaning. The choice of litter material is important. Some cats prefer a plain clay litter material without any odor control matter added. Other cats may prefer fine clay litter materials that clump and allow for frequent, easy litter box cleaning. Cats may be reluctant to use the litter box if it has been recently deodorized or if the cat dislikes the odor of the cleansers (so rinse well after cleansing).

If the same litter box has been used for several years it may hold a residual odor. Discard the old one and obtain a new one. Another factor that may need to be changed is the type of litter box. If the cat has always used a covered litter pan, a change in body composition or mobility may make removing the cover important. If a cat has become overweight, it may no longer fit comfortably in a covered pan. An elderly cat that may have musculoskeletal changes such as arthritis may also find climbing into an uncovered pan, or a litterbox with lower sides, much easier. A covered pan may allow other cats to ambush a cat as they exit. And, covered pans may hold in odors that are associated with infrequent cleaning.

The location of the litter pan can often be important for cats that do not use their litter box. Some cats may be unwilling to use a box that is difficult or inconvenient to access, or if the box is located in an area that the cat finds unappealing or unpleasant. For example, a box that is in the far recesses of the basement or near a furnace or washing machine may be undesirable. Older cats can find stairs an obstacle and be unwilling to go into the basement to use the litter box.

When there are multiple cats in the home, multiple pans in multiple locations may be needed. It is speculated that cats may not share the space they have equally, and be unwilling to go to some locations to use the litter box. If the relationship between cats is not harmonious, one cat may feel threatened when trying to get to the litter box and choose to go elsewhere. Most cats prefer privacy when they eliminate. If the litter box is located in a high traffic or noisy area in the home, the cat may avoid it. Moving the pan to another quieter location may encourage the cat to return to litter box use.

How can I stop the cat from eliminating on spots in the home?

A cat may not use the litter box if it prefers another location. This can often be determined by a careful history into where the elimination is found. If it is always found in one place, this indicates a location preference, while elimination on one particular surface type or texture (such as carpeting or tiled floors), indicates a substrate preference. For treatment, if it is happening in only one or two places, the cat should be prevented from being in that location without supervision. When no one is home, or you are asleep, the cat may need to be confined. When you are at home, you should always know where the cat is. This can be accomplished by watching the cat or by using a bell on an approved cat collar or a leash and harness. Alternately, the location could be made aversive to the cat using devices mentioned in other sections. If the cat does not like where the litter box is due to disruptions in that location, moving the box to a quieter, more secure location may also aid in getting the cat to return to regular litter box usage. The surface can be made less appealing by changing the surface texture (remove the carpeting), or by making the surface uncomfortable (double-sided sticky tape, a plastic carpet runner with nubs up, remote punishment or booby-traps). In some cases, access to the area can be permanently prevented by closing off doors to the area, by putting up barricades, or confining the cat away from the problem area. The appeal of the surface can also be reduced by eliminating all odors that might be attracting the cat back to the area by cleaning and then by applying commercial odor neutralizers. Sometimes changing the function of the area by turning it into a feeding, playing, sleeping or scratching area may reduce the cat's desire to eliminate in the area.

How can we make the litter area more appealing?

Besides making the location where the cat has eliminated aversive or inaccessible, the litter box needs to be made attractive to the cat. From the history, it may be possible to first determine some of the reasons that might be deterring the cat from using its litter box or litter area and these can first be resolved to increase the appeal of the litter. For example, more frequent cleaning, or switching litter materials may be all that is needed. Then, try to determine what litter, location, and type of box might be preferable to your cat.

How can I tell what my cat would prefer?

To determine the most suitable litter for your cat, first determine what type of litter your cat seems to be avoiding and what type of surface your cat prefers to use. Then set up two boxes that are identical and fill the boxes with two different types of litter. Some cats may prefer a clumping litter, cedar shavings, recycled newspaper, or plastic pearls. For cats that prefer solid or hard surfaces, an empty litter box, or one with minimal litter might do. A carpeted ledge around the box, artificial turf or some discarded or shredded carpet might help to increase the appeal for cats that prefer to eliminate on carpets, while some potting soil or a mixture of sand and soil, may be preferable for cats that eliminate in plants or soil. Making a good choice may require a little imagination and should be based on the type of surfaces in the home on which the cat is eliminating. If you prefer scented brands of litters, make sure this is also acceptable to your cat by comparing to an unscented brand. In your preference testing, if you find one litter type that is a clear favorite, discard the second type and continue your testing with other products. For cats that use hard surfaces you could also try an empty litter box, while cats that prefer carpet, may do better with some carpet strips, artificial turf or a carpeted ledge around the box.

To determine the most suitable box for your cat, you might want to look at the design of the box and find different types for preference testing. Use the litter type that was most preferable to the cat and try it in a variety of boxes to determine what the cat prefers. You might consider boxes with hoods and no hoods, a very large box, such as a plastic storage container, a box with lower sides or a ramp for access, boxes with or without litter liners and perhaps even self-cleaning types of litter boxes (appealing to some cats and frightening to others).

To determine if the cat has a clear location preference, you might begin by a litter box in the location where the cat eliminates. If the cat uses the box in that location, it should be left there for one week. Then the box can slowly be moved to a new location. This needs to be done very carefully to be sure that the cat follows the box and continues to eliminate in the litter box as it is moved. Most importantly, the box should be moved only 6-8 inches at a time. Then it should be left in each place at least one day. When trying to go from one room to another, or up or down stairs, longer distances can be covered as long as the cat follows the box and continues to use it. A room with better access or lighting or an area with more or less privacy from owners and other pets might be preferred. By altering the location of the litter box you might even be able to find something that has been deterring the cat (toilet, furnace etc) in the previous location.

I've made the litter more appealing and the house-soiling areas less appealing but the cat continues to eliminate in inappropriate areas. What next?

Even after making the litter area more appealing, decreasing the appeal of the soiled areas, and perhaps anti-anxiety drugs for anxiety induced or marking problems, the habit may persist. Confinement to an area with

bedding, water and a litter box (and away from the areas that have been soiled) is often necessary to re-establish litter box use. Generally a small room such as a laundry room, extra washroom, or bedroom where the cat has not previously soiled should be utilized. Also be sure to confine your pet in an area where the litter box and litter area are appealing, where there are no obvious deterrents, and that has surfaces that the cat is unlikely to soil. In rare cases where the cat will not use its litter box at all, confinement in a cat cage with perches or a large dog cage with a floor pan covered in litter and a ledge for perching and sleeping may be

needed to get the litter use restarted. Most cats will require confinement to this area for one to four weeks, (the longer the problem the longer the confinement period) to re-establish good litter use. Confinement however, may not be required all of the time. For example, if the cat only eliminates out of its box at night, or when the owners are preparing for work, then these are the only times that the cat may need to be confined. Many cats, when supervised will not eliminate in the inappropriate areas so that these cats can be allowed out of confinement when the owner is available to supervise. It may also be possible to allow cats out of confinement with minimal supervision for the first few hours after the cat has eliminated in its litter box. Allowing release from confinement and some food treats immediately following elimination may also serve to reward use of the litter box. Over time, cats that have been confined are gradually given more freedom and less supervision. However, there will be some cats that will use the box in confinement but once back out in the home revert to elimination in other locations.

I am finding the urine on vertical surfaces like walls and backs of furniture. What does that mean?

When cats urinate on vertical surfaces, it is known as spraying. This is a feline marking behavior. Usually the cat backs up to a vertical surface, raises their tail, treads with their back feet, the tail may quiver and a stream of urine is directed backwards. Marking includes spraying urine on vertical locations as well as elimination of small amounts of urine in multiple locations and occasionally defecation. A behavioral history should help differentiate marking behavior from other elimination behavior problems. A cat may mark due to the presence of other cats both inside and outside of the home. Many behaviorists feel that cats mark their environment in response to "stress" or anxiety. Spraying and marking cats are covered in 'marking behaviors in cats'.

What are the general treatments for elimination problems?

Treatment focuses on modifying both the environment and pet to re-establish regular litter box usage. Commonly the cat will need to be confined when it can't be supervised. The litter material, box and location may need to be made more appealing (or remove those factors that are reducing the appeal). The cat will need to be prevented or deterred from returning to the soiled areas, and if there is an anxiety or marking component drugs may be useful. Litter trials (using two or more litter types), location trials (using two or more locations) and litter box trials (using two or more different box types) may be useful for determining the cat's preferences (see 'house-training – using the litter box' for details).

Are drugs useful in treating this problem?

Drug therapy can be a helpful adjunct where stress, anxiety, marking or a medical component is involved. It requires a thorough understanding of the indications, contraindications and potential side-effects of the various drugs. An accurate diagnosis is needed to determine if such therapy will be helpful and which drug to choose. If the behavior is due to a surface substrate preference, location preference or any type of aversion, drug therapy is unlikely to be helpful. Commonly used drugs include buspirone, anti-depressants and benzodiazepines.

My cat is defecating outside of the litter box, what should I do?

Much of the same information as for a urination problem is needed to make a diagnosis in defecation problems. If the defecation is found in a linear pattern be sure to ask about intercat aggression (the cat is defecating while fleeing) and possible constipation. Cats may defecate outside of the litter box if they are mildly constipated, so this should be evaluated, especially in older cats. If medical problems are ruled out, the same diagnostic and treatment considerations as in urine house-soiling will need to be considered.

INTRODUCING A KITTEN TO A NEW HOME

How best should I introduce my new kitten to my home?

Your interaction with your new kitten begins on the ride home. Cats should always be transported in some kind of carrier in the car. By teaching your kitten to ride in a confined location you are providing safety for your cat in future car rides. Upon arriving at home, place the kitten in a small, quiet area with food and a litter box. If the kitten is very tiny, a small litter box with lowered sides may be necessary at first. If possible, duplicate the type of litter material used in the previous home (see 'house-training – using the litter box').

The first place you put your new kitten should be inspected for nooks and crannies where a kitten might hide or get stuck. All kittens and cats will need to investigate their new surroundings. For a new kitten this is a more manageable task if you limit space available and initially supervise the kitten. When cats do investigate they use a random method of search. Be sure the room is effectively cat-proofed, which includes anywhere the cat can jump or climb. Potentially dangerous items such as electric cords and owner items that might be chewed or swallowed (such as thread, rubber bands, paper clips, children's toys) should be booby-trapped or kept out of reach (see 'controlling undesirable behavior in cats'). After your new kitten has had some quiet time in a restricted location, slowly allow access to other areas of the home under your supervision.

Kittens are natural explorers and will use their claws to climb up onto anything possible. In the first few weeks slow access to the home will allow exploration as well as the ability to monitor the kitten's behavior.

What should I do if I have other pets?

Although some kittens may show fear and defensive postures toward other pets in the home, most young kittens are playful and inquisitive around other animals. Therefore, it is often the existing pets that can pose more of a problem. If you know or suspect that your adult dog or cat might be aggressive toward the kitten, then you should seek behavior advice before bringing introducing the pets to each other.

The kitten should be given a safe and secure area that provides for all of its needs and introductions with the existing family pets should be carefully supervised. At the first introduction there may be no immediate problems so that reinforcement of desirable responses may be all that is required. If there is some mild anxiety on the part of your dog then introductions should be controlled, gradual, supervised and always positive. Your new kitten could be placed in a carrier or on a leash and harness so that it will not provoke your dog. Then using a leash for control, favored rewards and your training commands, encourage your dog to 'sit' or 'stay' calmly in the presence of the cat. Calm investigation should then be encouraged and reinforced. A leash and head halter could be used to further improve control and safety. Any initial anxiety should soon decrease and the kitten should quickly learn its limits with the dog including how to avoid confrontation by climbing or hiding. If you are not positive that you can safely leave the dog and kitten together, then a basket muzzle could be placed on your dog while you monitor the situation. If, on the other hand there is the possibility of aggression or injury then a behavior consultation would be advisable. Most adult cats are fairly tolerant of kittens, so that keeping the kitten in its own area, and then allowing introductions when the cats are eating or playing, should help to decrease any initial anxiety. A leash and harness or a crate can be used to control one or both of the cats during initial introductions. A synthetic cheek gland scent may also be useful for easing introductions. Most cats and kittens will soon work out their relationship on their own, without injury. However, if there is a threat of aggression, then details of a gradual introduction program can be found in 'territorial aggression'.

How can I prevent problems from developing?

The key to preventing behavior problems is to identify all of the needs of the cat and provide appropriate outlets for each. This is especially important for the indoor cat since all of its play, predation, exploration, scratching, elimination and social needs will need to be channeled into acceptable indoor options, while sexual motivation can be reduced by neutering. Interactive play with wand and movable toys can provide an opportunity to chase and play hunt, while small plastic or fleece toys that can be batted and chased or retrieved can keep the cat occupied when the owners are away. Toys can be stuffed with food or coated with catnip and paper bags, cardboard boxes and hidden food treats can provide opportunities for exploration. Highly social and playful cats may also benefit from having a second social and playful cat in the home. A comfortable blanket or rug for napping, counters, shelves or play centers for perching, posts for scratching and a proper litter area for elimination round out a number of the cats needs. One important rule of thumb is that each cat is different so you must choose the types of play and toys that are most appealing to your cat and most appropriate for your household.

Can I prevent my cat from becoming overly fearful?

Most kittens are highly social but sociability and social play begins to wane after two months of age. Therefore as soon as the kitten is obtained you should make every attempt to introduce the kitten to a wide variety of people (ages, races, infirmities) a wide variety of environments, other pets, and as many new stimuli (e.g. noises, car rides, elevator) as possible. One way to help insure a positive relationship with each new person, pet, place and event is to give the kitten one of its favored treats or toys with each new meeting and greeting.

How can I teach my cat to enjoy handling?

Depending on the personality and early experiences as a kitten, your cat may enjoy, accept, or dislike, certain types of handling from petting to bathing. In order for the cat to learn to accept and enjoy a variety of types of physical contact from humans, it is critical that the human hand only be associated with positive experiences and that all physical punishment be avoided. Begin with those types of handling that the cat enjoys or is willing to accept, and provide small treats at each of the first few sessions. Once the cat learns to associate food with these sessions, slightly longer or intense sessions can be practiced. This type of handling can be used to help the cat become accustomed to, and perhaps enjoy, patting, grooming, teeth brushing, nail trimming, and even bathing. Never force this type of handling upon your cat as any negative experience will only make the problem worse and the cat more resistant to further handling.

It is important to remember that physical discipline is inappropriate. It can scare your cat and make him or her afraid of being picked up or held. If required, kittens should be discouraged from repeating inappropriate behaviors, by the use of punishment devices such as, remote control devices and booby-traps (see 'controlling undesirable behavior in cats').

I want to get a cat but I live on a very busy main road so I am thinking of keeping it indoors. Is that cruel?

For many people the thought of keeping a cat totally indoors seems to fly in the face of everything that the species stands for and certainly there is a lot to be said for cats having the freedom to roam around a wider territory and to come into contact with other cats and with natural prey. However, there are many certain circumstances in which keeping a cat indoors may be safer for the cat and therefore, arguably, better for the cat. Indoor cats are at lower risk for injuries associated with the outdoor environment (cars, trains, dogs, predators, humans, etc.) and are at far less risk of contracting parasites and more serious diseases such as feline leukemia, feline infectious peritonitis and feline immunodeficiency virus. Studies have consistently shown that urban cats that go outdoors have far shorter life spans (averaging two years), while most indoor cats live over 15 years. Keeping cats indoors also prevents killing of wildlife, fouling of neighborhood yards, and fighting with other cats. Depending on your cat's personality, it may be safer for other cats and wildlife in the neighborhood if you keep your cat indoors.

If you decide to keep your cat as an indoor pet, you will need to be very aware of the extra responsibility that an indoor cat brings. You must take the time and trouble to ensure that the indoor environment offers the cat the opportunity to express as many of its natural behaviors as possible.

What do I need to do to make my indoor cat happy?

The most important thing for you to consider when you decide to keep a cat indoors is how you are going to provide for its behavioral needs. Obviously you will have thought about the need for food, water, elimination, and warmth, but have you considered your cat's need to hunt, its need to be able to retreat and hide and its need to feel in control. Providing for the behavioral needs of a cat is not difficult but it does require some time, some thought and some commitment.

Why does my cat need to hunt when I feed it so well?

The feline desire to hunt is not connected to the sensation of hunger and no matter how well you feed your cat it will still react to the sight and sound of prey with an instinctive stalk. Obviously indoor cats are unlikely to come across natural prey, but anything that moves rapidly or squeaks in a high pitch can trigger the same behavioral response. Toys are therefore essential for an indoor cat and you need to make sure that the ones that you buy are attractive to your pet. Those that squeak and can be moved rapidly and unpredictably are probably the best. You can also select toys that mimic real prey in terms of size, texture and color. Small toys, and it is worth remembering that small toys that resemble mice rather than rats, are usually more successful! Play sessions for indoor cats need to be frequent and regular and if your cat is interested and willing you should aim to give your cat at least three play sessions of 10 minutes, every day. You can have hours of fun playing with your cat, but remember that the independent action of hunting is important, so do not be tempted to get too involved in the play sessions and give your cat plenty of opportunity to catch its prey. If you do not want to induce your cat to ambush your hands and ankles later on, it is also worth avoiding any predatory play with human flesh, so hands and feet under the covers and running fingers across the back of the sofa are not advisable.

How do I ensure that my cat has enough to occupy its time?

One of the most important considerations for an indoor cat is how you are going to occupy it 24 hours a day. Of course cats are famous for their desire to sleep and it is certainly true that your cat will be happy to wile away many an hour in front of the fire or next to the radiator. However, indoor cats do need access to activity that will stimulate both their mind and their body and provide the exercise that they would naturally engage in if they were out and about. Cat aerobic centers offer climbing, hiding and playing opportunities and can be ideal for indoor cats. Your cat needs to have easy access to the center and to be able to get at it from a number of different angles. If possible, you should put it in the middle of a room rather than in a corner or under the stairs. Scratching posts are also essential, since there is no opportunity for your cat to condition its claws on the shed roof or the fence post. You need to make sure that the post is tall enough to allow your cat to get a good position on the scratching surface.

Should I feed my cat at specific times or should I leave food down in the bowl all of the time?

Cats are not social feeders and therefore set meal times are not of any inherent benefit to them. Ad lib systems that allow the cat to eat when it wants to and to consume small amounts frequently, are most natural. It is important to remember that wild cats need to hunt and kill their prey before they can eat and that the whole feeding process takes some considerable time. On average 1 in 15 hunting expeditions will be successful per day and in order to acquire enough food to survive most cats need in excess of 100 hunting expeditions a day. This can take between 6 and 8 hours a day and it is not hard to see how simply providing ad lib food in a bowl is likely to leave most cats with a lot of time on their hands! Cats that have access to outdoors will compensate by spending time hunting insects, but for an indoor cat there has to be another approach. One solution is to put a proportion of the cat's daily food ration in a puzzle feeder, which the cat needs to work at in order to gain access to the food, and another is to scatter the food around the house and let the cat hunt it out. Puzzle feeders do not need to be expensive and you can easily make your own from an old plastic drink bottle. All you need to do is cut holes in the bottle which are just a little larger than the diameter of the dried cat food, and then file the holes so that there are no sharp edges that could harm your cat. Fill the bottle with dry food and then watch your cat play with the bottle and get rewarded as the food falls through the holes. Commercial toys that deliver food when chewed or manipulated are also available.

Does my cat need to climb?
The picture of a cat stuck in a tree or stranded on a roof top is a familiar one but the fact is that cats need to climb. Getting up high is an important way to relieve stress in the feline world and when your cat is feeling under pressure its instinct will be to move upwards. It is therefore very important to have accessible high up resting places and while built-in wardrobes may be great in terms of space saving for people you need to realize that they are not so good for your cat! Tops of fridge freezers, bookcases and stereo hi-fi cabinets are all popular resting places for cats, but if all of the furniture in your house is built-in you will need to make special provision for your cat in the form of shelves and radiator cradles. High vantage points allow your cat to observe the world from a place of safety. When it is not allowed the option of escaping through the cat flap these vantage points become all the more important.

If my cat hides on top of the furniture or spends its time behind the sofa should I be concerned?
Hiding is an important coping strategy for cats and when a cat is spending considerable amounts of time hiding it is important to examine why. In a cat that has recently moved into a home hiding may be a perfectly normal response to the overwhelming amount of new information. In a cat that has been resident in the house for some time hiding is likely to be a sign that all is not well. If it is possible to identify the reason for the hiding then it is important to treat that first. In many cases no clear cause can be found and in these situations you need to resist the temptation to bring the cat out to face the world. Hiding serves a purpose for the solitary hunter who needs

to assess potential danger from a safe haven and simply denying the chance to hide will make things harder for the cat. Instead you should allow your pet to withdraw into safety, at least in the short term, and then work to make the home so appealing that it cannot resist the temptation to join in. If hiding persists and is accompanied by lack of appetite you should consult your veterinarian for advice.

I would like to give my cat some fresh air but I am not sure if it will walk on a lead is there any alternative?

Some cats may need to be kept permanently indoors and this can work as long as owners are aware of the responsibility that it brings. For others access to outdoors needs to be restricted, but owners would like to offer some contact with the world outside and in these cases there are a number of alternatives. The harness and lead approach is certainly one, but you are right to mention the fact that not all cats will learn to walk in this way. Introducing harnesses as early as possible will help and making a kitten accustomed to the lead will minimize resistance to its use as an adult. If you have tried introducing your cat to the harness and you have been met with overwhelming resistance you may wish to consider the use of an outdoor pen. Since cats can climb, the pen will either need a roof to prevent escape or have the sides angled inward at the top to prevent climbing over. There are a number of commercial cat containment products for both indoor and outdoor use. Ideally the pen will be accessed from the house via a cat door flap and will offer the cat access to outdoors while offering you complete peace of mind. If a pen is to be used successfully it should mimic the outside world as closely as possible and cat furniture, tree trunks, toys, scratching posts and high up resting places should all be available within the pen.

MARKING BEHAVIORS

What is spraying?

Spraying is the deposition of small amounts of urine on vertical surfaces. The spraying cat may be seen to back into the area, the tail may quiver, and with little or no crouching the urine is released. Although much less common, some cats will also mark their territory by leaving small amounts of urine or occasionally stool on horizontal surfaces.

Why do cats "mark" with urine?

Cats mark the locations where they live or where they frequent in many ways. Cats will mark with scent glands on their feet, cheeks, face and tail as well as with urine. Cheek rubbing (bunting) and scratching (with both the odor from the glands in the footpads and the visual mark) are both forms of marking. Deposition of an odor communicates that the animal was in a location long after that animal has gone. Cats will mark their territory to signal "ownership" and to advertise sexual receptivity and availability. Marking can occur due to other cats in the vicinity either outdoors, or among cats that live in the same household. Cats will also mark their territory when they feel threatened or stressed. This can occur with a change in household routine, compositions, living arrangements, new living locations and other environmental and social changes. In these cases the marking pattern may be related to new objects brought into the household, or the possessions of family members, especially those with which there is the greatest source of conflict or insecurity. Because marking is a method of delineating territory, urine is often found in prominent locations, at entry and exit points to the outdoors such as doors and windows and around the periphery. When outdoors, cats might tend to mark around the periphery of their property, prominent objects on the property, new

objects (e.g. a new tree) introduced into the property, and locations where other cats have marked.

Which cats are more likely to urine mark?

Both male and female cats can mark with urine. Urine marking is most common in intact (non-neutered) male cats. When an intact male sprays urine, it will have the characteristic "tom cat" odor that is strong and pungent. Neutering will change the odor, and may reduce the cat's motivation for spraying, but approximately 10% of neutered males and 5% of spayed females will continue to spray. While cats in multiple cat households are often involved in spraying behaviors, cats that are housed singly may spray as well.

Instead of spraying, I am finding multiple locations of small amounts of urine. What does that mean?

Some cats will mark their territory with small amounts of urine (and on rare occasions, stool) in various locations. These locations can be similar to those for spraying, i.e. near doors, windows, new possessions in the home or favored locations, but may occasionally be found on owner's clothing or other favored possessions. However, small amounts of urine deposited outside of the litterbox is more commonly due to litter box avoidance which could have many causes including diseases of the lower urinary tract. Similarly stool found outside of the litter box can be due to a multitude of causes including colitis, constipation and any other condition leading to difficult, more frequent or uncomfortable elimination. As with any other elimination problem, a complete physical examination and laboratory tests are necessary to rule out each physical cause.

How do I treat a spraying or marking problem?

As with all behavior problems, the history will help determine treatment options. The location of the urine marking, the frequency, duration and number of locations are important. The number of cats both inside and contacts outside of the home should be determined. Changes in environment, social patterns of humans and animals, and additions (people, pets, furniture, renovations) to the home should also be examined.

If the cat is not already neutered, and is not a potential breeder, castration is recommended. A urinalysis should be performed to rule out medical problems. The location of the urine spots should be determined. Is the urine found on walls, 6-8 inches up from the floor, or are there small urine spots found in multiple locations?

Treatment is aimed at decreasing the motivation for spraying. It has been shown that spraying may be reduced in some cases by reviewing and improving litterbox hygiene. Ideally the minimum number of litter boxes should equal the number of cats plus one, the litter should be cleaned daily and changed at least once a week, and proper odor neutralizing products should be used on any sprayed sites. In addition any factors that might be causing the cat to avoid the use of its litter should be considered (see 'house-soiling in cats' for more details).

If marking appears to be stimulated by cats outside of the home, then the best options are to find a way to deter the cats from coming onto the property or prevent the indoor cat from seeing, smelling or hearing these cats. See 'controlling undesirable behavior in cats' and 'behavior management products' for remote control devices and booby-traps that can be used to deter outdoor cats and to keep indoor cats away from the areas where they are tempted to mark. It may be helpful to house your cat in a room away from windows and doors to the outdoors, or it may be possible to block visual access to windows. When you are home and supervising you can allow your cat limited access to these areas. It also may be necessary to keep windows closed to prevent the inside cat from smelling the cats outside, and to use odor neutralizers (see 'behavior management products') on any areas where the outdoor cats have eliminated or sprayed.

If the problem is due to social interactions inside the home, it may be necessary to determine which cats do not get along. Keep these cats in separate parts of the home with their own litter and sleeping areas. Reintroduction of the cats may be possible when they are properly supervised. Allowing the cats together for positive experiences such as feeding, treats and play sessions, helps them to get used to the presence of each other, at least on a limited basis. However, when numbers of cats in a home reach 7-10 cats you will often have spraying and marking.

I've cleaned up the spot but the cat keeps returning to spray. What else can be done to reduce the problem?

Since the "purpose" of spraying is to mark an area with urine odor, it is not surprising that as the odor is cleaned up, the cat wants to refresh the area with more urine. Cleaning alone does little to reduce spraying. Cats that mark in one or two particular areas may cease if the function of the area is changed. It is unlikely that cats will spray in their feeding, sleeping or scratching areas. It has also been shown that cats that mark an area with cheek glands are less likely to mark in other ways such as with urine. In fact it might be said that cats that use their cheek glands are marking in a more calm, familiar manner while those that urine mark are doing so in a more reactive, anxious manner. A commercial product containing synthetic cheek gland scent has proven to be an effective way of reducing urine marking in some cats. When sprayed on areas where cats have sprayed urine or on those areas where it can be anticipated that the cat is likely to spray, it may decrease the likelihood of additional spraying in those areas. The scent of the pheromone may stimulate cheek gland marking (bunting), rather than urine spraying. In Europe the product is also available as an aerosol room diffuser. It has also been used to calm cats in new environments including the veterinary hospital and to help familiarize the cat with a new cage or cat carrier.

Where practical, a good compromise for some cats is to allow them one or two areas for marking. This can be done by placing a shower curtain on the vertical surface, tiling the area, or by taking two plastic litter boxes and placing one inside the other to make an L-shape (with the upright surface to catch the marked urine). Another option is to place booby-traps in the sprayed areas, but spraying of another area may then develop.

Are there any drugs that are available to treat this problem?

Over the years many pharmacological means have been tried to control spraying behaviors. The choices have focused on the theory that one of the underlying causes for spraying and marking behaviors is anxiety. For that reason, anti-anxiety drugs such as buspirone and the benzodiazepines, antidepressants such as amitriptyline, clomipramine, fluoxetine and paroxetine, and female hormones have all been tried with varying degrees of success. None of these are presently approved for use in cats. Dosing, cost, and the potential for side effects will all need to be considered in selecting the most appropriate drug for your cat (see 'behavior drug therapy').

MOVING WITH YOUR CAT

Will my cat be upset by the move?
Some cats seem to take moving in their stride, but for others the loss of their familiar territory can be very traumatic and settling in to the new home can pose problems for owners and cats alike. Cats are territorial creatures and when your cat is the new kid on the block it may find itself being less than welcomed by the local feline residents. Cats that are kept entirely indoors may adapt more easily to a new home, since their territory still contains familiar people, animals and objects, and integration into an existing feline population is not an issue. However, indoor cats can develop behavioral problems following a house move and whether your cat lives indoors or out, the way in which you prepare it for the move and deal with the first few days in the new home can be very important.

Preparing for the move
Feline territory is divided into three main zones: the core, the home range and the hunting range. The core territory is where the cat eats, sleeps and plays and in the wild this area is very stable and secure. For the domestic cat the core territory is usually represented by the house, although for some cats it may be smaller and consist of one or two rooms within the house, and disruption within this area can be very distressing. Minimizing changes and upheaval within the core territory is important and when you are preparing for the house move it may be advisable to keep the boxes and suitcases out of view so that the home remains as constant as possible for your cat. Obviously there comes a point where the packing cannot be hidden. At this point, if your cat seems overly anxious or if conflict induced behavior problems (such as excessive grooming or urine marking) begin to emerge then it might be best to put your cat in a kennel, rather than allow it to watch the dismantling of its territory.

How should I introduce my cat to the new house?
Once you have moved into your new home it is advisable to wait until at least one room in the house is completely unpacked before bringing your cat into the house. This ensures that the environment that your cat comes into

is as stable as possible. Restricting the cat's access to the rooms where the unpacking has been finished is a sensible precaution, since the packing boxes and suitcases are likely to be a symbol of disruption and signal to your cat that this new environment is less than secure. Introducing your cat to one room at a time will also prevent problems of overwhelming it with too much new territory too quickly. Therefore, even if you are a very efficient unpacker and have all of your rooms up and running within days, it can still be beneficial to restrict access to one or two rooms for the first few days.

Using scent signals

One of the ways in which you can increase your cat's acceptance of its new territory is to make it as familiar as possible. The first room you place your cat into should perhaps be one that will have some furniture that is familiar to the cat from the previous home. Putting your cat's bedding and food bowls from the old house into the room should also help. In addition you may find it beneficial to a synthetic feline facial scent, to the room. This product, which is available from your veterinarian, acts to make the environment appear familiar to your cat and will help it to settle in. It would be sensible to apply the product to the room at least 30 minutes before your cat goes inside and to top up the scent profile by applying the product once a day for the first week. As you expand your cat's territory within the home by giving it access to more and more rooms you should use the product in each new area.

How long will my cat take to settle in at the new house?

There is no easy answer to this question as every cat is an individual and will react differently to the challenge of a new home. Most cats start to relax within a few days of moving, but there are others that take weeks to adjust to their new environment. One of the most important coping strategies for cats when they face a new challenge is hiding and it is important to resist the temptation to bring your cat out from his hiding places. It can be distressing for owners to see their cat huddled on the top of a dresser or peering out from under the table, but you need to give your cat the opportunity to observe its new home from a safe vantage point and to come to terms with the changes in its own time. Forcing cats to come out to meet the world (or to do anything for that matter) can seriously back fire and make the settling in process far more drawn out in the long run. Obviously if your cat shows no signs of adjusting, or if it refuses to eat for more than a couple of days, you will need to take action and you should consult your veterinarian for advice. The aim is to encourage your cat to come down from his safe haven. Work to make the home more attractive in feline terms using tasty food treats and special play to fulfill the cat's need for affection or attention. However, it is important to remember that cats need to feel in control and the treats or games should not be forced on the pet. Instead they should be provided as soon as the cat voluntarily displays any small progress (baby steps).

When can I let my cat out into the yard?

For owners of cats that go outside one of the hardest decisions to make after moving is when, if ever to open the door and let the cat out! There are a number of myths concerning this subject and various techniques have been suggested as ways of ensuring that the cat comes home again, such as putting butter on the cat's paws! Cats live in a scent-orientated world and they find their way from place to place by following scent gradients. This means that your cat will return home to where his scent signal is strongest provided there is no strong fear or anxiety associated with the new home. Therefore the practice of restricting your pet to the new home for a couple of weeks makes perfect sense. By staying inside the house for this period your cat will build up a strong scent presence and any fear or apprehension about the new household will have diminished or disappeared. Then when the cat eventually ventures outside, there will be a significant scent gradient to follow back to the house and no feelings of avoidance. A feline facial scent can also be used to assist in the forming of a stable scent profile and some sources suggest that it encourages cats to return to their new home, so that the amount of time your cat needs to be kept confined before letting it out for the first time can be decreased. It can help to give the first taste of freedom at a time when the cat is most likely to stay close at hand and waiting until just before mealtime can be a sensible approach. With the prospect of a meal looming your cat should be eager to stay near to the house and if you call it in for dinner just a few minutes after letting it out, you will be reinforcing the behavior of coming home.

What can I do to stop my cat from returning to my old house?

When owners move relatively short distances, one of the most common problems that they face is their cat returning to the old house. There are numerous tales of cats walking significant distances to get back to their old home and while some go straight to the house and demand to be let in, others seem content to sit in their old garden or wander round their old hunting ground. There are two possible approaches to this problem. Firstly, to increase the attraction of the new home, in feline terms, and secondly to decrease the reward associated with the old home.

It is possible to increase the bond to the new house and yard by ensuring that positive associations are made in the form of provision of valuable resources. Working to ensure that food, shelter, affection, and privacy are available in abundant supply will help to maintain the cat's interest in its home. However, the way in which these resources are offered is important and owners need to guard against being too overpowering with their pets. Too much human intervention in the form of oppressive affection and high levels of owner initiated contact may be too much for some cats and are likely to increase the likelihood of avoidance. In that case adopting an off hand attitude, that leaves the cat asking for more attention and affection, will be far more effective. Games with a fishing rod toy can be very helpful as they give you the opportunity to interact with your cat while still allowing it to engage in some independent play. Offering food treats without trying to make any direct interaction can be another way of rewarding your cat for staying home while allowing it to feel in control.

Decreasing the value associated with the old stomping ground can be a little more difficult, especially for a cat that is an efficient hunter! If the old patch had a good supply of prey, and the cat was frequently rewarded on its hunting expeditions, it can be very hard to convince the cat that returning "home" is not a good idea. However, if the reward appears to be strongly associated with the house, and with the warmth, comfort and security it offers, things can be a little more straightforward. Co-operation with the new occupants is essential, since they need to work to make the old home less appealing, and this is usually much easier if they are not particularly fond of cats! Making sure that there is no food available when the cat returns and using hostile interactions with sounds and water or avoidance devices (see 'behaviour management products') can help to make the old place much less appealing. This may sound simple but it is important that the hostility is consistent and is not simply connected with the new inhabitants, because cats can very quickly learn to only come by when the new people are out! Equally any hostility must not be harmful and people need to be prepared to use their brains as well as their brawn when trying to outwit a cat.

Obviously a combination of these two approaches will offer the very best chance of keeping the cat at the new house.

Will there be problems with other cats in the neighbourhood?

One of the major concerns for owners of outdoor cats is the potential conflict from other cats in the new neighborhood. It is certainly true that newcomers are not made particularly welcome in the feline world, but one of the most significant effects of neutering on feline behavior is to decrease hostility to outsiders. In an urban area where most of the cat population is neutered this certainly helps.

Integration into the local population is largely a feline matter and there is little that owners can do to smooth the process, but it can be helpful to talk to other cat owners in the area and work out a time share system for the first week or so. This enables the newcomer to explore the neighborhood without risk of attack and to leave some scent signals for the resident cats to read. Such indirect communication can smooth the way for the first face-to-face encounters since the incoming cat has a familiar scent.

NEUTERING

Most male animals that are kept for companionship, work, or food production (horses, dogs, cats, bulls, boars) are neutered (castrated) unless they are intended to be used as breeding stock. This is a common practice to prevent unacceptable sexual behavior, reduce aggressiveness, and prevent accidental or indiscriminate breeding. The intact male (tomcat) is likely to roam, fight with other males, and spray and is of course, strongly attracted to seek out and mate with intact females. Tomcat urine is particularly odorous. Overall the intact male cat can make a most unpleasant household companion.

How does castration affect behavior?

The only behaviors affected by castration are those under the influence of male hormones (sexually dimorphic behaviors). A cat's temperament, training, and personality are the result of genetics and upbringing, and are generally unaffected by the presence or absence of male hormones. Castration is unlikely to calm an overactive cat or decrease aggression toward people. Since the male brain is masculinized by the time of birth, castration will reduce some, but not all of the sexually dimorphic male behaviors. If performed prior to sexual maturity castration will help to prevent the development of secondary sexual characteristics such as penile barbs, large jowls and glands at the dorsal part of the cat's tail.

What is neutering?

The operation of neutering or castration of male cats is called an orchidectomy. The procedure involves general anesthesia, and an incision is made over each side of the scrotal sac so that each testicle can be excised. External sutures are not generally required. In males both testicles descend prior to birth from inside the abdominal cavity through the inguinal canal into the scrotal sac. In some cats one or both testicles do not descend fully into the sac and may either remain in the abdomen or anywhere along the inguinal canal path to the scrotal sac. These cats are called cryptorchid and a more extensive surgery will be required to locate the testicles and remove them. If these testicles are not removed they will continue to produce hormones and the behavior problems associated with intact male cats. Vasectomies are not performed in cats. It is both sterilization and removal of the male hormones that provide the behavioral benefits.

What are the benefits of neutering?

POPULATION CONTROL

Millions of cats are destroyed across North America each year because there are far more cats born than homes available. A single male cat can father many litters so that neutering of intact males is essential for population control. Although sexual desire will be greatly reduced by castration, some experienced males may continue to show sexual interest in females.

SPRAYING

The most common behavior problem in cats of all ages is indoor elimination at locations other than the litter box. A large number of these cases are cats that spray or mark walls and other vertical household objects. Adult male cats have an extremely strong urge to mark territory, both indoors and out. Neutering reduces or eliminates spraying in approximately 85% of male cats.

AGGRESSION

Cats, whether neutered or intact, can get into fights but most inter-cat aggression is seen between intact males. This is a direct result of competition between male cats, and because intact male cats roam and protect a much larger territory. If these fights lead to punctures that penetrate the skin abscesses are a common sequel. Neutering reduces fighting and abscess development in male cats.

ROAMING AND SEXUAL ATTRACTION

Intact males have much larger territories and wander over greater distances than females and neutered males. The urge to roam may be particularly strong during mating season. Castration reduces roaming in approximately 90% of cases. Neutering greatly reduces sexual interest, but some experienced males may continue to be attracted to, and mate with females.

PHYSICAL CHANGES

Male urine odor is particularly strong and pungent. Castration leads to a change to a more normal urine odor. Many owners claim that their intact males become much cleaner, less odorous, and better self-groomers after neutering. Abscess formation as a result of fighting is far less frequent and some of the secondary sexual characteristics such as the over-productive tail glands in the condition known as "stud tail" can be dramatically improved.

Does neutering lead to any adverse effects on health or behavior?

There are many misconceptions about the effects of neutering on health and behavior. Neutered males are no more likely to become fat or lazy provided they receive a proper diet and adequate exercise. With less roaming, fighting, mating, calorie intake may have to be reduced and alternative forms of play and activity provided. Behaviors that have developed independent of hormonal influences such as hunting are not affected. Regardless of age at which it is performed, neutering does not have any effect on physical development, (overall height and weight, urethral size). Although neutering prior to puberty appears to have similar effects to neutering post-puberty, every attempt should be made to neuter prior to puberty before the cat develops new problems, experiences and habits.

PLAY & INVESTIGATIVE BEHAVIORS

How does play develop in kittens?

Young kittens play using chasing and pouncing behaviors that seem to have their origin in predation. Predatory play is an integral part of feline play behavior and early learning. This play in a kitten is often aggressive and intense. Kittens begin social play as early as 5 weeks and continue at a high level until about 12 -14 weeks. Object play develops at 7-8 weeks when kittens develop eye-paw co-ordination needed to deal with small moving objects. Full development of locomotion occurs between 10-12 weeks and as a kitten becomes more coordinated play may become more intense. Kittens are attracted to moving objects and will chase and stalk them. Play is an important component of kitten development, and proper play and exercise should be encouraged.

What is the best way to play with my kitten?

Kittens use multiple objects as prey items when they play. This play behavior consists of stalking, pouncing, jumping, biting and clawing. Small objects that can easily be moved with paws and grasped in the mouth or between the feet are often preferred. Avoid objects that are so small that they could be ingested and cause intestinal blockage. Some kittens like to play with a linear object like string. This can cause severe intestinal dysfunction if eaten and should only be used under supervision.

Avoid playing with your hands as you interact with your kitten. This can be dangerous and lead to human injury. The moving hand can become an appealing play object and attempts at correction could aggravate the situation. Although young kittens may not inflict damage, as it ages and continues to use the owner's body for play, serious injuries can result.

Cats are stimulated by simulated prey so that wands and toys that can be pulled along or dangled in front of the cat and laser lights are generally most effective. Fishing rod type toys and long wands with prey type toys (feather toys, catnip mice) on the end can be used to encourage play without contact with the owner's body. Some cats are also attracted by the light from a laser toy. Young kittens will often fetch small fleece toys, or bat them across the floor.

Why is my cat always getting into mischief?

Another important part of the development of young animals is the need for exploration and investigation of new objects and new environments. These behaviors can lead to damage to the home as well as injury to the kitten. Preventing these problems is quite simple; you accept your cat's needs to play and investigate. When the owner is not around or available to supervise, the cat can be provided with a variety of toys that can be batted, chased or pounced upon. Toys stuffed with food or catnip, toys that release food when manipulated, battery operated or mechanical toys that the cat can paw or chase, and toys that can be dangled from doors or play centers are just a few of the self-play toys that are enticing to some cats. Your cat should also be provided with suitable opportunities and outlets for scratching, climbing, perching and relaxing. These could include posts and toys designed for scratching, shelves, counters, windowsills and play centers for perching, and paper bags, cardboard boxes or hidden treats for exploration. Cats that chew and scavenge might be provided with higher bulk foods, chew toys, dental foods, dental toys or even a small herb garden to try and satisfy this need.

How can I prevent damage when I am not available to supervise?

When the cat cannot be supervised leave it in a cat-proof area, with soft comfortable bedding and a litter box for elimination. Although a large dog kennel may be an acceptable form of confinement for short departures, most cats can be confined in one or a few rooms that have been effectively cat-proofed. This allows the cat some freedom while preventing damage and injuries. Child locks and secure containers can be used to keep your cat out of cupboards or garbage cans. Any of your possessions or household objects that might be clawed, pounced on, explored, or knocked flying, should be either kept out of the cat's reach or booby-trapped. Remember that with their excellent ability to jump and climb, damage prevention may also be needed far above floor level.

Booby-trapping can be used to teach your cat to "stay away" from specified areas by making the sites unpleasant. Before making an area unpleasant, the cat must have access to appropriate outlets to meet its innate needs. The cat should be provided with a post for scratching, some ledges or shelves for climbing and perching, and a few play toys that can be swatted, batted, or chased. Cat toys on springs and those that are hung from doors or play centers, ping-pong balls, "whole walnuts", or catnip mice are often fun for cats to chase and attack. Cat play centers can be purchased or constructed to provide areas for perching and scratching in a relatively small compact area. Some cats like to explore new objects, so a few empty boxes or paper bags (never plastic) will keep some cats entertained until the owner has time to play. Sometimes the best solution is to get a second cat for companionship and play. Be certain that the second cat is young, sociable and playful.

Although some people think of confinement, cat-proofing and booby-trapping as unnecessary or cruel, they are precautionary measures to keep the cat safe and prevent damage to the household when the owners are not available to supervise. Common owner complaints such as chewing on plants, scratching, climbing or playing in inappropriate locations, or elimination outside of the litter area, are just a few of the potential problems that can best be prevented with a little planning and forethought. Then, when a family member is home and available to supervise, your cat should be given more freedom to explore and become accustomed to those areas of the home where problems might otherwise occur.

How can I successfully booby-trap areas where problems persist?

Booby-trapping areas may be a simple matter of making the area less appealing by placing a less appealing surface in the area (such as a sheet of plastic or tin foil) or an uncomfortable surface on the area (double-sided sticky tape, plastic carpet runner with nubs up). Home made booby-traps can be constructed in a Rube-Goldberg set-up, by placing a stack of cups or empty soda cans that tumble down, balloons set to pop, or a water container poised to spill on the cat when disturbed. Commercial products such as motion detectors, mats that emit an alarm or mild electronic stimulation on contact, or mousetrap trainers are also available (see 'behavior management products').

What problems are associated with play?

There are a number of behavior problems that arise out of over-exuberant and inappropriate play. Some examples are cats that rambunctiously tear around the household, those that swat at or pounce on the owners (sometimes escalating into bites and injuries), and those that grasp, nip, bite or swat at the owners throughout the night.

How can over-exuberant play and play attacks toward people be prevented?

Before any attempts at stopping or interrupting the behavior are attempted, provide sufficient opportunities and outlets for play. Choose play toys and activities that are appealing to the individual cat. Since play that is initiated by the cat could potentially escalate into overly aggressive play, the owner should select play toys and initiate all play sessions. Sessions initiated by the cat should be ignored or interrupted using a distraction device, such as the ones listed below.

How can over-exuberant play and play attacks toward people be interrupted?

Although interruption devices may be effective, physical punishment should be avoided. First, pain can cause aggression. If you hit your cat you may increase the aggressive behavior. Second, painful punishment causes fear and owner avoidance. Third, owners that attempt to correct the playful aggression with physical contact may actually serve to reward the behavior.

For punishment to be effective it must be timed to occur while the behavior is taking place. Punishment should be species appropriate. Noise deterrents are often effective in cats. For very young kittens, a "hissing" noise may deter excessive play behavior. The noise can be made by you, but if not immediately successful a can of compressed air (used for cleaning camera lenses) may be more effective and less likely to cause fear or retaliation. Some cats need an even harsher noise. Commercially available "rape" alarms or air horns make extremely loud noises that will startle the cat and interrupt the behavior. What is most important in using these techniques is the timing. You must have the noisemaker with you so that you can immediately administer the correction (see 'controlling undesirable behavior in cats' and 'play aggression').

SCRATCHING & DECLAWING

Why do cat's scratch?

Scratching is a normal feline behavior. Although scratching does serve to shorten and condition the claws, the primary reasons that cats scratch are to mark their territory and to stretch. Some cats may increase their territorial marking (e.g. scratching, urine marking) in situations of anxiety or conflict. Cats may also threaten or play with a swipe of their paws.

For cats that live primarily outdoors, scratching is seldom a problem for the owners. Scratching is usually directed at prominent objects such as tree trunks or fence posts. Play swatting with other cats seldom leads to injuries because cats have a fairly thick skin and coat for protection. When play does get a little rough, most cats are pretty good at sorting things out between themselves. Occasionally, rough play or territorial fighting does lead to injuries or abscesses that would require veterinary attention.

Cats that live primarily or exclusively indoors may run into disfavor with their owners when they begin to scratch furniture, walls, or doors, or when they use their claws to climb up, or hang from the drapes. Claws can also cause injuries to people when the cats are overly playful or don't like a particular type of handling or restraint. With a good understanding of cat behavior and a little bit of effort, it should be possible to prevent or avoid most clawing problems, even for those cats that live exclusively indoors.

Cats that go outdoors may be content to scratch when outside, and leave the walls and furniture intact when indoors. Cats that spend most of their time indoors, however, will usually require an area for indoor scratching, climbing, and play.

How can I stop my cat from scratching?

It is impractical and unfair to expect cats to stop scratching entirely. Cats that go outside may be content to do all their scratching outdoors, but the urge may still arise when the cat comes back indoors. Cats that spend most of their time indoors will of course, need some outlet for their scratching and marking behaviors so don't be surprised if you come home to objects strewn all over the floor, scratches on your furniture, and your cat playfully climbing or dangling from your drapes. Therefore, while it may not be possible to stop a cat from scratching, it should be possible to direct the scratching, climbing and play to appropriate areas indoors. Building or designing a scratching post, providing appropriate play toys, and keeping the cat away from potential problem areas will usually be adequate to deal with most scratching problems.

How do I design a scratching area for my cat?

Since cats use their scratching posts for marking and stretching, posts should be set up in prominent areas, with at least one close to the cat's sleeping quarters. The post should be tall enough for the cat to scratch while standing on hind legs with the forelegs extended and sturdy enough so that it does not topple when scratched. Some cats prefer a scratching post with a corner so that two sides can be scratched at once while other cats may prefer a horizontal scratching post. Special consideration should be given to the surface texture of the post. Commercial posts are often covered with tightly woven material for durability, but many cats prefer a loosely woven material where the claws can hook and tear during scratching. Remember that scratching is also a marking behavior and cats want to leave a visual mark. Carpet may be an acceptable covering but it should be combed first to make certain that there are no tight loops. Some cats prefer sisal, a piece of material from an old chair, or even bare wood for scratching. Be certain to use a material that appeals to your cat.

How can I get my cat to use its post?

A good way to get the cat to approach and use the post is to turn the scratching area into an interesting and desirable play center. Perches to climb on, space to climb into, and toys mounted on ropes or springs are highly appealing to most cats. Placing a few play toys, cardboard boxes, catnip treats, or even the food bowl in the area should help to keep the cat occupied. Sometimes rubbing the post with tuna oil will increase its attractiveness. Food rewards can also be given if the owner observes the cat scratching at its post. Products have been designed to reward the cat automatically by dispensing food rewards each time the cat scratches. It may also be helpful to take the cat to the post, gently rub its paws along the post in a scratching motion, and give it a food reward. This technique should not be attempted, however, if it causes any fear or anxiety. Placement is important when trying to entice your cat to use a scratching post. Because scratching is also a marking behavior, most cats prefer to use a post that is placed in a prominent location. It may be necessary to place the post in the center of a room or near furniture that the cat was trying to scratch until the cat reliably uses it and then move it to a less obtrusive location. For some cats, multiple posts in several locations will be necessary.

What can I do if the cat continues to scratch my furniture?

Despite the best of plans and the finest of scratching posts, some cats may continue to scratch or climb in inappropriate areas. At this point a little time, effort, and ingenuity might be necessary. The first thing to consider is partial confinement or "cat-proofing" your home when you are not around to supervise. If the problem occurs in a few rooms, consider making them out of bounds by closing off a few doors or by using child-proofing techniques such as child locks or barricades. The cat may even have to be kept in a single room that has been effectively cat proofed, whenever the owner cannot supervise. Of course the cat's scratching post, play center, toys, and litter box should be located in this cat-proof room.

If cat-proofing is not possible or the cat continues to use one or two pieces of furniture, you might want to consider moving the furniture, or placing a scratching post directly in front of the furniture that is being scratched. Take a good look at the surfaces of the scratched furniture and ensure that the surface of the post is covered with a material similar to those for which the cat has shown a preference. Some scratching posts are even designed to be wall mounted or hung on doors. Placing additional scratching posts in strategic areas may also be helpful for some cats. Another option is to try using a feline facial scent on scratched surfaces. This may help to reduce scratching at these sites but the cat will still need alternate areas to scratch. Keeping the cat's nails properly trimmed or using plastic nail covers, are also useful techniques for some owners.

How do I punish my cat for inappropriate scratching?

All forms of physical punishment should be avoided since they can cause fear or aggression toward the owners, and at best, the cat will only learn to stop the scratching while the owner is around. Indirect, non-physical forms of punishment may be useful if the owner can remain out of sight while administering the punishment. In this way the cat may learn that scratching is unpleasant even when the owner is not present. Water rifles, ultrasonic or audible alarms, or remote controlled devices are sometimes useful.

Generally, the best deterrents are those that train the pet not to scratch, even in the owners absence. If the surface or area can be made less appealing or unpleasant, the cat will likely seek out a new area or target for scratching, which will hopefully be its scratching post. The simplest approach is to cover the scratched surface with a less appealing material (plastic, a loosely draped piece of material, aluminum foil, or double-sided tape). Another effective deterrent is to booby-trap problem areas so that either scratching or approaching the area is unpleasant for the cat (e.g. motion detectors or a stack of plastic cups that is set to topple when the cat scratches). Of course, neither remote punishment nor booby-traps will successfully deter inappropriate scratching, unless the cat has an alternative scratching area that is comfortable, appealing, well located, and free of all deterrents.

When should declawing be considered?

Declawing is a drastic but permanent solution for scratching problems, but for most households the techniques discussed previously are generally quite successful. There are some homes however, where declawing may be the only option if the pet is to be kept. In fact, in one study it was estimated that as many as 50% of cat owners who declawed their cats would not have otherwise kept the cat. This might be the case where the cat continues to damage the furniture, or where the cat causes injuries to people during play or handling. Even the slightest scratch can have serious consequences (cat scratch fever) when a member of the household suffers from a severely debilitating disease. In some cases the issue comes down to whether the owner should be able to keep their cat and have it declawed, or whether it should be removed from the home. Although it has been estimated that approximately 25% of cats are declawed in North America, declawing is illegal in many countries outside North America.

What is the effect of declawing on the cat?

Many authors have written of dire behavioral and surgical complications of declawing, but these reports are based on myths and anecdotes. In the past few years, a number of veterinary behaviorists and pet psychologists have studied the effects of declawing on the cat, the owner, and the cat-owner relationship. Some 10 scientific studies, have examined the consequences of declawing on the pet and on the pet-owner relationship. These studies show that declawing does not alter the cat's behavior. In fact, cats may continue to scratch furniture after declawing, but cause no damage. There is no increase in behavior problems. Declawed cats are not at greater risk of getting bitten or injured in cat fights. Owners of declawed cats report a higher number of good behaviors than the owners of clawed cats. Quite surprisingly the only recognized concern is a few days of post-surgical discomfort. Therefore be certain to discuss pain management options with your veterinarian prior to surgery.

When owners of declawed cats are asked to assess the effects of declawing on the cat owner relationship, declawing always met or surpassed their expectations, and over 70% indicated an improvement in their relationship with their cat. Declawing allows people to keep their cat and stop household damage. Normally, only the front claws need to be removed to prevent furniture damage.

What is a tendonectomy and how does it compare to declawing?

Another surgery to reduce scratching is a digital flexor tendonectomy which cuts the tendon on each claw so that it cannot be used for scratching. The surgery resulted in less post-operative pain for the first two days in comparison to declawing. However, after the tendonotomy you will need to regularly trim your cat's nails as they will continue to grow and may catch on furniture because they will no longer be conditioned and worn down by scratching. Therefore with special attention to pain management, declawing may be the preferable surgery for owners who cannot properly maintain their cat's nails.

SOCIAL BEHAVIOR & SELECTION OF A NEW KITTEN

What is socialization?

Socialization is the process during which the kitten develops relationships with other living beings in its environment.

What is habituation?

As cats develop, there are numerous stimuli (sounds, smells, sights and events) that when they are unfamiliar, can lead to fear and anxiety. Habituation is the process of getting used to and not reacting to those stimuli by continuous exposure under circumstances that have no untoward consequences.

What is localization?

Localization is the process during which the kitten develops attachment to particular places.

Why are these terms important?

Cats that receive insufficient exposure and contact with people, other animals and new environments during their first two months may develop irreversible fears, leading to timidity or aggression. Expose your kitten to as many stimuli (people, places and things), when they can most effectively socialize, localize, and habituate to these stimuli. The first 1 to 3 months of life are the most critical periods in the social development of the cat.

Are cats a social species?

Although they are fairly independent and can do well on their own, cats are quite social. Although feline social behavior has not been as extensively studied as for the dog, the domestic cat is much more social than has been traditionally reported. There are many situations where cats live together in groups and interact in a friendly manner. The composition of these groups differs from dog groupings. Usually they consist of mothers, daughters, aunts and grandmothers; female cats that are related. In large colonies, there may be many smaller related groups sharing the same space. Male cats will leave the group but return for breeding. Males that have been neutered join the group in much the same way as females. Colonies of feral (wild) cats will be found in areas where food is abundant and shared, such as barns, dumpsites or around fishing ports. The cats in the group will allogroom (lick each other) and allomark (rub against each other). They will share the raising of kittens, fostering others from different litters.

Do cats have "personalities"?

Research has shown that it may be possible to classify cat "personalities" similar to what has been done for dogs. One such study identified cats that were shy, timid or fearful and those that were confident. The timid cats took significantly longer to approach persons and be held by them. Another study identified cats that were "shy" and those that were "trusting". That research noted that trusting cats were trusting regardless of where they encountered people; while shy cats were more fearful the further from home they were encountered. Based on these and other studies there are two common personality types: (a) sociable, confident and easygoing; (b) timid, shy and unfriendly. Some other research has also indicated an active aggressive type as well. What influences the development of personality type? Not surprisingly studies have confirmed that not only is personality inherited from the mother, but that friendliness specifically is, in part, inherited from the father.

How does the mother cat (or queen) teach her kittens?

Cats are very good at observational learning. This occurs when an animal watches a behavior being performed by another. The queen starts to teach her kittens at a young age. From the queen, kittens learn elimination behaviors and predatory behavior. Kittens will begin to spend time in the litter box at about 30 days of age and will learn appropriate litter usage through observation of the queen and certain olfactory (smell) cues. If allowed access to prey, the queen will begin to bring them to her offspring at about 32 – 36 days of age and teach them to hunt. The kittens will also begin to be weaned and eat solid food at the same age. The choice of food is also influenced by the queen. Play between kittens is also an important part of social development, particularly for those kittens that will be housed with other cats later in life.

What can I do to improve my chances of having a social non-fearful cat?

a) **Selection:** The genetics of an individual cat plays a critical role in how sociable, playful, fearful, excitable, or domineering a kitten will become. The first issue in helping to ensure that a kitten will be friendly and social when it grows up is to choose an appropriate kitten for your family. Since cats have a variety of personality types, the question is whether these personality types can be determined at the time of selection. As kitten socialization begins to decline at about 7 weeks of age, selection testing may become increasingly more accurate after this age. Therefore assessing older kittens and adult cats may provide more accurate information.

In addition to genetics, early handling and the situations, people and other animals that your cat is exposed to during development, (especially during the primary socialization period), are important factors that contribute to your cat's adult personality. Therefore, knowledge of the breed, assessment of the kitten's parents and evaluation of the kitten's environment and upbringing are important considerations when selecting a kitten. Some important questions to ask are: Has there been adequate exposure to people, both adults and children? Has the kitten been handled frequently, preferably on a daily basis for at least 15 minutes? How does the kitten behave when picked up by prospective owners? Does it hiss, bite or scratch, or does the kitten purr and solicit affection? Does the kitten approach people or does it stand away? What has been the historical behavior of the queen and tom? Did they hunt and/or have access to prey? Do they have a good history of litter usage, and what type of litter material is used? What are the feeding habits and preferences of the parents? General observation of the temperament of both the kittens in the litter and the parents is helpful. Are they outgoing, shy or timid? Assessment of young kittens is likely of limited value if the kittens are still progressing through the primary socialization period, and the assessment of the parents may provide just as much information.

b) Early handling: Kittens that are stimulated and handled from birth are more confident, more social, more exploratory, faster to mature and are better able to handle stress as they develop. Early handling of kittens decreases their approach time to strangers and increases the amount of time that they stayed with them. The more handling the better but even 15 minutes a day will help to improve later behavior. Regular and frequent handling from birth increases the likelihood that the kitten will relate well to people when placed into a home after weaning at 6 to 9 weeks of age. Therefore, kittens obtained from a breeder or home where they have had frequent contact and interaction with the owners are likely to be more social and less fearful as they develop.

c) Socialization: Socialization of cats to people is variable. The two most important factors appear to be the cat's genetic personality, and the amount of socialization it receives during the sensitive period of socialization which is thought to be 3 – 7 weeks of age. Certainly, the greater exposure a kitten has to humans of all ages, other pets and novel situations, the better adjustment that kitten will have. Therefore the best options may be to obtain a kitten from a home where good socialization has already taken place, or to obtain a new kitten prior to 7 weeks of age and insure immediate socialization.

How best should I introduce my new kitten to my home?

Your interaction with your new kitten begins on the ride home. Cats should always be transported in some kind of carrier in the car. By teaching your kitten to ride in a confined location you are providing safety for your cat in future car rides. Upon arriving at home, place the kitten in a small, quiet area with food and a litter box. If the kitten is very tiny, a small litter box with lowered sides may be necessary at first. If possible, duplicate the type of litter material used in the previous home (see 'house-training – using the litter box').

The first place you put your new kitten should be inspected for nooks and crannies where a kitten might hide or get stuck. Often in a new environment, a kitten may look for a secluded place to hide. However, all kittens and cats will need to investigate their new surroundings. For a new kitten this is a more manageable task if you limit space available and initially supervise the kitten. When cats do investigate they use a random method of search. After your new kitten has had some quiet time in a restricted location, slowly allow access to other areas of the home.

Kittens are natural explorers and will use their claws to climb up onto anything possible. In the first few weeks slow access to the home will allow exploration as well as the ability to monitor the kitten's behavior.

TRAVEL RELATED PROBLEMS

Why are cats so reluctant to travel?

Cats are highly attached to territory, and movement away from that secure base is not something that is undertaken lightly! Travelling in cars, planes and other forms of human transport can be a very stressful experience for all concerned, in part, because the cat is no longer in control of its own experience. For some cats, being confined in a travel container adds insult to injury and the cat's fear of leaving its familiar surroundings is compounded by its fear of being enclosed.

My cat seems to get worse with every journey – why doesn't he get used to it?

For most cats travel is a relatively uncommon experience and there is simply not enough opportunity for any significant level of habituation to be achieved. Unlike dogs, who come to see the car as a chance to accompany their owners on what might be a fun and adventurous outing, most cats see travel as an entirely negative experience and the likely destinations of feline transport confirm this. Visiting destinations such as veterinary clinics, boarding kennels, and unfamiliar or new homes are probably the most common destinations for a travelling cat and none of these give much scope for teaching cats that transport is fun!

I want my cat to travel happily in the car – can I teach it?

Cats can certainly learn to enjoy car travel and there are cats that actively seek the inside of the family car and sit purring on the parcel shelf for the entire journey. In most cases these cats have been taught to travel and the best time to teach them is when they are very young. There is a period in the kitten's life when it is most open to new ideas and when it can come to accept just about anything as being normal, provided that it is fun! Unfortunately this period is very early in kittens and therefore the responsibility for introducing kittens to car travel would need to be undertaken by breeders, but few breeders have the time to ensure that all of their charges are taken for daily trips in the car. Realistically it will be the new owners who need to start the introduction process and, even when the primary period of sensitivity to habituation has passed, short frequent car trips that are pure pleasure will still be very valuable. Taking along a few treats or play toys and insuring that the first few trips are to pleasant destinations can help to insure only positive experiences. Although cats perching in the back window of a car may look cute it is important to ensure that your cat is under control during a journey and in most cases this will mean confining the cat to a carrier of some sort while it is in the car.

My cat reacts badly to the carrying basket – what can I do?

One of the major sources of stress for cats during travel is confinement within a cat carrier and the fact that the carriers are only used when the cat needs to go somewhere is highly significant. For many cats the destination is not particularly pleasant and very rapidly the cat will develop a strong negative association with the carrier, seeing it as a signal of the impending veterinary clinic or cattery. Training kittens to enjoy being in their carrying boxes can make these outings far less traumatic for all involved, but even when cats are older it is possible to break down the negative image of the carrier and work to make it a safe haven rather than a prison cell. The first step is to select the right sort of carrier for your cat and there are a number of things to consider. The ease of cleaning and the way in which you put the cat into, and take it out of, the carrier are factors that are likely to be determined by your own preferences, but the level of security that the carrier will offer to your pet will depend on the cat's personality. Some cats are far more relaxed when they can see what is going on around them and the wire basket is better for them, but others feel more secure when they are totally hidden from view and a solid cat carrier will be a better choice for these individuals. Whichever type of cat carrier you purchase the most important step in introducing it to your cat is keeping it on permanent display. If it is hidden away between uses there will be no opportunity for your cat to learn to like it, but if you keep it easily accessible you can increase its positive image by lining it with a warm blanket and putting cat treats inside for your cat to find. The idea is to let the cat explore the carrier without any interference from you so that he learns that being in it is fun.

I do not have time to introduce my cat to its carrier in this controlled way – what can I do to make the car trip next week more bearable?

If you have not had time to introduce your cat to its carrier it is important to take steps to make the confinement as stress free as possible. Putting familiar bedding inside the carrier, together with a favorite toy, can be useful. The idea is to make the carrier smell familiar and therefore reassure the cat that it is safe. Another possible way in which to increase the familiarity of the carrier is to apply a synthetic feline facial scent. This scent is believed to help the cat to relax during the journey and, in trials, it has been shown to significantly decrease the signs of stress in cats during car travel. In order to be most effective it must be applied to the interior of the carrier 30 minutes before you need to put your cat inside. This is important since the smell of the carrier for the product can disturb some cats and you need to leave time for this to evaporate.

I am going to have to take my cat by airplane – should I use a sedative?

Sedating cats for travel is certainly an option, but cats can react very differently to sedative medication and selecting the right tablets for any individual is not always easy. You also need to be aware that sedation may not last for the entire duration of your plane trip and therefore medication should not be used as an alternative to the behavior therapy approaches discussed above. Your cat will still need to be prepared for its travel by being introduced carefully to the carrier and the feline facial scent should also be used within the carrier to make the journey less stressful. This applies to long car journeys as well as for plane travel. If you feel that medication is necessary, because of the severity of your cat's reaction to travel, you will need to discuss this in detail with your veterinarian It may be useful to use a trial dose of the sedative prior to travelling to determine the effects that it has on your cat and the optimum dose. Anti-anxiety drugs are another option you might discuss with your veterinarian. They are a better choice for reducing anxiety but some cats will travel better with a more sedating drug.

VOCALIZATION – EXCESSIVE

Why is my cat persistently crying?

Most owner complaints about feline vocalization are either to do with the intensity and persistence of the vocalization, or the fact that it occurs at night, when family members or neighbors are trying to sleep. Attention getting behaviors, sexual (estrus or male) behaviors, play behavior, medical problems, discomfort and aggressive displays are the most common reasons for feline vocalization. Of course, since some cats are quite active at night, it is not surprising that many owners are concerned about their cat's nighttime vocalization and activity. Some breeds, such as the Siamese are much more likely to be vocal than others.

What can be done to prevent undesirable vocalization?

Providing sufficient play and exercise during the daytime and evening may help to schedule the cat so that it sleeps through the night. For details on feline play see 'Excessive nocturnal activity in cats'. Never reward vocalization by providing food, attention, or play, when the cat vocalizes. Mild outbursts of vocalization can either be ignored or interrupted with remote punishment techniques such as a water gun, compressed air, loud verbal no, or an alarm device, but never through physical punishment.

How can excessive vocalization problems be treated?

UNDERSTANDING THE PROBLEM

The cause of the cat's vocalization, those stimuli that are associated with the onset of the behavior as well as all factors that might be reinforcing the behavior, must be understood. For some cats, especially those that are middle aged or elderly, veterinary examination is recommended to rule out potential medical causes of vocalization such as pain, endocrine dysfunction and hypertension. Some older cats may begin to vocalize as their senses or cognitive function begins to decline (senility) – see 'behavior problems of older pets' for more details.

MODIFY THE ENVIRONMENT

If the cat can be denied exposure to the stimuli for the vocalization (e.g. the sight or sounds of other cats), or prevented from performing the behavior (e.g. keeping the cat out of the owner's bedroom at night), the problem can often be successfully resolved.

MODIFY THE PET

The most important aspect of a correction program is to identify what may be serving to reinforce (reward) the behavior. Many owners inadvertently encourage the behavior by giving the cat something it values during vocalization. Attention, affection, play, a treat, and allowing the cat access to a desirable area (outdoors, indoors) are all forms of reinforcement. Reinforcement of even a very few of the vocalization outbursts perpetuates the behavior. Although removal of reinforcement (known as extinction) ultimately reduces or eliminates excessive vocalization, the behavior at first becomes more intense as the cat attempts to get the reward. This is known as an extinction burst.

PUNISHMENT

Physical punishment should never be utilized in cats. Not only is it ineffective at correcting most behavior problems, it can also lead to fear and anxiety of the owner, people in general or being handled and petted. Although ignoring the vocalization, so that the cat receives no reward for the behavior, is the best solution, in the long run it can be difficult to do. Punishment devices can be used to interrupt the behavior immediately and effectively. A spray of water, an ultrasonic device, an audible alarm or a quick puff of compressed air (from a computer or camera lens cleaner) is often effective at stopping the behavior, and at the same time ensuring that the cat has received no form of reward. Punishment that is not immediately effective should be discontinued. With some ingenuity, remote control devices can be used to activate punishment devices and remove the owner as the source of the punishment. Some cats might be successfully fitted with a remote citronella collar so that they can be immediately interrupted.

What can be done for cats that vocalize through the night?

For those cats that vocalize through the night, it is first necessary to try and reschedule the cat so that it stays awake and active throughout the daytime and evening. Food, play, affection and attention should be provided during the morning and evening hours, and as many activities as possible must be

provided for the cat during the day (cat scratch feeders, activity centers, or even another pet). Drug therapy may also be useful for a few nights to help get the cat to adapt to the new schedule. Older cats with sensory dysfunction and geriatric cognitive decline may begin to wake more through the night and vocalize more frequently. These cases will need to be dealt with individually depending on the cat's physical health.

If the cat continues to remain awake through the night, there are two options that might be considered. The first is to lock the cat out of the

bedroom by either shutting the bedroom door, or confining it to a room or crate with bedding and a litter box for elimination. If the cat is ignored it may learn to sleep through the night, or it may be able to keep itself occupied if there are sufficient toys, activities or another cat to play with. Do not go to the cat if it vocalizes (even to try and quiet it down) as this will reward the behavior. If the cat must be allowed access to the bedroom, inattention, and punishment devices such as an ultrasonic alarm, compressed air, or a water sprayer, can be used to decrease or eliminate the cat's desire to vocalize.

Will neutering help?

If your cat is an adult male or female and not yet neutered, then some forms of vocalization are associated with communication, especially with regard to estrus cycles and mating. Cats in estrus are particularly vocal "calling". Neutering should help to reduce vocalization in these cats.

Neutered animals still may wish to go outside and roam. If there are other cats in the neighborhood that frequent the home territory, this may encourage your cat to vocalize. Blocking visual access, and providing "white noise" may help if you are unable to get the outdoor cats to leave your property.

Index

Index

Note: General topics are indicated by page numbers; page numbers followed by a c indicate canine behavior; page numbers followed by an f indicate feline behavior.